The SAA Handbook

A Practical Approach to IBM®'s Systems Application Architecture

Dennis Linnell

Addison-Wesley Publishing Company, Inc.

Reading, Massachusetts   Menlo Park, California   New York
Don Mills, Ontario   Wokingham, England   Amsterdam   Bonn
Sydney   Singapore   Tokyo   Madrid   San Juan

Many of the designations used by manufacturers and sellers to distinguish their products are claimed as trademarks. Where those designations appear in this book and Addison-Wesley was aware of a trademark claim, the designations have been printed in initial capital letters.

Library of Congress Cataloging-in-Publication Data

Linnell, Dennis.

    The SAA handbook : a practical approach to IBM's Systems Application Architecture / Dennis Linnell.

        p.   cm.

   ISBN 0-201-51786-8

   1. IBM computers--Programming.   2. Computer architecture.

I. Title.

QA76.8.I1015L56   1989

004.2'525--dc20   89-17826

                                                              CIP

ISBN 0-201-51786-8

Managing Editor: Amorette Pedersen

Set in 10.5-point Palatino by Benchmark Productions

ABCDEFGHIJ-MW-943210

First Printing, October 1990

To Victoria

Table of Contents

Preface

Systems Application Architecture (SAA) is IBM's sweeping effort to standardize nearly all facets of application software design. Though comprehensive, SAA is complex, obscure, and potentially difficult to learn. This book describes the key architectural features and the products that implement them. I try to demystify the architecture by explaining the SAA lexicon in plain English, without using much hyperbole or marketing rhetoric.

If you need a technical understanding of SAA, this book is for you. I've assumed you are familiar with computer programming and application design. If you have experience with IBM products, you may appreciate the subtle humor hidden in the text. Otherwise, IBM knowledge isn't necessary; the book provides the necessary background and context.

The first chapter speculates about the reasons for SAA and the final chapter speculates about the future. Chapter 2 contains my analysis of the past two decades of IBM computers. The rest of the book is mostly factual. You should know that my forecasts are correct about 50% of the time; my opinions should be taken with a grain of salt.

The book covers the architecture at three levels of detail. Chapters 1 and 20 are at the executive level; they mostly discuss technology trends, problems, and strategies. Chapter 4 provides a succinct technical overview of the architecture. Chapters 5 through 19 burrow into progressively greater detail about the SAA components. The lowest possible level of detail, concerning the mechanics of programming, is absent from this book. The bibliography lists the dozens of IBM manuals that cover the programming details.

Our IBM consultant relations representative, Alfred B. Jackson, cheerfully furnished photographs of equipment. I thank IBM Corporation for providing the IBMLink on-line service, which was invaluable for researching and verifying facts. Conversations with Stephen L. Gray formed the basis for Chapter 1. Victoria Linnell deserves special recognition for drawing most of the pictures in the book and reviewing the manuscript many times. I am grateful for the patience and diligence of Amorette Pedersen in the production of the book. James A. Shields and Michael T. Wilcox contributed many improvements to the manuscript and helped me in many other ways.

Chapter 1

IBM Strategies and Issues

This book is about a new standard for application programming, Systems Application Architecture (SAA), which IBM Corporation introduced in March of 1987. In the highly competitive computer industry, it is hard to find two people who agree on any particular topic, and many people are suspicious of new standards. IBM wants to "sell" the SAA standard to its customers and to others in the computer industry. The mission of this book is to explain the thinking behind the standard to a skeptical audience that wants an objective view.

IBM is the largest computer vendor in the world, with revenue five times that of its nearest rival. The company's strategies, both stated and implied, influence the entire computer industry, including customers and competitors. IBM's broad product lines meet a wide range of customer needs while competing with almost every other vendor's offerings.

IBM tries hard to explain its product strategies to its customers. This process is complicated by the sheer number of products offered and the technical nature of each product. Because most people in the computer industry are specialists, few people fully understand the "big picture" of the IBM world. Until IBM developed SAA, nothing explained how the pieces of the big picture fit together.

The pieces don't always fit. IBM needed to guide its development teams to build well-integrated products. Furthermore, customers buy many non-IBM products, which also must be integrated. In SAA, IBM standardizes the interfaces of many key products, solving several problems discussed in this chapter.

Single Versus Unified Architectures

In the 1970s, IBM could have decided to use the successful System/370 architecture in all its computers. Instead, the company offered several diverse computer architectures, each intended to serve different customer needs. This decision made it difficult for customers to switch from one computer family to another. Software developers had trouble building products that worked with multiple IBM computer families because each family was different.

While many IBM computer product lines were successful in the marketplace, others ultimately failed. Although IBM support sometimes seems everlasting, no company can support a failing product forever. Some notorious products, such as the 8100 information system, had unique architectures that many customers adopted. When IBM phased out these products, they became orphans. Customers had difficulty converting their applications to newer systems.

Figure 1-1: Single Versus Unified Architecture

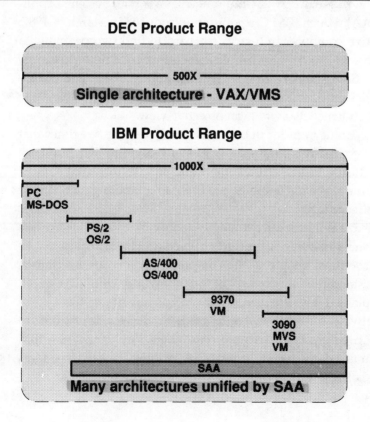

IBM's archrival, Digital Equipment Corporation, took a different approach. Digital reasoned that a single architecture could be used in its entire product line, spanning the full spectrum of computing power. Introduced in the late 1970s, the VAX architecture propelled Digital to industry leader status. This architecture is comparable to, but not compatible with, IBM System/370 architecture.

The single architecture strategy worked well for Digital and other vendors such as Wang and Hewlett-Packard. Customers wondered whether IBM's motley collection of architectures would meet their long-term needs. Competitors argued that IBM's strategy was fragmented, leaving customers stuck with orphaned products. They pointed out several product lines, such as the 8100, where this had happened.

The single architecture strategy is flawed, but few vendors admit it. This strategy dictates putting all their eggs in one basket. How do vendors take advantage of the latest technology, which may not fit into their architecture? What happens when an architecture becomes obsolete? How do vendors tell customers it is obsolete? Some vendors who were using a single architecture failed, and others might fail in the future.

IBM could not easily switch to a single architecture strategy because many of its disparate product lines had been so successful. The company sold thousands of System/370, System/36, and Personal Computer products. Although System/38 wasn't a great sales success, customers liked the product. If IBM abandoned these architectures, customers might abandon IBM. Nevertheless, something had to be done.

IBM picked the most important architectures and unified them through a common user interface, programming interface, and communications. The new AS/400 computer family is the fusion of the old System/36 and System/38 products. The Personal System/2 followed the Personal Computer, and Enterprise Systems Architecture (ESA) added new functions to System/370. SAA pulls these hardware environments together under one umbrella. Although SAA doesn't mandate a single computer architecture, it is IBM's best response to its competitors.

Portability

Portability has been an issue ever since engineers built the world's second programmable computer. SAA is concerned with portability of three assets:

- Application programs
- Programmer skills
- User skills

Portability makes it easy to move these assets from one computer environment to another. If all SAA hardware had the same architecture, portability wouldn't be difficult. However, the three SAA hardware architectures are very different, so SAA's portability features must address many problems.

Many customers outgrew the capacity of their IBM systems and learned how difficult conversion could be. This was a special problem for System/36 customers, who often are small businesses. They could choose between two IBM product lines, but both required tricky conversions. System/370 offered plenty of growth potential, but had few application software products intended for small businesses and System/38 offered suitable software, but much less capacity than System/370. Customers who outgrew System/38 faced an arduous conversion to System/370.

SAA is supposed to cut software conversion effort when growth dictates moving to another hardware platform. At first, this was a primary selling point for the new architecture. After customers asked many pointed questions about software portability, IBM retreated. SAA won't provide full portability of application source code, so software writers must tailor their code to run on each platform, which might raise development cost by 10 to 20 percent. Programmers should avoid using unique features of each SAA hardware platform. This "least common denominator" approach may simplify application design, but it also may degrade performance.

Each IBM computer architecture demands different sets of programmer skills. A System/38 programmer must be retrained to work on a System/370, which could take months and cost thousands of dollars. By providing a standard application programming interface, SAA lets developers focus on the logic of applications, rather than the details of the computer environment. Today, SAA falls short of isolating the programmer from each system's foibles. If IBM succeeds in its goal of programmer portability, the possible benefits are huge for both users and vendors.

User skill portability may be SAA's most important benefit. The standard user interface makes it easier to move users between computer environments. Real users of applications often are not computer professionals; computers tend to intimidate many people and resistance to change is a common problem. People make more errors during the "learning curve" for applications; such errors can be devastating or merely expensive. SAA's objective is to reduce the time spent retraining people to use new applications.

Cooperative Processing

In pure mainframe environments, nearly all application processing takes place in the central processors. Users are located at non-intelligent terminals, that are connected through communication links to the central processors. Although this approach has worked well for many years, it isn't always the least expensive or most efficient way to run applications.

Figure 1-2: Central Versus Cooperative Processing

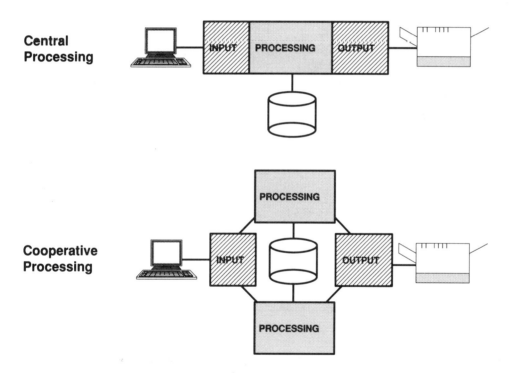

Mainframe computers always have been expensive. Minicomputers were cheaper, based on the cost per computation, but they could not be used for many applications because they were not powerful enough. In the late 1970s, IBM and other vendors tried to divide the processing between mainframes and minicomputers. This effort, called *distributed processing,* worked well for some applications, but the cost of networking the machines often exceeded the cost savings in hardware. To put it kindly, distributed processing technology matured very slowly.

Figure 1-3: Distributed Database Technology

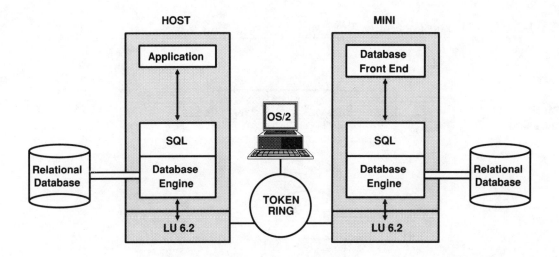

Microprocessor technology offers further cost advantages. The computing power is packaged into smaller units, but today's best microcomputers are almost as powerful as an average mainframe of 1976 vintage. Microcomputers are common in mainframe environments. The economic reasons for dividing the processing between microcomputer and mainframes are even stronger than they were for minicomputers. However, the technical problems of networking remain difficult.

The term distributed processing developed a well-deserved bad reputation, so IBM called the same idea *cooperative processing* in SAA. Cooperative processing divides a task among multiple SAA computers, which are connected by a network. Programs running on a PS/2 interact with the user, while transaction programs and database functions run on a System/370 or AS/400. The technology encourages widespread access to centrally managed databases. Another variation on this idea is *distributed database*, which connects the database systems, rather than the applications.

If IBM builds useful cooperative processing products, customers will benefit. Cooperative processing takes advantage of the low cost of computing on micro-computers, but recognizes that many important applications need more powerful machines. The technology could make better use of the personal computers in-stalled in most large organizations, and raise demand for mainframes. This solves marketing problems for IBM, which is interested in keeping control of the lucrative mainframe arena while expanding its share of the minicomputer and microcomputer markets.

Figure 1-4: Two-tiered Cooperative Processing

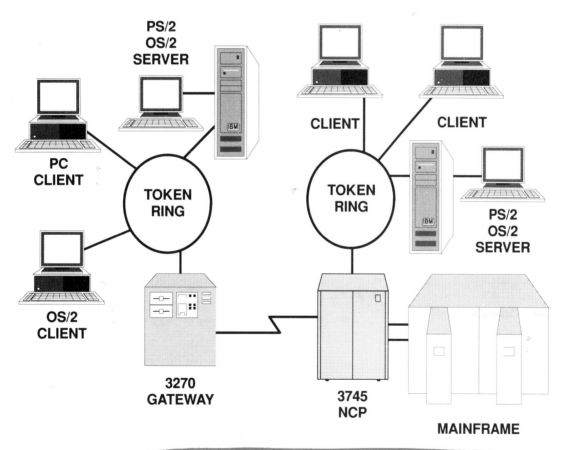

It isn't a secret that cooperative processing is the primary sales pitch for SAA, it is just a restatement of the old arguments in favor of distributed processing.

Because computer and communication technology is better and less expensive, cooperative processing is worth considering now, even though it didn't make much sense in 1979.

Software Pollution

Pollution is a dirty word in the software industry—it describes environments that have become polluted by overlapping or conflicting products. Some examples are:

- MVS versus VM versus VSE
- JES2 versus JES3
- CICS versus IMS

IBM's practice of creating diverse product families prevails in both software and hardware. Within a single hardware platform, IBM offers several similar software products. The differences among these products seem minor to outside observers, but not to devoted customers. It's like comparing Thunderbird and Cougar cars: they are built by the same company, they look and perform somewhat alike, but they don't appeal to the same customers. Unlike cars, however, differences among IBM software products can cause real problems for customers.

The problems begin with operating systems. In System/370, IBM offers a choice of three products: MVS, VM, and VSE. IBM also has other System/370 operating systems, including AIX/370 and TPF, but they are more specialized and less popular. Application software must be written specifically for each operating system; for example, source code for VSE applications must be changed substantially to run under MVS.

VSE is the entry-level system, which is the least powerful, but has the largest number of installations. VM operates best on medium-sized System/370 computers and MVS is used by the largest customers on the most powerful hardware. Each of these operating systems has unique strengths. For example, VM offers excellent interactive time sharing, while MVS works well for medium-volume transaction processing and heavy batch processing. All three products, however, are general purpose operating systems, and therefore have roughly the same functions.

An MVS customer can choose between JES2 and JES3 (Job Entry Subsystems) for batch workload scheduling. JES2 is the simpler and more popular of the two products, but JES3 handles large computer complexes and heavy tape workloads especially well. Job Control Language (JCL) dialects are different between JES2 and JES3. Hence, batch jobs with JCL designed to run under JES2 may not operate correctly under JES3, and vice versa.

For transaction processing, an MVS customer can choose between IMS and CICS. These products differ in database integration: IMS has a built-in hierarchical database, but CICS mainly uses conventional files. A CICS customer can buy a database product separately from IBM or another vendor. CICS and IMS are incompatible at the source code level. CICS is the market leader; IMS also is popular. Some customers use both products.

Pity the application software vendors! They might have customers with every possible combination of IBM system software. One customer has MVS, JES3 and IMS; another has VSE and CICS; a third has MVS, JES2 and CICS. A financial software vendor might need three different versions of its general ledger package to support these three customers. Imagine the cost and difficulty of developing, testing, and supporting software in these diverse environments.

Why did software pollution occur? Some possible reasons are:

- IBM didn't closely control its software development groups.
- IBM had to support an existing customer base while adding new functions to its products.
- When IBM originally developed the products, nobody knew how they would grow.

Some people think that IBM has a master plan that is executed like clockwork by legions of professionals wearing blue suits. This view is inaccurate. IBM software groups often operate independently, without central coordination. IBM encourages internal competition, so the groups might not know each other's plans. They might not agree, even if they knew what their co-workers were doing—they could be in different countries and speak different languages.

"Customers control our development plans," said one IBMer. IBM delivers initial software releases and then solicits customer suggestions. Although customers may wait years for product improvements, their ideas are taken seriously. However, this approach moves software products in unpredictable directions. Products such as IMS and CICS might diverge because their customers wanted different features, or they might converge.

IBM had to make its product offerings more consistent. One approach might have been to prune some of the redundant product offerings, however, this would create problems for customers who were running or building applications using those products. In the past, when IBM abruptly dropped important products, customers became upset. IBM needed to reassure customers that their software investment was protected. The company knew it had to shift its strategy smoothly.

Another lesson from the past is that architectures are good tools for making product lines more consistent. IBM standardized its communication product lines by introducing Systems Network Architecture. Although SNA took many years to mature, it added consistency to IBM's diverse communication product groups. By heavily promoting the architecture, IBM forced its own development staff to follow the rules. Customers began to insist all products conform to the architecture. The same scenario is now being repeated with SAA on a larger scale.

Standardizing the "Look and Feel" of IBM Products

Perhaps the two most frustrating problems for users are different styles of user interaction in software and differences in keyboards. These slow down experienced people, but stop beginners dead in their tracks. The art and science of human-to-machine interaction has probably reached the point where some consistency is needed—SAA provides this consistency.

While some vendors have taken legal action to keep others from copying the "look and feel" of their software, IBM has adopted an open approach, and encouraged others to follow its lead. Any effort to reduce the barrier between users and their computers is worthwhile, because it will encourage more people to use computers, and it might raise productivity. If computer interaction were consistent, each person would learn only one user interface.

SAA represents a compromise in look and feel, reflecting current hardware technology and past practices. It is a reasonable starting point, that can be refined as technology improves. Adopting a standard, no matter how imperfect, is better than the current state of chaos surrounding human-to-machine interaction techniques.

Strategic Interfaces

For many years, IBM and its customers have focused mainly on products. The company has *strategic products*, which are sold aggressively and are expected to have a bright five-year future. By saying which products are strategic, IBM bolsters its sales while helping customers in their planning. Although this approach has worked well for hardware, it hasn't been ideal for software. Software products don't fit the strategic product model, because they are:

- Derivative in nature
- Inexpensive to manufacture
- Easy for competitors to imitate
- Hard for vendors to protect their development investments

Figure 1-5: User Interface on Programmable Workstations

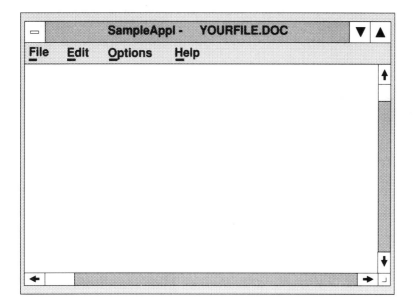

SAA represents a new way of thinking about software. Interfaces, rather than products, are strategic, and they will last over ten years. These interfaces are documented and can be used by anyone. IBM software products, such as OS/2, ISPF, and DB2 expose the interfaces. Customers will make commitments to the interfaces, not the underlying products. Strategic interfaces will be easier for IBM to protect and manage.

Figure 1-6: User Interface on Non-Programmable Terminals

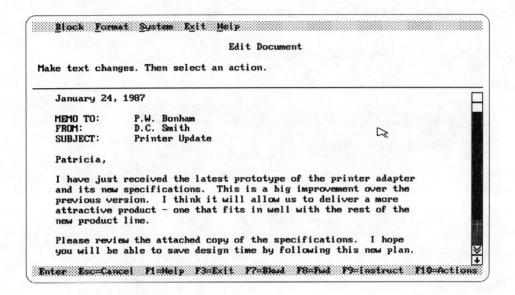

Deflecting Criticism

SAA is an effort to solve problems faced by the entire computer industry, not just IBM. The architecture is IBM's response to a crescendo of criticism that began in the early 1980s. While SAA lacks many features, and it is not at the cutting edge of technology, it is an obvious solution to many real problems.

Even if SAA doesn't solve problems immediately, it is a visible signal that IBM is working on tangible solutions. The issues raised by SAA will help sell a variety of IBM products and postpone the sale of competitive products. Whether customers will ultimately benefit from SAA is debatable, but IBM salespeople appreciate the architecture's merits now.

SAA Objectives

SAA's goal is to solve several major problems faced by the computer industry in general and IBM in particular. In announcing SAA, IBM didn't explicitly state its objectives. Most observers believe, however, that the objectives include:

- *Cooperative Processing Orientation* Enable development and usage of diverse applications that share information through a network
- *Simplicity* Simplify the user interface and make it consistent among applications. The architecture must let programmers create software quickly by providing powerful application programming interfaces
- *Unification* Unite several key hardware product lines and operating systems, so new applications can operate across several platforms
- *Versatility* Provide useful services for diverse hardware and software environments ranging from microprocessors to mainframes
- *Performance/price optimization* Let customers select the hardware and software platforms that minimize cost while providing adequate capacity for applications
- *State-of-the-art* Take advantage of the latest achievements in computer, communications, and user interface technology
- *Ease of migration* Make it easy for customers to implement SAA without changing current applications, but let new applications use the full power of the architecture
- *Stable structure* Define manageable, mass-produced, and general-purpose building blocks for application developers that vendors can augment as technology matures
- *Portability* Promote easy movement of applications, programmers, and users between computer environments

On the surface, these goals are so obvious that they might appear in any computer vendor's literature. They will be difficult to achieve, however, for reasons mentioned above. Meeting the goals will require new technology outside IBM's traditional strengths. SAA will add at least one new layer of software to a base that is already complicated. The architecture will dictate major changes in application design, requiring programmers to learn new techniques. This will take a long time.

Significance of SAA

Just considering IBM's strong advertising and promotion of SAA, the architecture is significant to some degree. In its first three years, SAA has motivated IBM's competitors to clarify their visions of application architectures and to voice some conflicting views. This dialog is important to the computer industry, and it may help advance the technology.

The marketplace will determine the commercial significance of SAA. In 1977, three years after the introduction of SNA, nobody knew whether the architecture would be significant in the long term. The same logic applies to SAA today. IBM plans its architectures for at least a ten year future. Some architectures, such as SNA, succeed—while others fail. Most architectures continue with acceptable but not spectacular results. Events that occur in the fifth to tenth years after introduction will determine SAA's place in the history books.

IBM Computer Environments

In any field of human endeavor, we stand on the shoulders of those who preceded us. This idea is pervasive in the IBM world and is perhaps the dominant theme in Systems Application Architecture. Nearly everything in SAA has evolved from previous IBM or industry practices. Furthermore, SAA pulls together several product lines, which developed separately but now are being unified. In Chapter 2, we review IBM technology and the sequence of events that led to the development of SAA, emphasizing IBM's mainframe roots.

Mainframe Computers

We've come a long way since the early 1960s, when the fundamental concepts embodied in today's mainframe computers were developed. The announcement of the IBM System/360 in 1964 was a landmark event that shaped the future of large computer systems, affecting every vendor and corporate user. Many IBM people view this event as the dawn of civilization in the computer industry. Ironically, System/360's early technical troubles were highly publicized, and the product could have easily failed in the marketplace. Instead, it was a great success.

While IBM may not have invented the idea of upward compatibility, the company certainly elevated the concept to high art in subsequent generations of its large computers. Many programs written for System/360 can be executed on today's newest IBM computers without modification. Such compatibility tends to protect a user's investment in software and thus has become a fundamental tenet of the computer industry. On the other hand, this philosophy has led to complex systems with hundreds of features built-in to ensure compatibility, some of which seem strangely out of place in a modern product.

The computer architecture of IBM large systems evolved from System/360 and is now called System/370. This architecture defines the operation of the latest systems, including the IBM 3090, 4381, and 9370 product lines. IBM's midrange computer product lines, including Series/1, System/36, System/38, and AS/400, are incompatible with System/370 architecture. Each of these product lines evolved independently, with different system software and applications satisfying different customer needs.

System/360

System/360 represented a dramatic departure from the computer systems of the past. In one bold stroke, IBM rendered 10 years of software development obsolete, and established the dominant large computer architecture for the next 25 years. The System/360 product family had a wide range of central processing units (CPUs, or processors), which were identified as model numbers 20 through 91. All System/360 models conformed to the same basic architecture, but certain features were not implemented in all models. Any program written for one of the lower models could be executed on a higher model without modification, thus providing upward compatibility.

The performance of the System/360 product line spanned a wide range. The System/360 model 20 could execute a few thousand instructions per second and was used widely as an intelligent remote job entry (RJE) terminal. The models 30, 40, and 50 performed small- to medium-sized data processing tasks. The model 65, which operated at about 1 million instructions per second (1 MIP), was the standard large system. Models 75 through 91 were expensive, high performance systems which were typically used for scientific computing in research laboratories and universities.

System/360 architecture mandated a 32-bit word length with an instruction set that contained both byte-oriented and word-oriented instructions. The instruction set was optimized for business applications, including extensive decimal arithmetic, character editing, and data conversion functions. System/360 also provided fixed point and floating point arithmetic for scientific applications. Its advanced Input/Output (I/O) architecture made the system attractive for high volume commercial data processing applications.

System/360 I/O architecture was novel. It defined three types of channels that connected the processor to peripheral devices and control units. Such channels are still used on modern IBM large systems. The latest System/370 channel interfaces are also compatible with peripherals of the System/360 era.

The three channel types are *selector, block multiplexer*, and *byte multiplexer*. In theory, each channel may be connected to a maximum of 256 devices, but in practice, the number of devices is limited by workload and channel data rates. A System/360 processor could have up to 16 channels. Today, the latest System/370 architecture specification allows 256 channels. Each channel operates at 50 kilobytes per second to 4.5 megabytes per second, depending on channel and device type.

System/360 Operating Systems

Two of the initial operating systems for System/360 have withstood the test of time: Disk Operating System (DOS/360) and Operating System/360 (OS/360). DOS/360 was intended for the less powerful System/360 models; OS/360 was more sophisticated, intended primarily for the largest systems. Both operating systems were designed to perform batch processing, but transaction processing and time-sharing functions were added later. DOS/360 and OS/360 are the ancestors of two current operating systems: Virtual Storage Extended (VSE), and Multiple Virtual Storage (MVS).

In the late 1960s, a time-sharing operating system called CP- 67/CMS was developed for the System/360 model 67. This system implemented a novel concept called the *virtual machine*, which created the illusion that each user had a dedicated computer. The virtual machine function let customers run multiple System/360 operating systems, including DOS/360 and OS/360, concurrently in the same computer. CP-67 was renamed to VM/370 in 1972, but it languished in obscurity until the late 1970s, when its popularity soared.

System/370

In 1970, IBM started the second generation of mainframes by announcing System/370, which replaced the System/360 family. Generations of IBM computer technology usually span seven to 11 years, with few exceptions. System/370 architecture offers practically all the features of System/360, thus it was easy for customers to convert to the new system.

The System/370 models were numbered using the same concept as their predecessors; processor speed and capacity increased with model number. The System/370 models were more reliable, had greater memory capacity and allowed more I/O channels than their System/360 counterparts. The top models established new levels of performance.

New models were added until the product line reached the end of its lifetime in the late 1970s. The mature product line included multiprocessor (MP) and attached processor (AP) options for some System/370 models. The model 168MP, the most powerful multiprocessor in the product line, operated at an instruction rate of approximately 5 MIPS.

In 1977, IBM announced the IBM 3033 processor complex, which became the most powerful machine using System/370 architecture. Subsequently, IBM introduced the less powerful 3031 and 3032 processor complexes, which replaced the upper echelon of the older System/370 models. This family of machines was called 303X, and its technology closely resembled the older System/370s. Although IBM implemented many technical improvements in the 303X product line, this series was essentially a refinement of System/370 hardware technology and it did not represent a new generation of computers.

Although some observers treated the 303X family as a single consistent design, it was not. The 3031, 3032, and 3033 had different internal designs and were created by separate engineering teams. It was not possible to upgrade a CPU from a 3031 to a 3032, or from 3032 to a 3033; a customer had to replace it with a larger model. The 3033 was the most successful design. IBM eventually developed a low-end 3033 model which replaced the 3032. The 3031 was replaced by the successful 4300 computer family.

IBM 4300 Small Mainframe Computers

The IBM 4300 product line was a versatile small mainframe family. Introduced in 1979, the 4300 heralded the start of the third generation of IBM mainframe hardware technology. The product had some of the characteristics of a mid-range computer, but it was intended for placement in a traditional computer room and it supported System/370 architecture. The 4300 series:

- Operated faster, with less power and cooling than its predecessors
- Provided upward compatibility with earlier System/370 models
- Used high performance, high density, but low cost circuit technology
- Supported the full range of System/370 operating systems
- Utilized standard System/370 peripherals

The product line included the following processors:

- IBM 4321 (1980)—entry level system—superseded by the 4361
- IBM 4331 (1979)—low cost, small system—superseded by the 4361
- IBM 4341 (1979)—small mainframe—superseded by the 4381
- IBM 4361 (1983)—low to mid-range system—replaced by 9370
- IBM 4381 (1983)—small mainframe—2 to 8 MIPS

By the late 1980s, all the 4300 models except the 4381 had become obsolete. The 4300 family was actively marketed from 1979 through 1989—quite a long lifetime for an IBM computer product line. In 1986, IBM announced the successor to the low end of the 4300 series, the 9370. The 9370 is priced lower and is more suitable for an office environment than the 4381. Although the 9370 is compatible with System/370 architecture, in other respects it is not a mainframe.

Figure 2-1: IBM 4381 Processor Complex

IBM 3081, 3083 and 3084 Large Systems

Announced in 1980, the IBM 3081 became the standard third-generation large IBM mainframe. This product was the most important advance in IBM large system technology since the introduction of the System/370 in 1970. It offered better reliability, higher performance, and quicker installation than the 303X product line. IBM extended the product line downward with the 3083, and upward with the 3084. Unlike the 303X family, a customer could upgrade from the entry-level 3083-CX model (3 MIPS) to the top-of-the-line 3084-QX model (29 MIPS) without replacing the system.

The 308X series used large scale integration (LSI) hardware technology. The major hardware structure was the thermal conduction module (TCM), which provided up to 133 high density chips mounted on a multiple layer substrate inside an envelope filled with helium. The TCMs were cooled by chilled water. The integrated circuit technology was transistor-transistor logic (TTL). The system provided a full set of microcode assist packages for the major operating systems, especially MVS and VM. Three processor configurations were offered: uniprocessor (3083), dyadic (3081), and four processor (3084).

Enterprise System/3090

Speculation about "Sierra," the code name for IBM's latest processor series, began shortly after the introduction of the 3081 in 1980. By the time IBM announced the 3090 in 1985, most observers expected the new product to represent a major leap forward in technology. Instead, the biggest improvement was a twofold increase in basic processor speed. The product had few new features. The 3090 is a continuation of third-generation IBM mainframe technology.

The 3090 is now IBM's most powerful general purpose computer. The base 3090 series had four models: 150, 180, 200, and 400. In 1987, the 3090 "E" series was announced, including models up to the 600E. In 1988, the "S" series superseded the "E" series, becoming the third refinement of 3090 technology. Finally, in 1990 deliveries began for the "J" series, which probably will be the last of the 3090s.

The first digit of the model number indicates the number of processors. The processor configurations are similar to those of the 308X series: single, dyadic, and four-way, but IBM added three-way, five-way, and six-way configurations. The latest 3090 models have all the features of the 308X, plus:

- Expanded storage facility, which speeds access to system data
- Optional integrated vector instructions, for scientific use
- Enterprise Systems Architecture, with 16-terabyte data spaces

The 3090 uses TCM technology with emitter coupled logic (ECL), rather than the TTL used in 308X products. The product line is upgradable from the entry-level 120E (7 MIPS) to the powerful 600J (117 MIPS).

Figure 2-2: IBM 3090 Processor Complex Model 600E

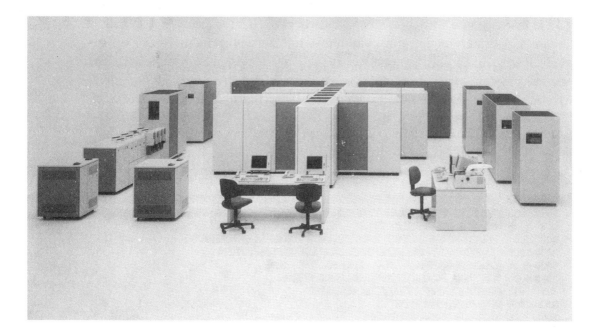

Mainframe Strategies

The progression of IBM mainframe products illustrates several important points about IBM's approach to technology and marketing. The most important concept is that all IBM mainframe computers built since 1964 conform to essentially one architecture. Although IBM has built a large number of mainframe models, the company has introduced only three generations of technology. Products that contain minor improvements are released every year or two, but products that represent milestones (such as the 4300 family) appear every seven to 11 years. Hence, most IBM products are evolutionary, and they are guided in the long term by architectures.

Mainframes dominate IBM thinking for one simple reason. They represent a large share of the company's revenue and a disproportionate share of profits. IBM has garnered a 76 percent share of the large systems market and continues to gain in market share. The company has nearly perfected the technology to manufacture high-quality mainframe computers, and can build the machines at relatively low cost. IBM controls the market for basic systems software (such as operating systems and communications functions) for all System/370 computers. No other company has been able to attain more than a small share of these markets.

Figure 2-3: MIPS Estimates for Popular System/370 Models

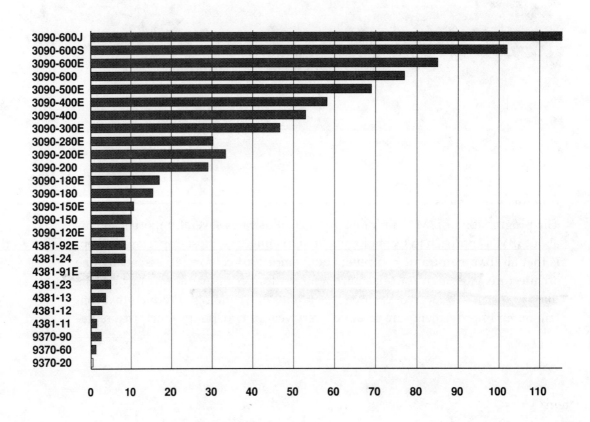

Trillions of dollars have been spent on software for System/370. Few people in the computer industry are willing to admit that inertia plays a major part in computer purchase decisions. Yet over 500,000 programmers work every day to produce more applications for System/370. If IBM dropped System/370 architecture today, these applications would continue to run in the twenty-first century. But IBM has no intentions of dropping System/370 architecture.

In fact, IBM continues to improve System/370 mainframe hardware products. Much of the refinement is related to IBM's traditional strengths: database and transaction processing applications. Many such applications can only be performed on mainframes, primarily due to application size and complexity. Many analysts think IBM is repositioning mainframes to act as huge database and transaction servers, operating at the center of networks of mid-range and micro computers.

Mid Range Computers

Enterprise System/9370

Unlike many IBM products, the Enterprise System/9370 has a very narrow focus: it is a departmental processor intended for work groups within a large organization. It fills the gap between PCs on the desktop and large 3090 processors in the corporate data center. The product shares the same basic System/370 architecture with the 3090, and its hardware facilitates the attachment of PCs using a variety of interconnection strategies and protocols. The product was announced in October, 1986, and was delivered in 1987.

Connectivity is an important part of the product's design. The 9370 offers at least 10 ways to connect to PCs and six ways to connect to larger System/370s. New IBM products often fail to deliver in this crucial area, however, because the 9370 implements the System/370 architecture, practically all the connectivity options for System/370 machines are instantly available. Many of these options can be implemented in a practical and economical manner, using standard product features.

The 9370 is not a single computer, but a series of seven models based on System/370 architecture. All models feature modular, rack-mounted components, ambient air cooling, IBM's one million-bit memory chip technology, and high density logic circuits. The systems are physically much smaller than other System/370s, and they can be located in normal office space. The model 20 is the size of a small file cabinet, needs no special air conditioning, and can be plugged into a standard wall outlet. Models 40 through 90 offer an upgrade path that provides up to five times the performance of the model 20, which cannot be upgraded. New rack-mounted disk units, tape drives, and communications controller boards are interchangeable.

The primary operating system is Virtual Machine (VM). VSE and MVS/370 are alternative operating systems. Advanced Interactive Executive/370 (AIX/370), IBM's adaptation of AT&T's UNIX, runs under VM. Practically any systems or applications software that executes under these operating systems will run on the 9370. IBM says that the top-of-the-line model 90 can support 70 to 145 concurrent VM users running typical applications development or office systems workload, with a two-second response time. The entry-level model 20 supports 15 to 30 users.

Figure 2-4: IBM ES/9370 Model 9375

The 9370 is not intended for a small business or first-time computer user. First, it is far too expensive. Second, most System/370 applications software products are not designed for small businesses. IBM offers two computer lines suitable for small business use: AS/400 and PS/2. The AS/400 is comparable in capacity and cost to the 9370, but it has a radically different (and, in some respects, more advanced) architecture. The PS/2 architecture is the least powerful.

Series/1

From its introduction in 1976, the Series/1 product family has offered an open system that allows third-party companies to provide additional hardware and software products. This was a remarkable departure from IBM's past practice. After successfully discouraging the use of plug compatible peripherals on its large systems, IBM opened Series/1 and provided a flexible, modular approach that allows system developers to tailor the hardware and software to their specific needs. IBM continues to manufacture the Series/1, but the product is near the end of its technological lifetime, and is not included in SAA.

The most interesting application of Series/1 has been in communications, both within IBM's SNA architecture, and outside, in the non-IBM world. The product can be used as a front end processor, terminal controller, distributed processing node, network gateway, and voice response unit. IBM's first implementation of the X.25 packet data network interface was announced for the Series/1 in 1980. Audio Distribution System (ADS) provides a voice mail capability for storing and forwarding telephone messages. This system features digital storage of voice messages, telephone retrieval of messages, and transmission of messages to other Series/1 systems. The system is often connected to the System/370 channel as a protocol converter supporting ASCII/asynchronous terminals.

Series/1 hardware includes a processor and I/O expansion slots that may be populated according to the user's requirements with communications controllers, peripheral interfaces, line drivers, and System/370 channel interfaces. IBM offers over 15 communications features, supporting asynchronous protocols and synchronous protocols including SNA/SDLC, HDLC, X.25, and BSC. A programmable communications subsystem is capable of attaching up to 32 lines using a mixture of data link protocols, data rates, and character sets.

Series/1 offers two unusual operating systems. Event Driven Executive (EDX) is mainly intended for conventional data processing applications. The Realtime Programming System (RPS) is used for more complex and sophisticated communications applications. Regardless of the choice of operating system,

Series/1 is intended for sophisticated users with expert programmers. It is a system builder's machine, not an entry level system for a first-time user.

System/36

System/36, IBM's evolutionary small computer system, was announced in 1983. It was the successor to System/34, which was preceded by System/3, developed in the 1960s. System/36 was marketed to new computer users, especially small businesses, and to departments in large organizations. The product interfaces well to System/38, Personal Computers, and System/370 host computers.

System/36 has an eight-bit multiprocessor architecture with virtual memory management. Software is available for creating text, printing, processing data, maintaining and distributing documents to local and remote users, maintaining mailing lists, and creating business graphics. System/36 was compatible at the source code level with its System/3 and System/34 predecessors.

The operating system, System Support Program (SSP), has help functions and prompted procedures. Operations Control Language (OCL) is the user interface for running jobs and programs. OCL is written in procedure form, stored in a user library, and provided to the application user as a menu. SSP allows applications to be written in COBOL, FORTRAN, BASIC, RPG II, or Assembler language. It supports concurrent batch and interactive execution and contains an optional spooler.

The System/36 is used principally for small business applications. The following IBM application software products are popular:

- Query/36, a data retrieval and report generation system
- Personal Services/36, electronic mail, and document distribution services
- DisplayWrite/36, a full function word processor
- Manufacturing Accounting and Production Information Control System (MAPICS)
- Retail Inventory Planning and Merchandising System

System/36 continues to be marketed, but the most powerful models have been superseded by the AS/400 product line. Although the architecture of the AS/400 is very different from the System/36, the AS/400 has an emulation mode, which allows System/36 programs to be executed without conversion.

System/38

System/38 was the first original architectural development by IBM since the System/360. It is intended for general-purpose data processing by small to medium size organizations. The product was announced in 1978 and first delivered in 1980. As with System/360, IBM had difficulty developing the product, but the customers applauded the result.

In the 1970s, IBM conducted an internal research project, called the Future System (FS) project, which defined a new mainframe architecture as the successor to System/370. Subsequently IBM decided not to adopt the new architecture, but instead, the company further enhanced the System/370 architecture. IBM's General Systems Division (GSD) revived the proposed architecture and used it to develop System/38. GSD later was eliminated in reorganization, but System/38 nevertheless became an important product.

The architecture of System/38 is highly influenced by database technology, and its advanced operating system contains a built-in relational database system. The system uses a 48-bit address, which implies an enormous potential address space. The operating system fully exploits this function. The system features flexible work management facilities, a high level of device independence for programs, and a new control language and data definition language that is used consistently throughout the system.

The CPF operating system, developed specifically for the System/38, contains the following features:

- Multiprogramming of batch and interactive tasks
- Integrated database support
- COBOL and RPG III languages
- Reentrant code in applications can be fully exploited
- Full SNA communications support

Many customers migrated to the System/38 from other IBM products, especially System/34 and 36. These systems use the same IBM 5250 terminals as the System/38, so it was not necessary to replace existing terminals during a conversion. Automated conversion software was available, but conversion was not easy, due to the differences in architecture and system software.

User satisfaction with System/38 was higher than with any other IBM computer line, including System/370. In 1986, the product line received its final enhancements, including new high capacity processors, additional memory, office automation features, advanced networking functions and many operating system improvements. In 1988, the product was superseded by the AS/400, which retains the features of the System/38, but offers a wider capacity range.

Application System/400

In June 1988, IBM announced the AS/400 and its operating system, OS/400 as the successors to the System/38 and selected System/36 models. AS/400 combines the major strengths of both System/36 and System/38 into a single product line. The hardware packaging resembles the 9370, and it uses the same disk and tape units. The product's innate architecture is similar to System/38 architecture. Further, it offers a System/38 emulation mode, which simplifies conversion for System/38 users.

Figure 2-5: Application System/400 Model B40

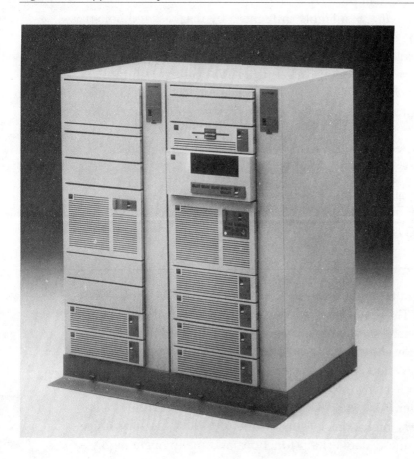

The AS/400 solves the problem of migrating applications from the System/36 by providing comprehensive communications facilities as well as emulation of the System/36 architecture. Portability is enhanced by the product's full support of Systems Application Architecture.

In its first year, shipments of AS/400 systems exceeded IBM's expectations. Many analysts forecast product shipments will grow in the 1990s. Although the AS/400 is a sharply focused product, the world-wide market for mid-range systems is huge, possibly exceeding $40 billion. While IBM does not enjoy monopoly status in the mid-range computer market, the AS/400 poses an important threat to competitors such as DEC, Wang, Hewlett Packard, and AT&T. OS/400 works with a broader selection of small business software than UNIX does, and it overshadows all proprietary minicomputer operating systems except DEC's VMS.

Personal Computers

When the IBM Personal Computer (PC) was introduced in 1981, it was immediately clear that the PC was going to become an important computer. Later, as sales of PCs skyrocketed beyond everyone's expectations, the PC became *the* standard for corporate desktop computing. This led to the development of several models, each with its own peculiarities. An enormous market developed for software products, compatible PCs, and add-on printed circuit boards which perform a wide variety of functions. Discussion of these developments has filled volumes, and is beyond the scope of this overview.

The obvious advantages of the PC are its low cost, ample processing power, and fast-growing software base. Though the PC is extremely useful by itself, it is nearly ideal as a workstation in a computer network. However, many customers have found it difficult to integrate the PC with their existing IBM computer systems. As a result, many hardware and software products have been developed by IBM and other vendors to address this need.

IBM has concentrated on providing interfaces among the PC, AS/400, 9370, and 3090 product lines. IBM has outlined a three-tier strategy of computer networking, having 370 processors at the top, AS/400s or 9370s in the middle layer, and PCs on the user's desk. These are connected by Local Area Networks or proprietary connection methods unique to each product line.

On April 2, 1987, IBM replaced the entire PC product line with the Personal System/2 (PS/2). The PS/2 offers a large degree of software compatibility with the PC, but not all models offer bus-level hardware compatibility. The PS/2 is more proprietary than the PC, and IBM has made the product difficult to imitate or "clone." Although the PS/2 operates with the standard Disk Operating System (DOS), IBM also released two new operating systems: OS/2, which greatly expands upon DOS, and AIX PS/2, which is compatible with UNIX.

Figure 2-6: Personal System/2 Model 30 286

Summary

IBM made an explicit decision in the 1970s not to put all its eggs into one architectural basket. This led to the development of several incompatible small computer architectures: Series/1, System/36 and 38, the Personal Computer, as well as several others that were less remarkable. IBM continued to refine its mainframe computer architecture at the top, but for many years the company did not attempt to provide a single architecture that covered the entire capacity spectrum.

In response to years of criticism, IBM finally did deliver single-architecture coverage in 1986 by announcing the 9370, which extends the System/370 line downward. The lack of demand for the 9370 shows that a single architecture strategy will not work for IBM. Hence, IBM offers three major computer lines with three distinct architectures and capacity ranges. With PS/2 as an entry-level system, AS/400 as the mid-range system and System/370 as the large system architecture, IBM believes that it can solve nearly all commercial automation problems. Systems Application Architecture provides consistency among these three disparate architectures.

Chapter 3

Architecture Concepts

An architecture defines the parts of a system and the interaction of those parts. It specifies technical details, including data formats, protocols, and programming interfaces to which hardware and software products must conform. This makes new products useful immediately because they share information and operate smoothly with existing products.

Architectures are important to both customers and vendors. Ideally, an architecture gives customers a wide choice of products and configurations that can expand easily as technology improves or as customer needs change. It helps guide a vendor's product development and informs customers about future product directions.

Architectures allow mass-production of hardware and software building blocks. Although interchangeable parts have been commonplace in most industries for the past century, the idea didn't exist in the software business until recently. Architectures let customers assemble an integrated system without requiring expensive custom-designed hardware and software interfaces.

People in the computer industry often use the term architecture as a euphemism for their incomplete plans. Some architectures are no more than design goals that developers try to achieve. Hence, architectures often expand. Just as successful products mature, so do architectures.

Architectures cover CPUs, I/O devices, operating systems, communications networks, and other esoteric subjects. They explain the operation of the latest technology, such as cooperative processing systems. Such systems usually have hardware and software pieces that were not explicitly designed to work together. For example, vendor A may never have tested its fourth generation language with vendor B's relational database. Without specific architectural guidance, it is likely that these pieces wouldn't work together.

Product developers are free to implement an architecture in any way they choose. There may be several different implementations of an architecture. The architecture itself doesn't depend on any particular product.

For example, IBM 3090 computers implement System/370 architecture. It isn't necessary, however, for a software product that uses System/370 architecture to run on a 3090; it can run on any System/370. Internally, not all System/370 implementations are the same as the 3090. Several companies build System/370-compatible computers that are much different in engineering from the 3090. Yet they all run the same software and produce identical results.

User needs, rather than exciting technological features, should drive the development of architectures. For example, a house's architecture ideally reflects the taste and lifestyle of its residents, rather than showing off the latest construction techniques. Architectures should achieve practical goals, besides defining engineering standards.

Developers of Architectures

As we have seen, the term architecture can mean almost anything to anybody. Hence it should not be surprising that many organizations are developing architectures. These groups have divided into three camps:

- Standards organizations
- Hardware and software vendors
- Customers, who buy hardware and software products

Increasingly, customers are developing their own architectures. Such architectures seldom have global significance, and they often apply to a single enterprise or to a particular industry. So we will concentrate on the other standards groups here.

Standards Organizations

The International Telephone and Telegraph Consultative Committee (CCITT), based in Geneva, has developed an elaborate set of data communications and computer network standards. CCITT is part of the International Telecommunications Union (ITU), which is an agency of the United Nations. CCITT has five levels of membership:

- Governments, which have voting rights
- Private communication carriers
- Industrial and scientific organizations
- Other international organizations
- Groups in other fields interested in CCITT's work

In many countries, including the United States, users routinely utilize CCITT standards, such as V.35, X.25, and X.400. This book refers extensively to the CCITT standards related to SAA.

The International Organization for Standardization (ISO) also has developed computer standards, some of which overlap CCITT's offerings. ISO membership is voluntary; each member is a national standards organization, such as the American National Standards Institute (ANSI). ISO coordinates its data communication standards work with CCITT. Many of ISO's subcommittees work closely with ANSI in such areas as encryption, packet data networks, and programming languages.

The most notable ISO work is the Open Systems Interconnection (OSI) reference model, which defines a seven-layer model for computer networks. Other ISO standards address non-computer topics, such as photographic film sensitivity.

The American National Standards Institute (ANSI) is a voluntary organization for standards in the United States. ANSI led the development of standards for programming languages such as COBOL, FORTRAN, and C. More recently, ANSI adopted standards for the SQL database interface. The institute represents the United States in the ISO. ANSI standards parallel those of the ISO, but they are not the same due to differences in U.S. market preferences. ANSI also coordinates with CCITT.

The Institute of Electrical and Electronics Engineers, Inc. (IEEE) is a respected international professional society. IBM incorporated part of IEEE's work in local area network technology into SAA. This organization has developed many other important standards, such as the IEEE 488 parallel interface.

The Electronic Industries Association (EIA) is a trade organization that develops standards for North America. As its name suggests, EIA concentrates on hardware electrical interface standards. The EIA 232 standard (called RS-232 in this book), first announced in 1962, forms the technical basis for most wide-area network physical connections today.

Hardware and Software Vendors

During the past 20 years, computer vendors have become prolific developers of architectures. IBM is the largest company in the computer industry and its contributions to the field of architectures are at least proportional to the company's size. Trying to emulate IBM's success, other companies developed their own competing architectures.

After IBM announced Systems Network Architecture (SNA), the first modern proprietary network architecture, Digital Equipment Corporation (DEC) created Digital Network Architecture (DNA). Though not compatible with SNA, DNA was successful in the marketplace. Digital also launched the VAX computer architecture, which was not compatible with System/370, but had similar technical goals. The VAX product line was a great success. DEC competed successfully with IBM's proprietary architectures, but not every vendor has enjoyed DEC's success.

Other vendors have created proprietary architectures that solved important problems in a novel manner without competing directly with IBM's architectures. For example, Adobe's PostScript is a page definition language mainly for laser printers. Such solutions have succeeded due to technical merit. Although some architecture developers are large companies such as AT&T, DEC, Xerox, Apple, Intel, or IBM, the industry also embraces innovations from smaller firms.

While some IBM products support proprietary architectures developed by other companies, the most important products mainly follow IBM and official (ANSI, ISO, CCITT, and IEEE) architectures. Ten years ago, IBM did little to acknowledge or support competing architectures. Today, the company is taking steps to make its products operate with competing architectures, such as PostScript and Ethernet. This reflects the trend away from single-vendor environments. IBM nevertheless didn't include other vendor architectures in SAA.

Chapter 4

SAA Components and Concepts

SAA has four components: Common User Access (CUA), Common Programming Interface (CPI), Common Communications Support (CCS), and Common Applications.

Common User Access, which defines a standard user interface for applications, includes rules and guidelines for:

- Screen layout and formatting
- Selection using the keyboard or mouse
- Meanings of specific keys
- Keyboard layout
- Fundamentals of the human-to-machine interface

CUA is complicated by the divergence of display technologies of IBM computer product lines. The PS/2, AS/400, and System/370 product families handle the keyboard and display differently. For example, PS/2s let programs use graphics efficiently and to respond individually to each keystroke. On the other hand, the IBM 3270 display terminals used on System/370 mainframes have limited graphics performance and cannot interact with the System/370 for each keystroke; instead they operate in block mode. These technologies necessarily require different styles of user interaction, and the CUA must define each style.

CPI defines the languages, application generators, database interface, graphics, dialog manager, and other tools needed to develop an application. CPI relies on ANSI standards for languages and databases, but patterns other services after proprietary IBM products.

CCS connects applications, systems, networks, and terminals. It relies on strategic IBM communications architectures, including SNA, which have been used extensively by customers, competitors, and third parties during the past decade. CCS simplifies the execution of cooperative applications on a network of heterogeneous IBM computers.

Common Applications satisfy general customer needs across all SAA environments. Examples are OfficeVision, which provides a general-purpose platform for office automation and AD/Cycle, which includes application development tools. This part of SAA hasn't developed as a real architecture; it supports IBM's marketing efforts for future products. Therefore, this book concentrates on the other three SAA components.

Figure 4-1: SAA Components

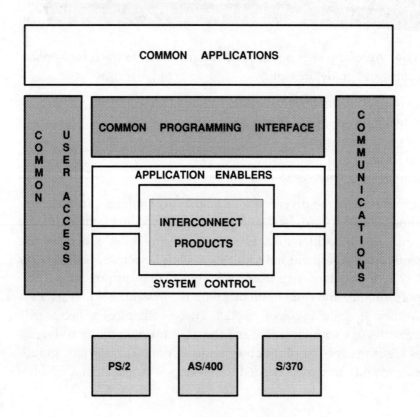

Common User Access

Common User Access defines the user interface to applications, which is a dialog between human and machine having three components: presentation language, actions language, and the user's conceptual model. An application provides access to data, performs computations, and translates information into a form understandable by the user. Its mechanism for giving information to the user is the presentation language. The user enters responses specified by the actions language, using a keyboard or mouse. The user's conceptual model reflects a person's understanding of the entire process of using an application, including assumptions about what a computer interface is, what it does, and how it works.

Consistency

CUA's conceptual model helps users to learn applications quickly. IBM is trying to make the user interface consistent across applications with respect to three dimensions: physical, syntactic, and semantic. *Physical consistency* refers to hardware: keyboard layout, placement of keys, and the use of the mouse. For example, the F1 key should always appear in the same location on all SAA keyboards.

Syntactic consistency refers to the presentation and actions languages, which define the appearance of items on the screen and the sequence of user requests. F1, for example, should always execute the HELP action.

Semantics define the meanings of elements in the interface. For example, the HELP action should display information about items on the screen.

Although consistency is desirable in theory, it is unattainable in practice because of historical constraints. During the past 15 years, IBM has sold millions of non-programmable 3270 and 5250 terminals, which are incapable of fast graphical presentation. PS/2s, on the other hand, offer good presentation technology at a low cost. It would have been unwise to use a least common denominator approach, with PS/2s emulating dumb terminals.

In CUA, IBM created two styles of presentation: one for programmable workstations (usually personal computers) and another for non-programmable terminals. These styles are similar enough to be recognized immediately by users. IBM originally named the non-programmable terminal standard *mainframe interactive (MFI)*. Programmable workstations first were called *intelligent workstations (IWS)*.

IBM describes the programmable workstation (PWS) style in the *SAA CUA Advanced Interface Design Guide* manual. The *SAA CUA Basic Interface Design*

Guide discusses the non-programmable terminal style. In an early version of this manual, IBM took the unusual step of including a diskette containing CUA demonstration programs. This diskette was useful in illustrating basic CUA concepts. In 1989, however, IBM changed CUA substantially, and rendering the diskette obsolete.

In the past, IBM offered a wide variety of keyboards, which was frustrating for people who switched frequently from one workstation to another. IBM selected the Enhanced Keyboard, first offered on the Personal Computer AT, as the SAA standard. The company now sells this keyboard with most computer and terminal product lines.

CUA supports concurrent use of the keyboard and a mouse, or any other pointing device that acts like a mouse. Applications must allow users to switch between a keyboard and a mouse at almost any point in the dialog without having to change application modes. Applications designed for intelligent workstations must support a mouse, but for non-programmable terminals, a mouse is optional.

CUA Concepts and Terms

CUA includes definitions of a few basic terms related to the design of the user interface. A *screen* is the surface of the workstation or terminal on which information is displayed to users. A *panel* is a predefined set of information arranged in a specific way and displayed on a screen. CUA defines several panel types, including menu, entry, information, list, and logo. Panels have three areas:

- Action bar with associated pull-down menus
- Panel body
- Function key definitions (optional)

The *action bar* appears at the top of a panel. This bar contains a list of action keywords, such as FILE, VIEW, or HELP. When a user selects a keyword, a pull-down menu appears. Acting as an extension of the action bar, the pull-down menu lets users make requests.

In CUA terminology, *request* means to initiate an action. Several methods can be employed to initiate the action: pressing a function key, typing a command, or selecting a choice in an action bar pull-down menu. The action bar itself doesn't actually initiate an action. The actions are listed on the pull-down, so users see what actions are possible before selecting one.

Figure 4-2: CUA Screen on a Programmable Workstation

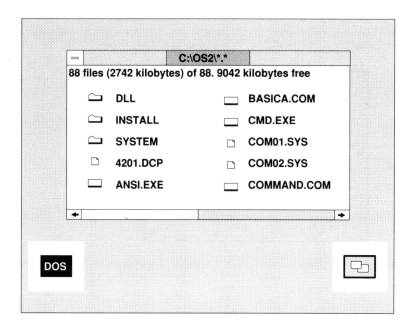

The action bar and pull-down menus provide a two-level hierarchy. A designer can provide additional levels using pop-up windows that appear when a choice is selected from a pull-down. Such windows may create one or two additional pop-ups during the processing of an action.

The mandatory *panel body* is located below the action bar. The designer may divide it into areas, to display or update several pieces of information simultaneously. Panels include elements such as titles, column headings, selection fields, and entry fields. The panel body may contain a command area for system or application commands and a message area. Although messages often appear in pop-up windows, they may appear in the message area to avoid obscuring other information in the panel body. CUA also defines symbols and visual cues, such as *radio buttons* and *check boxes*, which show users the available choices.

Figure 4-3: CUA Screen on a Non-Programmable Terminal

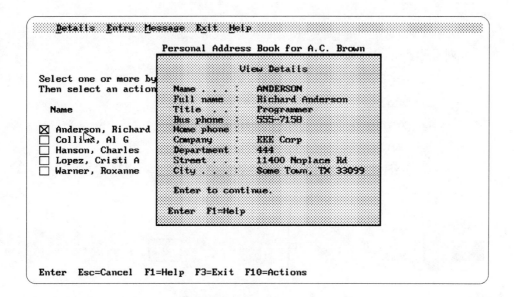

User Interaction Techniques

The object-action principle lets users select an object from the panel body first, and then to select an operation from the action bar or function keys to work on that object. Intuitively, this seems backwards. However, it allows the application to present only those actions that are valid for the selected object, and minimizes the need for modes, which might confuse users. CUA recommends using the object-action approach, but designers can also implement the action-object approach. The selection cursor, typically a bar of color, selects the object and highlights the user's choice.

Not everyone will appreciate the step-by-step prompting and visual cues that make CUA applications easy for the novice. Users who are accustomed to products such as ISPF, which have selection sequences like =3.2.7, appreciate CUA's fast path interaction techniques, including:

- Actions assigned to function keys
- Use of mnemonics and numbers for selecting choices and actions
- Areas for entering system commands

- Mouse techniques that speed up choice and action selection
- A quick exit action that zips directly out of an application

Figure 4-4: Navigation Within an Application

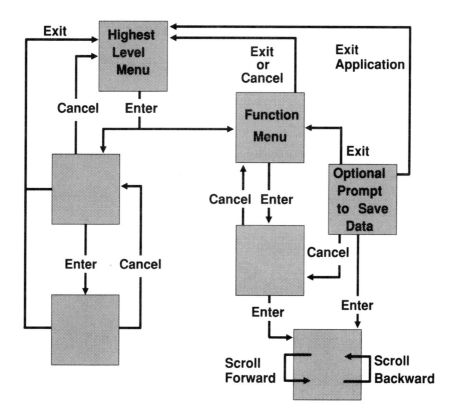

Navigation

Some applications contain dozens of functions, which logically constitute a hierarchy. This is common in mainframe applications. Besides executing application functions, users must navigate through a maze of panels to find the desired function. Hence, SAA dialogs have two parts: requests to process information and requests to navigate through the application.

Users navigate by requesting common dialog actions, which IBM standardized across all SAA applications. Such actions include:

- *Enter*   Executes the default action. This usually moves users to the next step of the dialog
- *Switch to Action Bar*   Moves the cursor to the action bar
- *Exit application*   Ends the application

The next step usually presents a new or substantially revised panel. Using the dialog interface, users can also transfer information from one panel to another. Figure 4-4 illustrates a typical application, including common dialog actions.

Figure 4-5: Primary and Secondary Windows

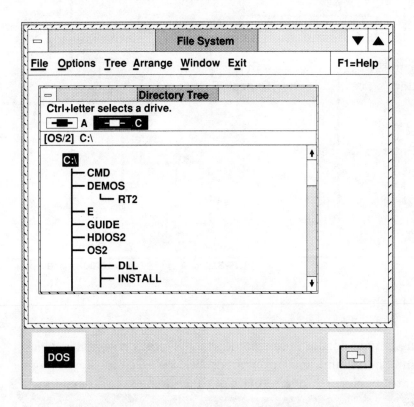

Windows

Systems with window functions let users divide the screen into multiple independent windows, each containing one panel. Users can scroll, re-size, and move windows. The operating system and related presentation tools usually provide all window functions. Not all SAA environments provide windows; some systems display one panel at a time.

CUA has primary, secondary, and pop-up windows. A primary window contains the main dialog; for example, edited text appears in a word processor's primary window. Window environments, such as OS/2 Presentation Manager, allow multiple primary windows.

A secondary window is subsidiary to the primary window, and allows a second dialog to be conducted in parallel with the primary dialog. In the word processor example, formatting options for the document in the primary window appear in the secondary window.

A pop-up window is an extension of a dialog that is running in either a primary or secondary window. Error messages, brief help information, or short prompts all appear in pop-up windows. Pop-ups may be fixed in size and position; users must complete their dialogs with pop-ups before continuing to use the underlying window. Pop-ups are mandatory, whether or not an application is running in a window environment.

Figure 4-6: Basic CUA Menu Panel

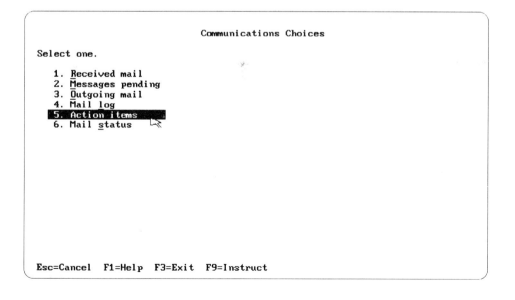

Customizing User Interaction

Users can customize portions of the user interface and control some aspects of a panel's appearance and interaction techniques. Options include panel colors, command area location, control of beeping, mnemonic usage, and suppression of logos and copyrights. Such customization may remain in effect from one application to the next.

CUA defines separate user interfaces for character and graphic applications. A graphic-mode application can take advantage of the graphic features of the interface, including icons, radio buttons, check boxes, pushbuttons, and scroll bars. Designers cannot mix character and graphic styles in the same application.

CUA also has rules for supporting languages other than English, including those in which writing is performed right-to-left. IBM set up the double-byte character set (DBCS) to handle languages that do not have Latin characters, including Japanese (Kanji), Korean, and Chinese.

Common Programming Interface

Languages and Services

SAA applications can be developed using many popular high level languages, including FORTRAN 77, COBOL 85, and C. IBM added Report Program Generator (RPG) and PL/I languages to the architecture to meet important needs within its customer base. Customers can use an application generator, Cross System Product (CSP), to shorten development time.

A procedures language, based on IBM's Restructured Extended Executor (REXX), acts as a command and macro language. SAA uses relational database services with the Structured Query Language (SQL) interface. Other services include:

- *Query Manager*   Casual database access and report writing
- *Presentation Manager*   Graphics and windows
- *Dialog Manager*   Keyboard and screen dialog management

In initially selecting the programming languages for SAA, IBM made the obvious and sensible choices: COBOL and FORTRAN, representing IBM's long standing constituencies—commercial data processing and scientific computing. Later, the company added RPG to meet the needs of AS/400 users. The selection of C is more remarkable, given its association with AT&T's UNIX, which indirectly competes with SAA.

Figure 4-7: OS/2 Programmer's View of SAA

Programming Interface			Application Generator	Procedures Language	Communications Interface
COBOL	FORTRAN	C	CSP	REXX	OS/2 Communications Manager
Query Interface			Database Interface	Dialog Interface	Presentation Interface
OS/2 Query Manager			OS/2 Data Base Manager	OS/2 Dialog Manager	OS/2 Presentation Manager

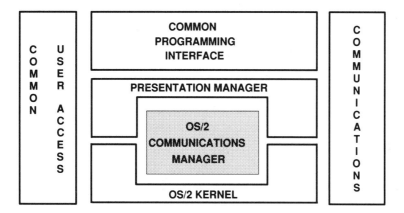

Nevertheless, C is a good choice from a technical perspective because it enables development of very sophisticated applications on the smallest to the largest computers. The capabilities of C complement, rather than compete with, COBOL and FORTRAN. COBOL and FORTRAN already are commonplace on System/370 mainframes, and compilers for C have emerged. PS/2 environments support all three languages; C is popular with application developers and it interacts especially well with OS/2.

Under OS/400, the picture is not so bright: some application use COBOL, but FORTRAN is a poor match for the AS/400 architecture. Most AS/400 customers have no experience using C. Here, RPG/400 is the logical choice.

Figure 4-8: Mainframe Programmer's View of SAA

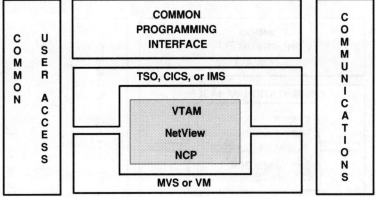

Programming Interface			Application Generator	Procedures Language	Communications Interface
COBOL	FORTRAN	C	CSP	REXX	CICS, VTAM
Query Interface			Database Interface	Dialog Interface	Presentation Interface
QMF			SQL/DS DB2	ISPF	GDDM

Application Generator

The application generator specification was derived from Cross System Product (CSP), which initially operated under MVS, VM, and the DOS compatibility mode of OS/2. IBM developed this tool for professional programmers, as an alternative to conventional programming languages. It reduces the level of detail in coding, possibly improving productivity. The product has been available for many years and, as its name suggests, was designed with portability in mind.

Customers have used application generators, including CSP, in the System/370 environment for the past several years with mixed satisfaction. Professional programmers can quickly build applications consistent with the design assumptions of the application generator. Many applications, especially those using low-level system interfaces, are not a good match for application generators, and should be developed using conventional tools.

Procedures Language

REXX, the SAA procedures language, contains statements in the operating system's command language, besides conventional programming logic. The procedures language is conceptually similar to batch (.BAT) files in DOS, but is more powerful. It has been available on System/370 under VM for several years.

REXX has been popular in the mainframe environment; programmers and end users alike have found it easy to master. Though primarily intended as a command or macro language, programmers have developed entire applications with it.

Database Interface

SQL provides interface services to define, retrieve, insert, delete, and update information in a relational database. With the relational data model, the user views the database as a set of tables. Data are organized into rows and columns, similar to records and fields. Applications access data through operations on tables. The physical structure of the database is defined separately from the application. Storage and management of data can be optimized independently, without affecting the portability of the application.

In SQL, users specify what is to be done by the database system, but not how it is done. SQL syntax resembles conventional programming languages. It performs arithmetic on retrieved values and has built-in functions for summation, grouping, ordering, and simple statistics such as means, minima, and maxima. Query functions allow selective retrieval from one or more tables, as well as sorting of the results. SQL statements can be entered interactively or imbedded into the source code of an application program. A precompiler processes the imbedded SQL statements and translates them into subroutine calls, then the program is compiled, linked, and executed.

SQL is included in Data Base 2 (DB2) in MVS, SQL/DS in VM, and the Database Manager in OS/2 Extended Edition. The SAA SQL specification was developed with consideration for the ANSI SQL standard X3.135-1986, and is mostly compatible with current DB2, SQL/DS, and OS/2 Database Manager products. Some database features haven't been implemented, for example, OS/2 doesn't have a full set of SQL security features.

Query Interface

The query interface provides interactive services to compose queries of a relational database and to create reports containing the answers. The first SAA-compliant query products were OS/2 Extended Edition Query Manager and Query Management Facility (QMF) for MVS and VM.

Using a series of menus, QMF accesses information, and then reports the results. On-line Help guides users in making their requests. Users can execute SQL statements directly or QMF will ask for all information to complete the query. Applications build and manipulate queries, procedures, and report specifications through a subroutine call interface. QMF can store results of queries, which other applications can access.

Figure 4-9: SQL and Query Manager Relationship

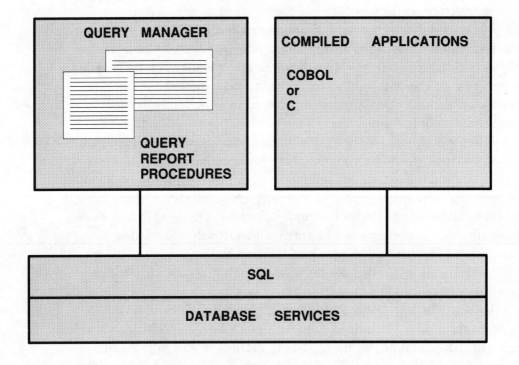

Presentation Interface

The presentation interface provides a comprehensive set of functions for displaying and printing information. Structured as a set of subroutine calls, it provides a window system, interaction via the keyboard and mouse, comprehensive graphics, fonts, image support, and functions for saving and restoring graphics. OS/2 Presentation Manager provides the full presentation interface, including windows and graphics.

Graphic functions are similar to those provided by IBM's Graphic Data Display Manager (GDDM). IBM derived the window functions from Microsoft Windows. GDDM will continue to be available under MVS and VM, but IBM hasn't announced an SAA window system for these operating systems.

Dialog Interface

The dialog interface promotes interaction between the user and the application by formatting the screen and by passing data and function requests from the keyboard or mouse to the program. It is similar in concept to *forms packages* used on minicomputers, or Basic Mapping Support (BMS) in mainframe CICS systems. The dialog manager displays on-screen panels containing menu selections, HELP information, data requests, and messages. It also assists the application in performing input field validation, issuing error messages, and navigating through the hierarchy of panels. The dialog interface manages pools of variables that contain information supplied or used by the application and it maps the contents of variables to the screen and keyboard.

Derived from a combination of Interactive System Productivity Facility (ISPF) for System/370, and EZ-VU II for PS/2s running DOS, the dialog interface is not totally compatible with these products. IBM's *SAA Dialog Reference* manual contains a detailed list of the differences, which are relatively minor. ISPF and OS/2 implement the SAA dialog interface specification.

Common Communications Support

Common Communications Support (CCS), SAA's communications component, includes data streams, application services, session services, network node capabilities, and data link controls. It contains subsets of Systems Network Architecture (SNA), related product features, other architectures, and international standards. As with the SAA programming interface, the components of CCS have been available in SAA environments during the past few years. A new component, Distributed Data Management, was added in 1988.

Unlike the programming interface, which today is largely unavailable, the components of CCS are available in nearly all SAA environments. IBM's approach for integrating the programming interface and communications support is specified in the Common Programming Interface for Communications (CPI/C). While application program interfaces (APIs) for communications in MVS, VM, OS/400, and OS/2 have differed in many ways, CPI/C describes exactly how applications should use SAA communications functions. However, APIs for some CCS features, such as Synchronous Data Link Control (SDLC), 3270 data stream, and Intelligent Printer Data Stream (IPDS), will remain nonstandard.

Nearly all facets of CCS are directly related to SNA, which defines sets of communications functions that are distributed throughout a network, and formats and protocols that relate these functions to one another. SNA sets the rules for interconnecting IBM (and, in some cases, non-IBM) computers, terminals, and applications. It is a huge architecture, with many possible subsets, some of which are now obsolete. SAA includes mostly modern SNA facilities and omits the obsolete ones.

Networking

CCS has three basic networking functions: Advanced Program-to-Program Communications (APPC, also called SNA Logical Unit 6.2) for communications between programs, possibly executing on different machine types, SNA node type 2.1 (also called Physical Unit 2.1 or Low Entry Networking) for peer-to-peer communications among low cost computers such as PS/2s and AS/400s, and SNA Management Services for centralized monitoring and control of communications networks. There are three types of data links: Synchronous Data Link Control (SDLC) for medium and high speed links in wide area networks, SNA-X.25 Interface for attaching SNA computers and terminals to packet data networks, and Token-Ring network for physical access and signaling on local area networks.

APPC is a fundamental communications protocol that forms the basis for many SAA features. It defines sets of verbs that enable conversations between pairs of applications. It is a single architecture that spans the entire IBM product spectrum from PS/2s to the largest System/370 mainframes, allowing communication between programs located on any machine in the network.

Figure 4-10: CCS Product Configurations

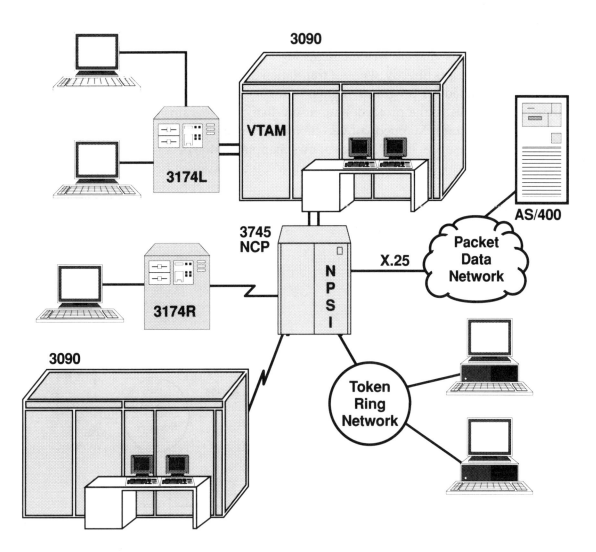

APPC operates on any SAA data link, including SDLC, X.25, and the Token-Ring local area network. The protocol uses network resources efficiently, allows programming in high level languages, and insulates applications from the technical details of the network. Unlike other SNA session protocols, APPC has standardized application interfaces including the protocol boundary and CPI/C. These are supposed to be consistent across IBM product lines.

APPC has two styles of conversations: basic and mapped. Basic conversations have access to the full set of APPC features, and are intended to be used by privileged programs, that are written in low level languages. Basic conversations exchange data records directly, without translation or mapping. Mapped conversations are intended for programs written in higher level languages; they hide some of the details of the protocol and ensure that the programs comply with certain protocol rules. Mapped conversations exchange information using the Generalized Data Stream (GDS), which allows mapping of the data from one format to another—for example, conversion from ASCII to EBCDIC.

Figure 4-11: APPC Configurations

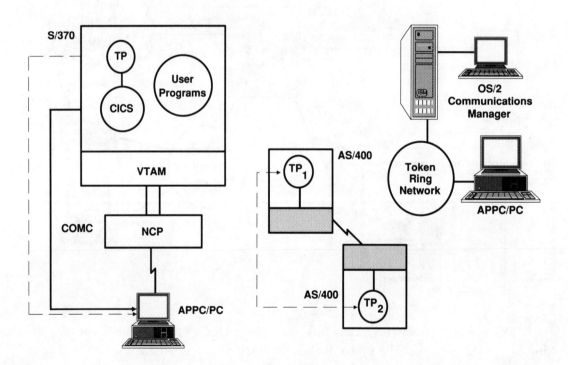

APPC can be used in all SAA environments plus many other IBM products. It is part of OS/2 Extended Edition Communications Manager. System/370 supports the protocol under MVS and VSE by CICS and VTAM, and under VM by APPC/VM. The communication features of OS/400 use APPC extensively. The architecture is also available in many non-IBM computer systems. Although IBM offers APPC in many operating system environments, very few applications actually use the architecture directly.

PU 2.1, also called Low Entry Networking (LEN), supports peer-to-peer communications. LEN allows multiple and parallel SNA sessions to be established between directly connected nodes. Thus, applications residing in different LEN nodes can communicate directly, using LU 6.2 or other SNA session protocols. LEN can be used on SDLC data links, X.25 packet data networks, or Token-Ring networks. Often, type 2.1 nodes operate as semi-intelligent cluster controllers in hierarchical SNA networks. In some networks, they operate in a peer-to-peer mode.

IBM's approach for managing communication networks is SNA Management Services (SNA MS). This architecture defines protocols that enable the network to monitor error and performance data from a central location. Network management data are collected locally at every SNA node. This information is forwarded periodically to a central network management facility located on a System/370 host computer.

IBM's NetView software product runs on System/370 and performs central network management functions, including:

- Automating operator functions and controlling the network
- Collecting and reporting error statistics
- Providing alerts to network operators about critical errors
- Monitoring actual response time, as viewed by users
- Testing SNA session connectivity and tracing session protocols

NetView/PC runs on remotely located PS/2s to collect information from non-SNA network components including Token-Ring networks, telephone PBXs, non-IBM modems, and multiplexers. A customer or communications vendor can write programs for NetView/PC to collect data from a wide range of network components. NetView/PC relays this data to NetView on the System/370 host. SNA Management Services are supported in all SAA environments.

Figure 4-12: Network Management Structure

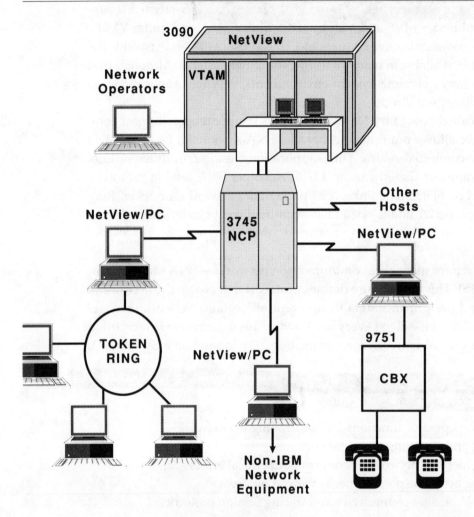

Data Links

Synchronous Data Link Control (SDLC), one of the three types of CCS data links, is a discipline for exchanging information across a serial-by-bit data link using a transparent, synchronous encoding system. It transports information directly from one SNA node to another. As the most popular SNA data link protocol, SDLC has always been an essential part of the architecture. It operates on links ranging in speed from 2,400 to 1,544,000 bits per second, and is available in all SAA hardware environments.

The second data link, the Token-Ring network, consists of a wiring system, a set of communication adapters (stations), and an access protocol that controls the sharing of the physical medium by the stations attached to the local area network. Although it offers nominal data rates of 4 and 16 megabits per second, it is limited in distance. The Token-Ring architecture is based on the IEEE 802.2 and 802.5 standards.

Figure 4-13: X.25 as an SAA Data Link

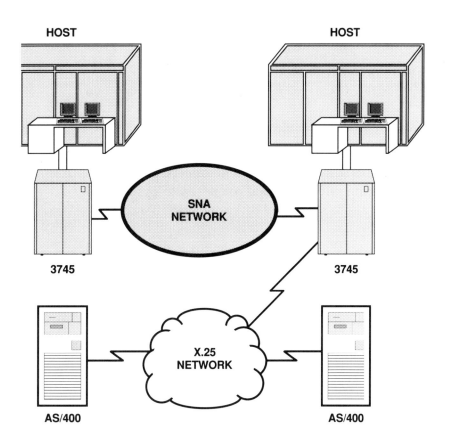

The third data link, X.25, is a CCITT (International Telegraph and Telephone Consultative Committee) standard for connecting computers and terminals to packet data networks. IBM has defined standard protocols for interfacing SNA networks to X.25. These protocols are documented in an IBM manual entitled *The X.25 Interface for Attaching SNA Nodes to Packet-Switched Data Networks: General Information*.

Using the SNA-X.25 interface, the packet data network typically appears as a series of conventional leased or switched lines to the SNA network. The interface contains the Qualified Logical Link Control (QLLC) protocol, which carries packetized SNA protocols transparently through the X.25 network. QLLC is supported in System/370, AS/400, and OS/2 Extended Edition.

Data Streams

CCS provides substantial services for formatting data:

- *3270 data stream* for non-intelligent display terminals and printers
- *Document Content Architecture (DCA)* for word processing documents and electronic mail
- *Intelligent Printer Data Stream (IPDS)* for electronic page printing

The 3270 data stream contains data, attributes, and orders for controlling and formatting information on IBM 3270 display terminals and printers. It has been a standard method of communicating with terminals connected to System/370 mainframes since the early 1970s and is supported by virtually all IBM computers including AS/400 and PS/2.

Document Content Architecture (DCA) defines the representation of a text document. It allows documents to be exchanged between dissimilar word processors and other office systems software. IBM supports DCA in nearly all recent word processing, electronic mail, and office automation products. It also has become an unofficial standard for document interchange among non-IBM word processing vendors, including Word Perfect, Microsoft, WANG, and DEC.

Intelligent Printer Data Stream (IPDS) is a page definition language that communicates with all-points-addressable (APA) printers. It handles pages containing high quality text, raster images, vector graphics, and bar codes. IPDS allows pages to contain a mixture of these elements, thereby easily printing *compound documents*. IPDS is IBM's equivalent to page definition languages, such as Xerox's Interpress and Adobe's PostScript. IPDS is most popular today in System/370 environments, but also operates in the other SAA environments.

Application Services

CCS offers three sets of application services:

- *SNA Distribution Services (SNADS)* Store-and-forward transmission of files and documents
- *Document Interchange Architecture (DIA)* Exchange of electronic mail and documents between office automation products
- *Distributed Data Management* Transparent access to files located on a remote system

SNA Distribution Services (SNADS) distributes data within an SNA network using a store-and-forward methodology and a decentralized user directory. Essentially, SNADS is a standard file transfer protocol for SNA. Its main application is within office systems products for document distribution and electronic mail. SNADS uses APPC and is implemented in DISOSS/370 (Distributed Office Support System), AS/400, and various office products.

Document Interchange Architecture (DIA) defines the protocols and data streams to exchange documents and messages through an electronic mail network. DIA has services for sending and receiving messages or documents, filing documents in a library, searching the library, and running applications that create or print documents. The architecture is implemented in DISOSS/370, Office-Vision/400, and Personal Services/PC.

Distributed Data Management (DDM) provides services for sharing files between systems across a network. It is conceptually similar to shared file systems provided by other vendors, such as Sun's Network File System (NFS). Typically DDM application programs are unaware that data is being accessed via the network. Applications use normal file access functions provided by the local operating system (such as read, insert, delete, and rewrite records).

Common Applications

IBM is developing Common Applications to satisfy general customer needs across all SAA environments. Initially, the development effort is focusing on office automation and application program development tools. Later, it will expand into industry-specific applications, marketed as integrated families of products. The office applications include document processing, document library, electronic mail, and personal productivity packages. For many years, IBM has been marketing products that address these needs, including Distributed Office Support System (DISOSS), which partially conforms to SAA, and Professional Office System (PROFS), which does not.

In SAA's first three years, IBM announced two major Common Applications. The office product family, OfficeVision, is the successor to PROFS, AS/400 Office, and related products. The AD/Cycle product family provides software development tools and a repository for central management of the application development process.

The manner in which IBM introduced these products suggests that Common Applications might be the most strategically significant area of SAA in the long term. It signals IBM's emergence as a major player in the applications software market. However, competing vendors could also release their own Common Applications, perhaps on non-IBM hardware, by conforming to the CUA, CCS, and CPI.

Chapter 5

PC and PS/2 Environments

At its debut in 1981, not many people imagined that the IBM Personal Computer would reshape the landscape of computing for the next decade. The PC was a modest computer, part of a routine product announcement by the world's largest computer maker. Yet, it defined the architecture that quickly spread throughout the computing world.

During the 1980s, IBM extended the PC product line using its traditional marketing strategies and tactics. They added newer and more powerful models, as the product's popularity soared. When third-party vendors successfully marketed clone PCs, IBM created a successor product line, the Personal System/2, which was more difficult to clone. It isn't surprising that most PS/2s can support the SAA environment, while most PCs and clones can't.

PC Product Evolution

To develop the PC in less than two years, IBM used ordinary off-the-shelf parts. While this approach is common among small computer makers, it is unusual for IBM. It was easy for third-party companies to build accessories and add-on circuit boards, thereby making the machine more useful and popular; on the other hand, the simple design was easy to imitate, which led to the development of clones. Such competition yielded a wide range of powerful, easy-to-use, and inexpensive machines from many vendors.

IBM Personal Computer

IBM designed the PC around a 16-bit CPU architecture, though most microcomputers previously had 8-bit CPUs. The company selected the Intel 8088 microprocessor, similar to the popular Intel 8086 that was introduced in 1978. The 8088 contains a single chip arithmetic and logic unit, which has 16-bit registers and an 8-bit data bus interface. Using a segmented addressing technique, the PC could access up to one megabyte of memory. IBM obtained the operating system, Disk Operating System (DOS) version 1.0, from Microsoft.

The PC is a desktop unit with a separate keyboard and video display unit. Printers, modems, and other devices are connected to the system, via cables, through adapter boards that are plugged into expansion slots on the system board. The system board contains up to 256K bytes of dynamic RAM (random access memory), a DMA (direct memory access) controller, an eight-level interrupt controller, a system clock, and a keyboard controller. The PC has a socket for an Intel 8087 numeric co-processor and has five expansion slots for the adapter boards mentioned above. Such expansion slots may also contain boards with additional memory.

During the next 18 months, competitors began to produce machines that were nearly 100 percent compatible with the PC. Some manufacturers improved on the design by offering more memory, extra I/O ports, and other features on the system board. They beefed up the PC's wimpy 63.5 watt power supply and began to offer hard disks. A few companies, including Compaq Computer Corporation, built an excellent reputation for providing the features that customers wanted. This put pressure on IBM.

IBM responded by releasing the Personal Computer XT in 1983. Although the XT has the same 8088 microprocessor, operating at the same clock rate, it has a 10 megabyte hard disk, eight expansion slots, and a 130 watt power supply. While the XT corrected the PC's major shortcomings, competitors had no trouble surpassing it. The XT's market leadership was very short.

IBM also released an improved operating system, DOS 2.0, which may have been more important than the XT itself. The new DOS supported hard disks through an enhanced file system with a tree-structured directory. The PC software business grew rapidly, and the power of word processor, spreadsheet, and database packages improved dramatically.

Figure 5-1: IBM Personal Computer XT

IBM Personal Computer AT

In 1984, IBM introduced a new machine that represented a major advance in technology. The AT was the first PC to use the 80286 microprocessor, which was introduced by Intel in 1982. The 80286 has a 16-bit instruction set and a 16-bit bus. When operating in *real mode*, it is compatible with the 8088, and thus allows a one megabyte address space. It also has a protected mode, with a one gigabyte virtual address space, which can reside in 16 megabytes of physical memory.

During the next two years, IBM improved the AT by raising the clock speed from six MHz to eight MHz, increasing the capacity of the hard disk to 30 megabytes, and enhancing the keyboard. IBM introduced the Enhanced Graphics Adapter (EGA), which provides high-resolution text and graphics (640 by 350 pixels, 16 colors). The AT and EGA quickly became standards in the corporate microcomputer market.

Compaq and many other vendors followed IBM in manufacturing 80286 machines. These machines improved on IBM's design, often at a lower price. Many knowledgeable corporate buyers preferred AT-compatibles to PC-compatibles. Although the market grew rapidly, some vendors couldn't keep up with the pace. This led to an industry shakeout, and many companies didn't survive.

Compaq Deskpro 386

Compaq not only survived, it prospered. In 1986, Compaq beat IBM in introducing the next generation of microprocessors, the 80386. The Compaq Deskpro 386 defined the category of the most powerful AT-compatible computers, offering five to 10 times the performance of the original AT.

Figure 5-2: Microprocessor Addressing Capacity

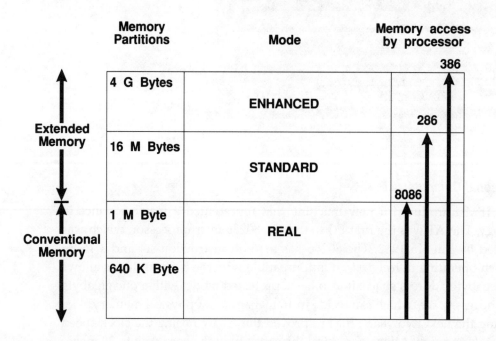

Announced by Intel in 1985, the 32-bit 80386 is upwardly compatible with the 80286 and 8088. The 80386 allows a virtual address space of up to 64 terabytes, with physical memory of up to four gigabytes and it also has a virtual 8086 mode, which allows simultaneous execution of multiple programs written for the Intel 8086 or 8088. Virtual machine technology, built into the microprocessor, isolates these programs from each other.

Unfortunately, the standard DOS operating system can't take advantage of the full power of the 80286, not to mention the 80386. The one megabyte addressing of the 8088 limits DOS's potential. While some software products take advantage of the latest generation of microprocessors, most are limited in complexity because they must run under DOS. The pace of operating system improvements has lagged behind the hardware innovations.

The IBM Personal System/2

Less than a month after the SAA announcement, IBM introduced the PS/2 computer family on April 2, 1987. Rumors had circulated within the PC industry for many months that IBM was ready to unleash the "clone killer." Although it didn't kill many clones, the PS/2 contained many surprises.

The most controversial surprise was the new Micro Channel Architecture (MCA) bus. MCA is incompatible with the AT bus, and therefore cannot use the same expansion boards. IBM announced a new generation of peripherals, expansion boards, and video displays designed for the new computer. Not all PS/2 models use MCA; the least expensive models still use the AT bus.

Another surprise was Video Graphics Array (VGA), a new display system, which has all the ingredients of a successful IBM innovation:

- Compatibility will previous standards (MDA, CGA, and EGA)
- New and better functions
- Reasonable cost
- Compatibility with existing hardware

VGA improves graphic resolution to 640 by 480 pixels and allows up to 256 colors on the screen, selected from a palette of 262,144 colors. IBM introduced a new family of displays, specifically for use with VGA. (Older IBM displays didn't work with VGA.) Even though VGA was only a modest improvement, it quickly became the standard for nearly all major vendors.

All PS/2 models have 3.5" diskette drives. Although Apple pioneered these drives a few years earlier, IBM was the first to offer them in PC-compatibles.

Despite their small size and excellent durability, the 3.5" diskettes created media compatibility headaches for many customers. IBM made the problem worse by providing a feeble 5.25" external drive that couldn't handle high-density diskettes properly. While some PC clone manufacturers followed IBM's lead by offering 3.5" drives as standard equipment, many have not.

The PS/2 family initially had four models: 30, 50, 60, and 80. The model 30 has an Intel 8086 processor, uses the AT bus, and provides better performance at a lower cost than the XT. Models 50, 60, and 80 represent the brave new world of the Micro Channel, which is supposed to offer big advantages, especially for the future. Models 30 and 50 are desktop machines, but models 60 and 80 have compact floor-standing cases. The model 50 uses an 80286 microprocessor and offers performance similar to an AT.

Figure 5-3: PS/2 Models 30, 50, 60, and 80

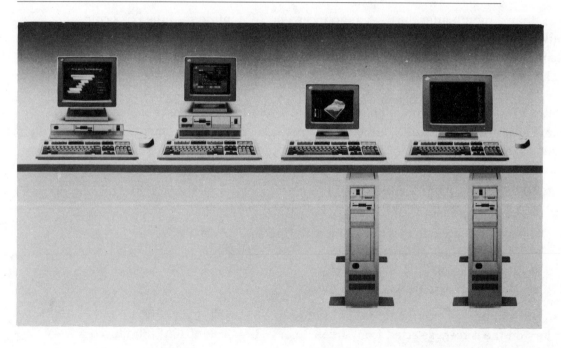

Entry-level PS/2 models

Later, the model 25, which was functionally similar to the model 30, integrated the display into the system unit. Its styling slightly resembles the Apple Macintosh. IBM targeted this model for schools and students; it is priced accordingly.

The model 30's successor, the model 30 286, has an Intel 80286 microprocessor, and offers better performance than an AT. The 30 286, introduced in 1989, keeps the AT bus alive in the IBM product line. This machine was IBM's response to the continued strong market for AT-compatibles. Five years after the AT's introduction, it still defines the most popular class of hardware for general corporate use.

Mainstream PS/2 models

IBM promoted the model 50 as the replacement for the AT. The processor is an Intel 80286, operating at 10 MHz, which is faster than the AT. Although the model 50 is compatible with most software designed for the AT, its internal architecture is much different. The model 50's Achilles heel is its 20 megabyte hard disk, which was too small and too slow. The model 50 probably isn't sufficient to run an SAA environment.

The model 50Z, introduced in 1988, fixed the major shortcomings of the model 50. IBM improved CPU performance by eliminating wait states for access to memory—hence, the "Z" in the model number means "zero wait states." IBM also offered the customer a choice between 30 and 60 megabyte hard disks, both of which were faster than the model 50's disk. The model 55SX uses the Intel 80386SX microprocessor, but otherwise is similar to the 50Z. Many observers regard the 55SX as the entry-level machine for SAA.

The floor standing model 60 went beyond the AT in expandability and performance. Like the model 50, it contains an 80286 operating at 10 MHz, but it offers more disk capacity and more MCA expansion slots. The model 65SX used the 80386SX microprocessor, thereby eclipsing the model 60.

IBM introduced the desktop model 70 386 in 1988. As the name suggests, this machine features an 80386 processor. Although the model 80 is considered the top of the PS/2 line, the model 70 is the speed king. This machine is ideal as a workstation for sophisticated users, and it may be a good choice for an SAA workstation.

IBM also markets an upgrade to the model 70 that includes an 80486 processor. IBM was the first vendor to introduce the 80486, but the company offered it only as an add-on circuit board to the model 70. The CPU performance of this machine is at the forefront of PC technology, but its I/O performance is no better than other top-of-the-line machines. Both the performance and packaging of the 486 version of this product limit its usefulness in the short term.

The model P70 represents the third generation of IBM portable computers. It weighs about 20 pounds and has an orange gas plasma display that supports VGA graphics. The P70's performance is competitive with other leading 80386-based portable PCs.

The model 80 is a floor standing system that uses an 80386 processor. It looks almost identical to a model 60, and it offers less CPU power than the fastest model 70. However, its greater disk capacity and expandability make it suitable as a file server, communication server, or a high-powered workstation.

PC Software

Many observers believe that application software has been the driving force behind the rapid growth of the Personal Computer business. The quick acceptance of spreadsheet software, first VisiCalc from Software Arts, then Lotus 1-2-3, was a major contributor to the PC's success. PCs have all but replaced dedicated word processing machines and have begun to do some of the work previously reserved for minicomputers and mainframes.

The most successful application software packages have been built for DOS, which is used on almost all PCs. Although it is a very significant operating system, *DOS isn't included in SAA*, perhaps because of its limitations, which fall into two major categories.

First, DOS conforms to the 8086/8088 architecture, and thus is subject to the hardware's one megabyte addressing limit. DOS restricts part of this address space, further reducing application memory to less than 640K bytes. Even when DOS is running on an 80286 or 80386, the addressing limit is still a problem. Many software products hit this limit, and while there are many ways of working around the problem, such techniques are awkward and inefficient.

Second, DOS normally executes one task at a time. A complex application might need to do *multiprogramming*, which allows several tasks to proceed in parallel. An application designer can create the illusion of multiprogramming under DOS, but this is awkward. Multiprogramming operating systems, such as UNIX, can do the job more easily and reliably.

UNIX, developed by AT&T, is a powerful alternative to DOS. IBM offers the AIX PS/2 operating system to customers who want UNIX compatibility. However, this system operates only on models 70 and 80, and is not included in SAA. Operating System/2 Extended Edition, announced with the PS/2, provides the SAA environment on selected PS/2s and PCs.

Disk Operating System (DOS)

DOS has been the primary PC operating system since the introduction of the PC. Although IBM initially offered PC versions of CP/M-86 and the UCSD p-system, users and software developers preferred DOS and it quickly became the standard PC operating system. It ran in 8K bytes of memory, and consisted of 4,000 lines of assembly language code.

IBM licensed DOS version 1.0 from Microsoft, which derived the operating system from SCP-DOS (according to rumor, its nickname was QDOS, Quick and Dirty Operating System). Microsoft licensed SCP-DOS from Seattle Computer Products. SCP-DOS was similar to Digital Research's CP/M-80, which was a popular operating system for 8-bit microprocessors used by hobbyists. CP/M evolved from early minicomputer operating systems.

Microsoft made DOS 1.0 highly compatible with CP/M-80. This was important because Microsoft wanted to make it as easy as possible to move existing microcomputer software to the PC. In hindsight, this decision was excellent from a business standpoint, but it eventually created technical nightmares. Future DOS versions had to be upwardly compatible with version 1.0; many old kludges had to be preserved.

DOS has a simple file system and I/O services for standard PC devices, including the diskette drive, keyboard, screen, and printer. The system has a command processor, called COMMAND.COM, which contains commands for routine functions such as copying, deleting, and renaming files. The command processor also loads and executes external programs, which do other utility functions, such as copying entire disks or formatting disks. Users could store predefined lists of commands, called batch files, which are useful for non-interactive functions, such as installing software.

DOS version 1.0 supported only diskette-based systems. A disk contained only one directory with a maximum of 64 files. This limitation was acceptable for the original PC because diskettes held a maximum of 180K bytes of data. A hard disk, however, holds much more than 64 files; having them all in one directory would be a mess.

In DOS 2.0, Microsoft developed a hierarchical file system. The first directory is the **root**, which contains files and other directories. A directory, in turn, may contain files and a tree-structured set of sub-directories. Microsoft also added a new I/O interface, and other UNIX-like features, such as I/O redirection and background printing. Installable device drivers, loaded during system startup, enabled DOS to work with third-party hardware devices without modifying the operating system.

When IBM released DOS 3.0 with the AT, everyone recognized that it didn't represent the great leap forward in technology that the AT did. The new features of DOS 3.0 were minor, including support for high density 5.25" diskettes, international keyboards and character sets, and a RAM disk driver. Four months later, DOS 3.1 added support for local area networks. Although this seemed unremarkable at the time, it became important when networks grew popular a few years later.

DOS 3.3 was released with the PS/2. As with DOS 3.2, it offered few remarkable new features. IBM continues to sell DOS 3.3 and it remains popular. DOS 4.0, which has a new user interface and supports very large hard disks, was not successful initially because of compatibility problems and bugs. Version 4.0 was the first time IBM enhanced DOS without help from Microsoft.

DOS incorporates 1970's technology, but now the product has gone through nearly a decade of evolution. It has an enormous software base, which grew at an unprecedented rate and created an entire industry. Although DOS is a good match for the power of many PCs, it doesn't take advantage of the full architecture of 80286, 80386, or 80486 machines. Many people at IBM, Microsoft, and in the user community thought that DOS's successor should be a "clean sheet of paper" design.

Operating System/2

IBM offers OS/2 in two editions. OS/2 Standard Edition contains only the OS/2 base operating system and the Presentation Manager, which provides a graphical user interface. Standard Edition is not a complete SAA environment. OS/2 Extended Edition, shown in figure 5-4, has all the features of Standard Edition plus communications, database, and query managers. Extended Edition promotes two-tiered cooperative processing, which puts an application's user interface on the PC, and executes major functions on the mainframe. IBM says Extended Edition will run on the IBM AT and PS/2 models with 80286 or 80386 microprocessors. In the real world, the minimum is a PS/2 model 55SX but, more realistically, a model 70 or 80. The operating system alone fills an entire 20 megabyte disk.

Figure 5-4: OS/2 Standard vs. Extended Edition

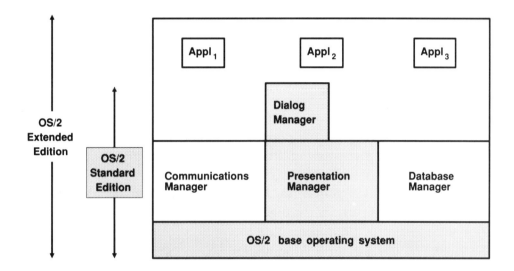

OS/2 Extended Edition follows an increasingly common marketing formula:

- Bundle the base operating system with a relational database, query facility, and communication features
- Promote the product as an essential part of SAA
- Price it below the sum of its parts

Until the last decade, IBM always maintained total control of the operating systems for its computers. But Microsoft developed DOS and OS/2 Standard Edition as part of a joint IBM/Microsoft effort. IBM developed the communications and database managers of Extended Edition; hence, IBM controls the parts of Extended Edition that qualify it as an SAA environment.

Developing Corporate Applications on PCs

Past IBM efforts to promote PCs for big corporate applications were ineffective. Some products, including TopView and the 3270 Personal Computer, were ill-conceived from a design standpoint and thus failed in the marketplace. IBM's latest response better addresses real customer needs and reflects the lessons learned from earlier products.

Developing complex corporate applications for the PC wasn't entirely practical under DOS. Such applications tend to be constrained by the operating system's 640K limit. Communications functions for mainframe connectivity also gobble up memory, often requiring applications to fit in less than 200K bytes. Furthermore, DOS does not offer the functions of *application enabling subsystems* such as CICS, IMS, or ISPF, which simplify an application's access to data and terminals.

OS/2 addresses this set of problems. Its 16 megabyte address space and multitasking features allow for truly large applications without forcing programmers to use overlays or expanded memory schemes. Unlike DOS, OS/2 has sufficient addressing capacity to run complex communication software without constraining large application programs. The Presentation Manager and the OS/2 Dialog Manager provide nearly all the functions of mainframe application enabling subsystems.

OS/2 expands the usefulness of the PS/2 by allowing it to work effectively as a communication, database, and application server. Although these functions are possible under DOS, they usually are awkward and perform poorly. OS/2 provides the foundation for future use of intelligent communications subsystems, in which a separate, dedicated processor handles communication protocols.

OS/2's inclusion in SAA offers real benefits to both IBM customers and third-party application developers. The consistent user interface defined by Common User Access simplifies learning new applications and reduces training costs. The standard programming interface encourages portable applications, letting a vendor develop one software product and market it for several IBM computer environments. The combination of the SAA programming interface and SAA communication features creates the foundation for cooperative processing applications.

Structure of OS/2 Extended Edition

The technology of OS/2 Extended Edition is similar to minicomputer and mainframe operating systems. The system has four major components: OS/2 base operating system, Presentation Manager, Database Manager, and Communications Manager. The base operating system and the Presentation Manager are the same as OS/2 Standard Edition, except for modifications to improve performance of communication and database functions.

Although many PC clone vendors offer OS/2 Standard Edition, only IBM provides OS/2 Extended Edition. IBM doesn't guarantee that Extended Edition will run on non-IBM computers. Nevertheless, it does operate on some clones. Customers who buy non-IBM personal computers take the risk that they won't be able to run true SAA environments on their machines.

The Database Manager uses the same Structured Query Language (SQL) interface as IBM's mainframe Data Base 2 (DB2) or SQL/DS software. The OS/2 Query Manager is strikingly similar to the mainframe Query Management Facility (QMF). Applications programs written in COBOL or C can use the services of the database and query managers directly, through the Applications Programming Interfaces (APIs). Pascal, which is not part of SAA, is also supported. Remote Data Services allow the Database Manager to access data residing on another workstation by using the services of Communications Manager over a local area network.

The Communications Manager contains many important features of IBM's Systems Network Architecture (SNA), including 3270 terminal emulation, file transfer, Server-Requester Programming Interface (SRPI), and Advanced Program to Program Communications (APPC). IBM 5250 terminal emulation, although not included in SAA, can be used with IBM mid-range computers. The Communications Manager supports the Token-Ring local area network, including the IEEE 802.2 and 802.5 data link control standards. The Communications Manager also supports other non-SAA protocols, such as NETBIOS and asynchronous terminal emulation for the DEC VT100 and IBM 3101. IBM supplies APIs for all communication protocols.

Aside from database query, terminal emulation, file transfer, and system administration, users must access Extended Edition functions through APIs. These APIs are crucial, because they support important cooperative processing applications. Many features of Extended Edition are not useful or accessible to the average end user. Hence, Extended Edition is mainly a run-time environment for complex corporate applications.

OS/2 Base Operating System

The OS/2 base operating system is the foundation of both OS/2 Extended Edition and Standard Edition. It is a single user, multiprogramming operating system for use on 80286, 80386, and 80486 personal computers. It works with all the IBM PC and PS/2 products that contain those microprocessors. It doesn't work with 8088 or 8086 machines, such as the PS/2 model 25. IBM doesn't guarantee that its versions of OS/2 will operate correctly with other AT-compatible computers, such as those made by Compaq. Some manufacturers, including Compaq, offer their own OS/2 versions.

OS/2 allows concurrent execution of many large programs. It takes advantage of the improved memory architecture of the 80286 processor. The OS/2 base operating system offers many new features:

- Multiprogramming
- Improved I/O services
- High level Applications Programming Interfaces (APIs)
- DOS compatibility
- SAA support

Multiprogramming

The most remarkable feature is OS/2's ability to run many large applications, each using more than 640K bytes of memory. OS/2 allows multiple sessions, and each session is an independent application. Hence, a user can start a word processor in one session, a compiler in a second session, and a terminal emulation program in a third. OS/2's memory management and multiprogramming functions isolate these programs from each other.

Like most modern operating systems, OS/2 has the multi-layer structure illustrated in Figure 5-5. Application programs constitute the top layer. They rely upon Application Programming Interfaces (APIs) (stored in Dynamic Link Libraries), which form the layer immediately below the applications. The kernel, which provides most operating system services, is below the APIs and uses device drivers as the hardware interface. For example, device drivers control the display, hard disk, and serial ports. Users and software developers can write their own APIs and device drivers, but they can't touch the kernel.

Figure 5-5: OS/2 Operating System Structure

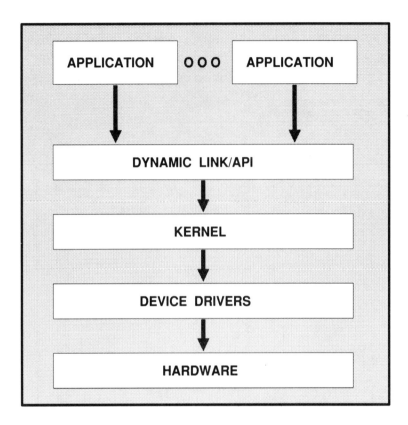

An application can be divided into multiple processes, which operate concurrently within a session. A process is an executing program and all the system resources, such as memory and files, that are assigned to it. Multiple processes can work independently, or they can cooperate by sharing data among themselves.

Processes contain *threads*, which are the basic units of work that are scheduled on the CPU. All the threads in a process automatically share the same memory and files. Figure 5-6 shows the relationships among sessions, processes, and threads. OS/2's Interprocess Communication (IPC) functions allow cooperation and synchronization between processes and threads, which the OS/2 Scheduler manages. IPC includes:

- *Pipes*   Pass information between processes and resemble files
- *Queues*   Allow more complex data structures than pipes
- *Semaphores*   Provide data objects that tell which thread is in control of a serially-usable resource. Semaphores insure that only one thread at a time modifies a critical resource
- *Signals*   Notify processes that an event has occurred

Figure 5-6: Sessions, Processes, and Threads

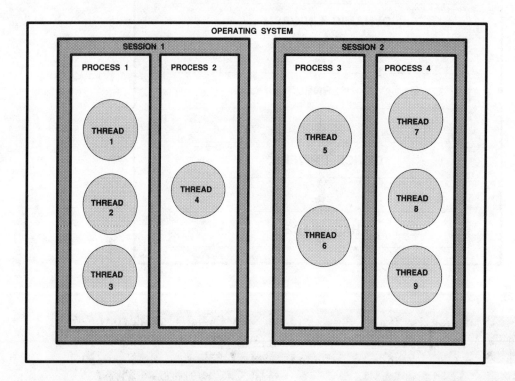

Application Programming Interfaces

Application Programming Interfaces (APIs) didn't originate with OS/2, but they are so prominent that they are impossible to ignore. The idea is very simple: provide a formal means for an application to request services from the operating system. In OS/2, APIs are always subroutine calls with parameters, rather than the software interrupts used by DOS.

OS/2's APIs are much easier to use than DOS's software interrupts. Programmers invoke DOS services through assembly language, but they access OS/2 functions simply by executing a CALL statement in a higher level language. The CALL passes control to a system program, which does the requested function and returns to the calling program. The procedure for calling the operating system is the same as calling an application's own subroutines.

The OS/2 system routines called by an application are automatically linked when the application is loaded. This *load-time dynamic linking* technique saves memory because routines are only loaded when needed and several programs can use the same copy of a routine. It saves disk space because copies of routinely-used functions aren't kept in executable files of applications. OS/2 routines are stored in dynamic link libraries (dynlinks or DLLs), which are easy to replace or expand.

Figure 5-7: Static vs. Load-Time Dynamic Linking

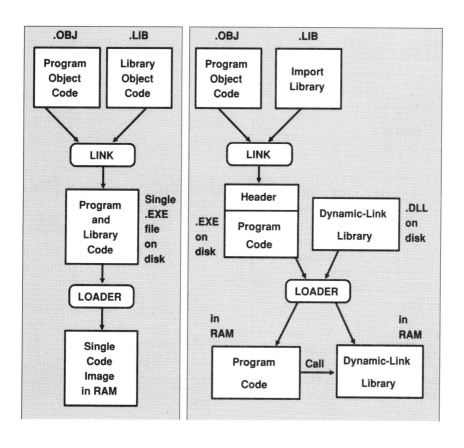

Applications designed for OS/2 usually don't operate under DOS. However, OS/2 offers a *Family API*, which works under both DOS and OS/2. Programs that use only the Family API will run under both operating systems. This API contains very limited services, which are useful mainly for utility software such as compilers, linkers, and very simple applications.

I/O Services

From a programmer's viewpoint, OS/2 has all the services offered by DOS plus many others. The standard file system is compatible with DOS, so users can easily switch between the two operating systems. OS/2 I/O services are easy to call from application programs and they operate like ordinary subroutines. These services are structured as APIs, which are stored in dynamic link libraries. Video, keyboard, mouse, and file system APIs each have a separate DLL.

Figure 5-8: OS/2 Device Drivers

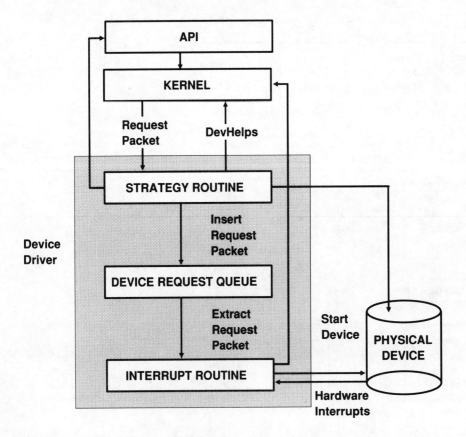

Device drivers in OS/2 are more complex than their DOS counterparts. They are interrupt-driven and they interact with the operating system kernel in complex ways. Because OS/2 has a DOS compatibility mode, all device drivers must work with both OS/2 and DOS applications. OS/2 device drivers have two different modes: one for character devices, such as keyboards, and another for block devices, such as disks.

OS/2 applications don't use the Basic Input/Output Support (BIOS) functions built into all PCs and compatibles. Only applications running in DOS compatibility mode use BIOS. Some PS/2 models also have Advanced BIOS (ABIOS), which supports OS/2 multiprogramming features and can be called directly from device drivers. Although ABIOS is not necessary for running OS/2, it reduces memory requirements for device drivers. OS/2 device drivers must be small and reliable, because they share the first 640K of addressable memory with DOS applications.

DOS Compatibility

In designing OS/2, IBM and Microsoft paid much attention to making the operating system run older DOS programs. The goal was to run nearly all DOS applications, regardless of whether they followed DOS programming rules exactly. Many applications "cheat" and bypass DOS services, for example, by writing directly to the screen buffers or by supplying their own interrupt handlers. Applications do this because many DOS services are weak or perform poorly. Hence, it is impossible to achieve 100 percent DOS compatibility while providing 100 percent integrity under OS/2.

The first OS/2 versions represent compromises in compatibility. The command language is nearly identical to its DOS counterpart. OS/2 runs many popular DOS programs, but requires customers to read the fine print about its limitations, which are:

- DOS device drivers don't work under OS/2. If a software product requires a driver, the vendor must furnish an OS/2 device driver.
- Applications that are time-dependent, such as communications software, don't always operate reliably.
- Certain mouse interfaces don't work under OS/2, and it isn't possible to share the mouse between OS/2 and most DOS applications.
- Misbehavior or failure of a DOS application could cause the entire OS/2 system to fail.

- DOS programs run about 10 percent slower than they would on a DOS 3.3 system
- At least 80K fewer bytes of memory are available to the application under OS/2's DOS compatibility mode than under DOS 3.3.

Figure 5-9: OS/2 Addressing and DOS Compatibility

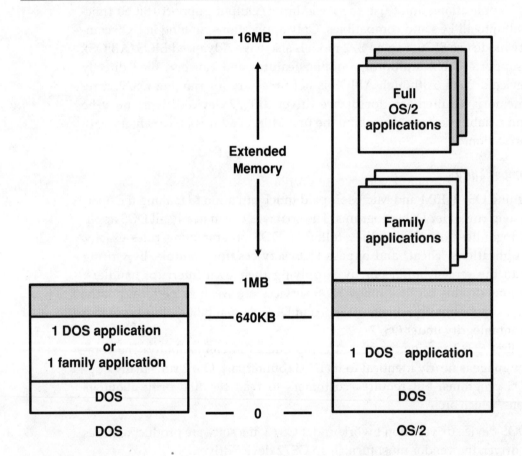

SAA Facilities

OS/2 provides an SAA-compatible user interface, which simplifies application execution, file management, and other routine tasks. OS/2 also preserves the command line interface of DOS. A help facility, accessible from menus or the command line, provides information about system functions and error messages.

OS/2 contains an interactive tutorial, which remains on the user's hard disk. The operating system supports SAA tools including the Dialog Manager and compilers such as C/2, FORTRAN/2, and COBOL/2.

The OS/2 Presentation Manager, which complies with SAA guidelines, is the major attempt to improve ease of use. Users select applications and functions using a "point and click" approach, rather than entering complex commands and operands. OS/2 lets the user view application output through multiple overlapping windows on the screen. The application controls such windows, and they can be moved, stretched, or removed from the screen by the user. Data entry requires a "fill in the blanks" approach through dialog boxes and pop-up windows.

OS/2 Presentation Manager

OS/2's graphical user interface, which resembles Microsoft Windows and the Apple Macintosh, is derived from research originally done by Xerox Corporation. This type of interface has become common in the computer industry, and is widely believed to simplify a person's interaction with a computer. Its main technical advance is that the user's screen continuously displays all-points-addressable (APA) graphics, and any program can use graphic elements at any time. Besides displaying graphics, Presentation Manager also stores, prints, and moves graphic objects between applications.

The Presentation Manager imposes some rules and restrictions on the use of the display, keyboard, and mouse. The product contains standard procedures for handling menus, requesting help, ending the application, and scrolling lists of items. This insures consistency among Presentation Manager applications. It also insures some consistency across IBM product lines, because SAA Common User Access standardizes many of these procedures.

When the Presentation Manager starts, the user interface shell appears on the screen. It manages both applications that run under the Presentation Manager, as well as programs that run separately (for example, Communications Manager or Query Manager). This shell contains:

- *Task manager* Selects applications and switches between running programs
- *Filing system* Lets users view and manage disk drives, directories, and files. It includes a window that loads and executes programs
- *Clipboard* Moves information between applications
- *Help facility* Gives information about using the shell

- *Startup editor* Creates lists of available applications, including prompts and icons that appear on the screen
- *Control panel* Sets system parameters such as cursor blink and double click specifications

Figure 5-10: Presentation Manager Screen Appearance

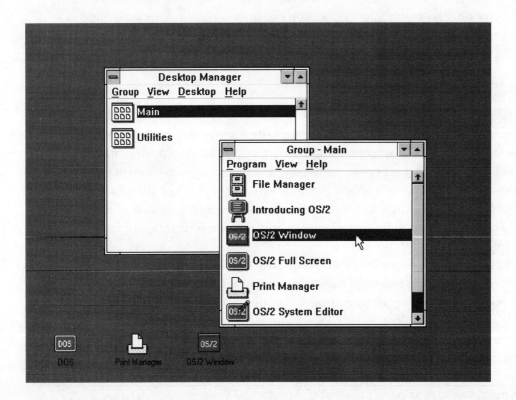

The Presentation Manager's API has the same structure as the other OS/2 APIs, but contains many complex routines. It allows applications to communicate with the keyboard, screen, mouse, printer, and other devices. It draws graphics, selects elaborate fonts, handles scanned images, and creates dialog boxes for data entry. The API is so complex that the classic 4-line "hello, world" sample program for the C language is five pages long in its Presentation Manager version.

Figure 5-11: Presentation Manager Structure

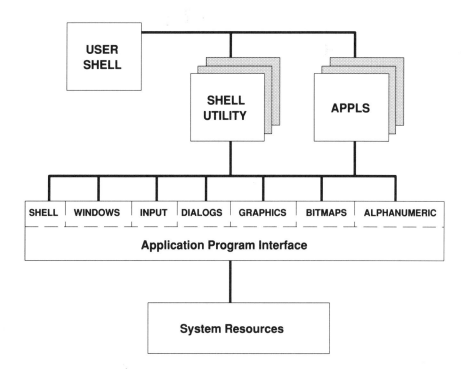

While this amount of coding might seem excessive, it could be worthwhile for complex applications because Presentation Manager programs are *device independent*. This means that the programs can be moved to different graphics hardware without any changes to the application. Ideally, all changes would be confined to the device driver, which would be furnished by the hardware vendor. Hence, a software vendor would not need to support the dozen or so graphic standards available in the marketplace, but instead could concentrate on application issues.

OS/2 Communications Manager

Communications Manager covers the bases in mainframe connectivity. Services include terminal emulation, file transfer, server/client relationships, and peer-to-peer program conversations. It supports the expected IBM features including:

- 3270 data stream
- Server-Requester Programming Interface (SRPI)
- Advanced Program to Program Communications (APPC)
- Network Basic Input/Output System (NETBIOS)
- Asynchronous communications
- 5250 terminal emulation

Communications Manager allows three types of data links:

- Conventional wide area network connections using synchronous or asynchronous modems
- IEEE 802.2/802.5 local area networks (LANs)
- CCITT X.25 packet data network interface

All these functions have been available under DOS. So what is unique about Communications Manager? The simple answer is: packaging and integration. In OS/2, IBM has provided consistent sets of Applications Programming Interfaces (APIs) for each of the major communication protocols. Like the other OS/2 APIs, they can be called directly from any application. Communications functions thus are more accessible and better defined. Furthermore, because OS/2 provides a 16 megabyte address space, much larger applications are possible. The memory usage of communication software does not constrain the size of applications.

Customers pay a price for these improvements. The OS/2 base operating system, including the Presentation Manager and DOS compatibility, requires about three megabytes of memory. The Communications Manager base, which is continuously resident, needs about 200K bytes. Each concurrent function (such as APPC, 3270 emulation, asynchronous terminal emulation, and file transfer) requires an additional 300K-400K. With three concurrent communications functions, the operating system alone requires 3.4 megabytes. Add the database and query managers (another 2 megabytes) and one megabyte of application code. Reserve some memory for a disk cache, which will be necessary to speed up I/O. Eight megabytes of memory fill up quickly.

For small applications, four megabytes is a good starting point. In OS/2, running out of memory is not a catastrophe, as it is in DOS. OS/2's virtual memory architecture allows the sum of the memory requirements of applications to exceed the total installed memory. When this occurs, segments are swapped between memory and the hard disk. With OS/2, the good news is that you can run the application, even though it is bigger than your machine. The bad news is that it might run quite slowly. For many communications applications, slow execution is not acceptable; ample memory is essential.

OS/2 Database Manager

Database Manager, a component of Extended Edition, brings both the strengths and weaknesses of mainframe data management to OS/2. It includes a powerful mainframe-like database engine called Database Services, and it also includes a weak Query Manager, which is patterned after Query Management Facility (QMF) on the mainframe. The interface to the database engine is Structured Query Language (SQL), which is part of SAA and is used with other IBM database products. Database Manager structures data according to the relational data model, in which users view data as tables and manipulate data using table operations.

IBM aimed Database Manager at users who are already using mainframe database products. It is very different from traditional microcomputer database managers, such as Ashton-Tate's dBASE III. Unlike such products, Database Manager is intended for professional programmers, and its user interface, Query Manager, is not as comprehensive as the competition. It does allow users to define a database, write rudimentary reports, create panels, and develop simple menu-based applications. However, most substantial applications must be written in a standard programming language, such as COBOL or C.

The database engine has extensive features for building large applications, including:

- A pre-compiler to convert embedded SQL into code acceptable to the C/2 compiler
- A binder to generate access paths to the data for each SQL statement
- Utilities for import and export of data
- Routines to create, delete, and recover databases
- Configuration routines to set system parameters

The Database Services engine allows concurrent access from multiple OS/2 processes, and can do medium-volume transaction processing. While all processes using the database must be on the same machine, IBM promises that distributed database features will be forthcoming. IBM plans to broaden the scope of this product to embrace the new client/server approach. In this model, front-end software, including user interface and application tools, can run on different computers connected over a network. Remote Data Services let the front-ends communicate with the database engine using the Communications Manager.

Figure 5-12: Client/Server Database Architecture

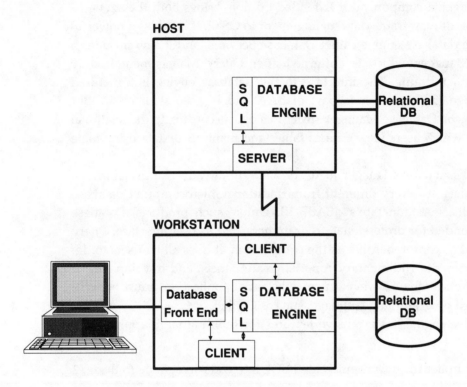

Query Manager is a menu-based interface to the Database Services engine. Users can create and define databases interactively in Query Manager more easily than in embedded SQL. The product also retrieves data, updates tables, defines reports, creates panels, and allows pre-programmed procedures. The format of the screen conforms with SAA Common User Access conventions, but uses a character-based user interface.

Chapter 6

System/370 Mainframe Environments

IBM achieved its 76 percent share of the large system market by providing high quality products that closely meet customer needs. IBM has developed these products over the past 25 years through evolution and stepwise refinement, using a variety of technical and marketing strategies. The products change continuously, and their relationships are complex. These characteristics are most evident in the System/370 product line.

The architecture and features of IBM mainframes are best understood from the historical perspective provided in Chapter 2. IBM developed the main ideas behind today's mainframe computers in the early 1960s. The basic computer architecture for such machines is called System/370, which defines the programming of the IBM 3090, 4300, and 9370 computer families.

System Architecture

System/370 architecture defines the machine language of modern IBM mainframes. From an application developer's viewpoint, the architecture has changed little since 1970. IBM's improvements in operating system and hardware performance have affected systems programmers and data center managers, but not application programmers.

Computer architecture defines the boundary between the processor logic (both hard-wired and microcoded) and the software executed on a machine, including the operating system. Architecture includes the instruction set of the processor, plus the interface between software and all I/O devices attached to the system.

Two computer architecture types are prominent today. Reduced Instruction Set Computers (RISC) have a small repertoire of simple instructions, most of which can be executed in one machine cycle. RISC is a recent innovation that has become popular on minicomputers and workstations. Complex Instruction Set Computers (CISC) have a wide variety of powerful instructions. System/370 is typical of the many CISC implementations available in the marketplace today.

Central Processing Unit

The central processing unit (CPU) performs the processing and control functions of System/370. Most modern implementations of the architecture use microcode to perform many complex instructions. The CPU provides facilities for:

- Addressing real and virtual storage
- Moving data between storage and registers
- Arithmetic and logical processing of data
- Executing instructions in a desired sequence
- Initiating I/O operations

System/370 does binary, decimal, and floating point arithmetic using a 32-bit word. Binary arithmetic can be carried out to 64-bit precision, and floating point numbers can be up to 128 bits long. Application programs use 16 general purpose registers and four floating point registers, which receive data from storage, hold it, and permit it to be operated upon. Such registers are used mainly for binary arithmetic, addressing, and logical operations.

The operating system has access to 16 control registers. These registers cannot be used by application programs. The CPU has an interruption handling function that allows it to respond efficiently to asynchronous events including I/O, virtual memory management, programming errors, and hardware malfunctions. A system may have multiple CPUs, which share a common operating system and workload. Alternatively, the CPUs may be logically or physically partitioned to support multiple operating systems.

Memory

System/370 processor storage sizes usually range from 16 megabytes (mega = 2^{20}, roughly 10^6) to 2 gigabytes (giga = 2^{30}, roughly 10^9). Some System/370 products can be equipped with optional expanded storage of similar size. A customer can select the processor storage size, subject to the limits of a particular machine model. For example, a 9370 model 90 can have a maximum of 16 megabytes of processor storage with no expanded storage, while a typical 3090 may have 256 megabytes of processor storage, plus 512 megabytes of expanded storage.

Figure 6-1: System/370 Storage Hierarchy

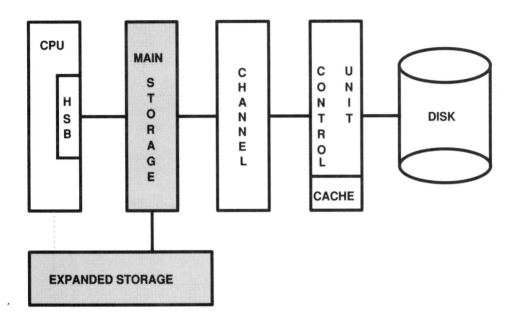

Performance of the storage subsystem depends on storage size, access width, cycle time, interleaving, high speed buffer (HSB) size, and program characteristics:

- *Access width* is the number of bytes transferred between the processor and main memory in each access. As access width increases, the quantity of data that can be transferred per second increases.
- *Cycle time* is the length of time that main storage is busy when it is referenced or changed.
- *Interleaving* is the number of simultaneous storage accesses that can be started in a storage cycle.

- A *High Speed Buffer (HSB)*, sometimes called a *cache*, contains the most recently used portions of processor storage. HSB storage is much faster and smaller than main storage. HSB size, which varies by model, has a great effect on system performance.

Virtual Storage

IBM's virtual storage architecture lets programmers develop programs that use one or more address spaces, each having a virtual storage capacity of 2 gigabytes. The total amount of virtual storage used by programs may exceed the amount of real storage installed on the system. Virtual storage is provided by dynamic address translation (DAT) and channel indirect data addressing, which are controlled by operating system software.

Figure 6-2: Virtual Storage Segments and Pages

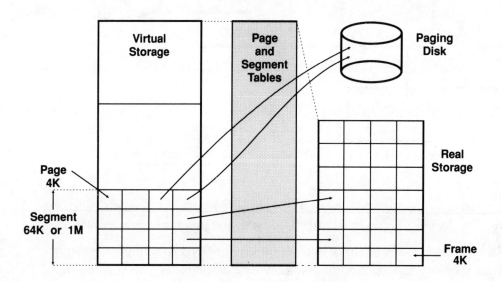

Virtual storage is a two-level structure that encompasses *segments* and *pages*. An address space has multiple segments of either 64 kilobytes or 1 megabyte. Segments usually are divided into pages of 4 kilobytes each; these pages contain instructions, data, or both. Application programs always use *virtual addresses*. The DAT hardware function translates virtual addresses to *real addresses*. When a program accesses a page that is not in processor storage, the operating system moves the page from disk or expanded storage to processor storage.

Input/Output Subsystem

Input/Output operations transfer data between main storage and an I/O device. An I/O operation is started by an instruction (such as Start I/O) that generates a command to a channel. A control unit receives the command via the I/O interface, decodes it, and starts the I/O device. Channels are the direct controllers of I/O devices and control units. They allow System/370 to read, write, and compute in parallel, by relieving the CPU of the task of communicating with I/O devices. Usually channels are physically packaged into the system cabinets.

Channels connect to peripherals through control units. In many peripherals, such as the IBM 3745 communication controller, the control unit is housed in its own cabinet. Other peripherals, including the IBM 3800 laser printer, contain built-in control units that connect directly to a channel. With most System/370 processors, up to eight control units connect to a channel via pairs of heavy *bus and tag cables*. These cables usually are routed below raised floors in a computer room.

Modern System/370 products have two types of channels: block multiplexer and byte multiplexer. A *block multiplexer* channel allows several I/O operations to be pending at any time, but it transfers a block of data to one device at a time, in *burst mode*. Burst mode is used with most devices, including disk and tape cartridge drives. When used with certain old peripherals, a block multiplexer channel operates in *selector mode*, which limits it to one I/O operation at a time.

A *byte multiplexer* channel transfers data to several devices concurrently, but it transmits one byte at a time. This *byte mode* is used by low speed, unbuffered devices such as card readers or IBM 2701, 2702, and 2703 communication adapters. Although byte multiplexer channels are required mainly by old I/O devices, most large System/370 processors have at least one such channel.

Figure 6-3: System/370 I/O Subsystem

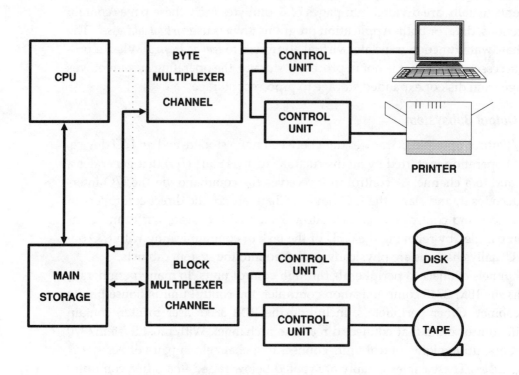

Any channel can be connected to a maximum of 256 devices, but in practice, the number of devices is limited by workload and channel data rates. Byte multiplexer channels operate at 50 kilobytes per second or less, and block multiplexers are limited to 4.5 megabytes per second in current IBM products. System/370 Extended Architecture (XA) permits up to 256 channels to be attached to each system, but most processor models support fewer channels.

Multiple System/370 processors can share the same data using a configuration technique called shared DASD. DASD is the acronym for direct access storage devices, or disks. With shared DASD, each processor is connected via DASD control units to shared strings of disk units. Each shared DASD unit can be accessed by any connected system.

DASD hardware has locking commands (called reserve/release) to protect the integrity of data. Each unit has only one lock, which prevents the hardware from locking individual files or records. This could hurt both performance and reliability, so various schemes in software have been developed to mitigate this problem. Shared DASD is commonplace because there are few efficient alternatives for sharing data at high speeds between different System/370 processor models.

Figure 6-4: Connecting IBM 3390 DASD to Channels

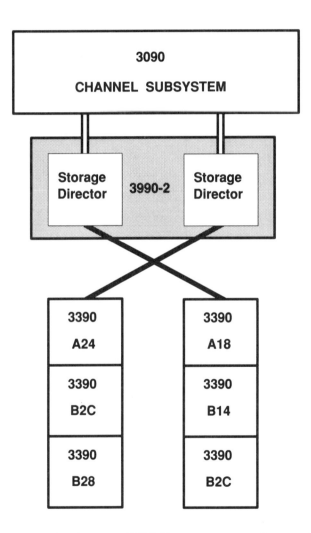

Channel-to-channel adapters (CTCA) connect two System/370 processors, enabling high speed transmission over short distances. Customers use them as an alternative to shared DASD or to circumvent some of shared DASD's limitations. As the name implies, a CTCA connects two block multiplexer channels, and each system appears as an I/O device to the other. The bandwidth of this connection is less than the maximum channel data rate, but can exceed 1 megabyte per second.

Figure 6-5: Shared DASD Architecture

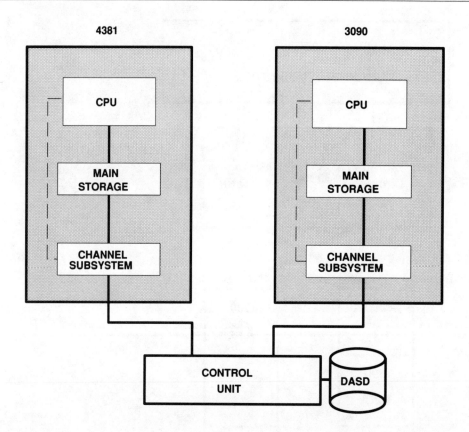

Multiple CTCAs can be attached to a processor, if necessary. The distance between processors is limited to 120 meters, but it can be extended to 2 kilometers, at lower speed, by using an IBM 3044 fiber optic channel extender. CTCAs are often used with communication software such as VTAM.

Multiprocessing

Multiprocessing refers to a system with two or more central processing units (CPUs) that share main storage. This technique became popular in System/370 in the mid 1970s, though it has been technically possible since the 1960s. The largest IBM systems today are multiprocessors, and several IBM computer product lines rely on multiprocessing to achieve high performance.

Multiprocessing offers several benefits:

- Workload is balanced among the CPUs. A single copy of the operating system runs in shared memory and maintains a list of user tasks to be executed. Each CPU selects tasks from this list and dispatches them independently. This strategy minimizes interaction among CPUs and promotes high throughput.
- System availability can be improved by doing maintenance while the system is operating; processing continues while CPUs, storage, channels, control units, and I/O devices are being repaired.
- Many multiprocessor configurations can be partitioned to run multiple independent operating systems.

Figure 6-6: Multiprocessor Architecture (Dyadic)

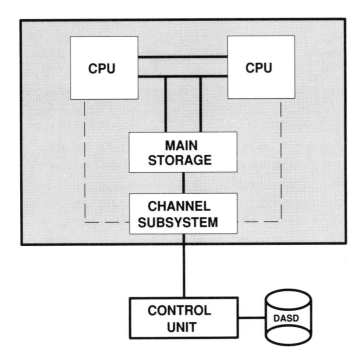

Although shared DASD is an alternative to multiprocessing, it can also be used in a multiple CPU configuration. A customer's application programs usually are not affected by a multiprocessor configuration, but they might be affected by shared DASD. Nevertheless, shared DASD is the only practical approach for customers who have several different System/370 processor models that must share a common pool of data.

Several multiprocessor configurations are possible:

- *Dual processor* systems have two identical CPUs that can be separated into two independent systems.
- *Dyadic* systems contain two equal CPUs in one physical box, with a shared channel subsystem and shared memory. Usually they execute one operating system and cannot be physically partitioned. If one CPU fails, the system can use the remaining CPU while the failed CPU is being repaired.
- *Four-way* processors (sometimes called *quad*) are two connected dyadic systems. Four CPUs can share memory, channels, and one operating system or they can be partitioned into two dyadic systems running two different operating systems.
- *Three-way* and *six-way* processors are variations of the dyadic and quad configurations. A *five-way* processor is a combination of one three-way and one dyadic processor.

Extended Architecture (XA)

In the early 1980s, IBM customers began to reach the limits of System/370 architecture in addressing and I/O. System/370 Extended Architecture (XA) significantly raised these limits. XA introduced a new 31-bit addressing mode, which lets new programs use address spaces of 2 gigabytes. It also has a 24-bit mode for compatibility with older System/370 programs.

IBM improved channel performance by moving some of the I/O scheduling functions from the operating system to microcode in the channel subsystem. XA redefined all I/O instructions, raised the maximum number of channels from 16 to 256, and increased the efficiency of paths between CPUs and I/O devices.

To receive the benefits of XA, a customer had to convert to a new version of the MVS or VM operating system. VSE customers could not use the new architecture. XA is supported only on 3081, 3083, 3084, 3090, and selected 4381 processors.

Enterprise Systems Architecture (ESA)

Even though many customers had not yet converted to XA, IBM introduced Enterprise Systems Architecture (ESA) in 1988. From a technical viewpoint, ESA is a modest architectural extension of XA. It is important though, because it enables big 3090 machines to handle large data objects more efficiently than earlier versions of System/370 architecture.

Figure 6-7: System/370 Architecture Evolution

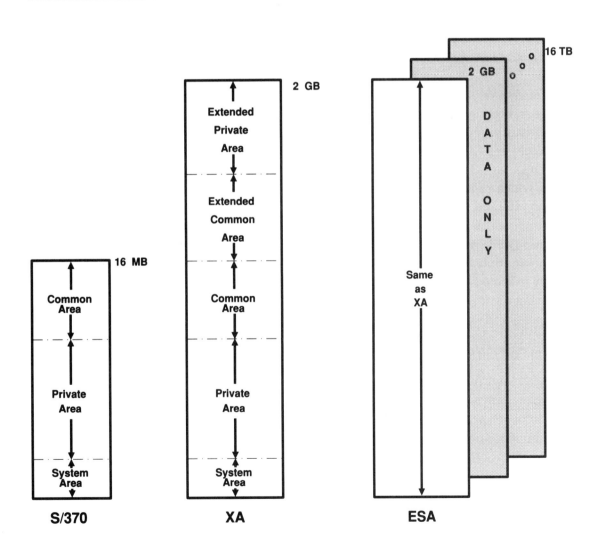

To receive the full benefit of ESA, customers may need to update their hardware, operating system, database, and application software. Such updating is straightforward for customers who are already running MVS/XA. (Chapter 7 discusses the differences between MVS/XA and MVS/ESA.) ESA is available only on 4381 E and 3090 E, S, and J processors.

The most important innovation in ESA is the *data space*, which is a 2-gigabyte byte-addressable space, similar to an address space. As the name implies, a data space contains only data, and does not contain executable code. The data space is kept in either real, expanded, or disk storage. The operating system automatically decides where to store the data space, so application programs need not be concerned with the physical storage of the data. Data spaces can be accessed by multiple address spaces, and they can only be used by assembly language programs.

A *hiperspace* is a specific type of data space that provides high performance storage and retrieval of data. It is accessed in 4,096-byte blocks through *data window services* by application programs written in high level languages such as FORTRAN or COBOL. Hiperspaces are backed by expanded storage or auxiliary (DASD) storage. IBM developed a special type of hiperspace for privileged programs, which resides only in expanded storage, and is not backed by central or auxiliary storage. This could improve the performance of subsystems such as database products.

The MVS Virtual Lookaside Facility (VLF) manages named data objects located in multiple data spaces. Library Lookaside (LLA) provides a cache for frequently executed programs. These features show that ESA has the potential of improving the large system performance by moving data from slow disks to fast storage.

System Software

Nearly all SAA functions are closely related to system software. In System/370, the term system software refers to the operating system and a large number of related software products. Together, these products provide an environment for programmers, operators, and end-users of the system. In this book, we arbitrarily divide system software into the following categories (with examples):

- *Operating systems* MVS, VM, VSE, TPF, AIX/370
- *Communication systems* VTAM, NCP, NetView
- *Application enabling systems* IMS, CICS, ISPF

- *Database*   DB2, SQL/DS, IMS
- *Utilities*   Compilers, text editors, sort programs

Nearly all customer systems contain products in each of these categories. Because IBM and other vendors offer hundreds of system software products, it isn't practical to describe them all. The next sections concentrate on the most popular IBM system software products.

Operating Systems

During the evolution of the System/360 and System/370 architectures, three primary operating systems emerged: MVS (Multiple Virtual Storage), VM (Virtual Machine), and VSE (Virtual Storage Extended). MVS and VM are full participants in SAA, but VSE only partially participates.

These systems evolved from OS/360, CP-67, and DOS/360, respectively. IBM has offered several other System/370 operating systems, but none has been as popular as these.

Multiple Virtual Storage

MVS (Multiple Virtual Storage) is IBM's flagship operating system. For marketing purposes, IBM named the system MVS/SP (MVS System Product), but most people call it MVS. It was introduced in 1974 to control the largest IBM systems. Today it is intended mainly for use on 3090 and large 4381 systems. Customers with heavy batch data processing or moderate transaction processing requirements prefer MVS.

MVS supports batch, transaction, and time-sharing modes. The operating system is justifiably famous for its excellent batch processing facilities. Customers choose between two Job Entry Subsystems, JES2 or JES3, which perform job scheduling and spooling. The MVS time sharing subsystem, TSO, reflects the compromises inherent in adding an interactive computing environment to a batch system. Transaction processing products, such as CICS (Customer Information Control System) or IMS (Information Management System), run under the control of MVS.

Time sharing is provided by TSO (Time Sharing Option), a standard MVS subsystem. IBM's formal name for this product is TSO/E (TSO Extended). TSO lets hundreds of terminal users share access to the system for interactive processing. Types of processing include: editing programs and data; compiling programs written in COBOL, FORTRAN, PL/I, and other languages; executing programs interactively; and submitting batch jobs and retrieving job output at a terminal.

Figure 6-8: Network Containing VM and CMS

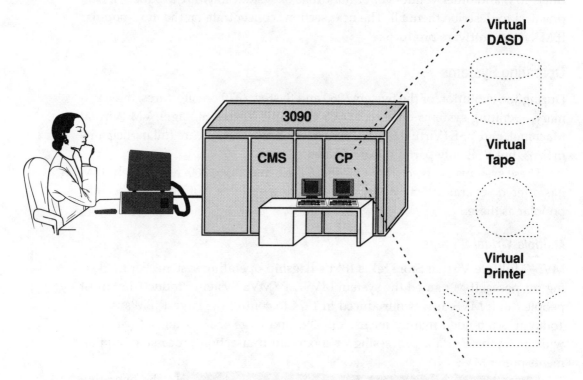

TSO is intended for professional programmers, but it can be used by people who have limited experience with computers. IBM offers the ISPF/PDF (Interactive System Productivity Facility/Program Development Facility) software product to simplify data editing and program development. It has a dialog manager that simplifies coding the user interface of applications that use IBM 3270 display terminals.

Virtual Machine

VM is a general purpose operating system that offers excellent time sharing facilities. It is arguably the most versatile IBM operating system, because it can be used on nearly all System/370 computers and it is compatible with other System/370 operating systems. Several versions of VM, each having slightly different product names (for example, VM/SP, VM/XA, or VM/SP HPO), are available today. This book describes VM/SP (Virtual Machine/System Product), but the other versions are similar.

VM has two components, CP (Control Program) and CMS (Conversational Monitor System). CP manages resources of the system and creates virtual machines where operating systems execute. A virtual machine has software and simulated hardware resources that run in a real computer under VM. A virtual machine can do almost anything a real machine can. Nearly all System/370 operating systems can run in a virtual machine, including MVS, VSE, and VM itself.

CMS is an operating system designed to run in a virtual machine. CMS supports only a single user and a single task; it cannot run on a real machine without CP. CMS lets the user run application programs from a terminal, and provides extensive facilities to manage files. The editor, XEDIT, has full-screen editing functions for preparing text, data, and programs. The REXX (Restructured Extended Executor) procedures language, which is included in SAA, contains powerful command procedure and programming functions.

CMS offers nearly the same functions as TSO, but is simpler and requires fewer system resources per user. Programs running under CMS sometimes are compatible at the source code level with MVS batch or TSO programs. However, CMS file formats are internally incompatible with MVS and TSO. Batch processing facilities in CMS are not as extensive as those provided by MVS or VSE.

Virtual Storage Extended

VSE is optimized for the performance needed by users of small System/370 processors, especially 9370s and small 4300s. It is a batch operating system, but it supports transaction processing and limited time sharing. Customers use VSE as the main operating system at more sites than MVS or VM, but VSE systems tend to be smaller. The system's 40 megabytes of virtual storage are used by tasks running in three address spaces, which may contain:

- *VSE/POWER* Spooling subsystem
- *VSE/ICCF* Interactive text editor, which provides limited time sharing
- *CICS* Transaction processing subsystem
- *VTAM* SNA communication subsystem
- *Batch jobs*

Users request VSE services through Job Control Language (JCL), which is incompatible with MVS JCL. The system has many high level languages and file organizations, including VSAM (Virtual Storage Access Method), which also is offered in MVS and VM.

Software written for VSE is not compatible with MVS or CMS. Conversion from VSE to MVS is straightforward but lengthy. VSE often is executed in a virtual machine under VM, which simplifies conversion and coexistence between the two systems. For many customers, VSE is an intermediate step to a more sophisticated operating system such as VM or MVS. Often VSE is used to supplement CMS's weak batch processing.

VSE was not included in IBM's original SAA announcement. As a result, some customers believed that IBM was not fully committed to VSE's future. In response, IBM added VSE to SAA, but the operating system is not a full participant in the architecture. VSE applications that run under CICS are included in SAA to the same extent as equivalent MVS applications. VSE does not have an IBM relational database. ICCF is not as powerful as TSO or CMS; therefore, it is not included in SAA.

Transaction Processing

System/370 workload divides into three broad categories: batch, transaction, and time sharing. In many commercial applications, the transaction workload directly supports the customer's business, and therefore is very important. Transaction processing has grown rapidly since its inception in the 1960s, and often is the largest component of a commercial installation's workload. CICS and IMS are the dominant tools for transaction processing. They are discussed in detail in Chapter 8.

Customers employ several strategies in processing transaction workload, depending on the volume and complexity of the transactions. There are many ways to process small numbers of transactions. If transactions are complex and time consuming, they can be executed under TSO or CMS (or partially in batch); otherwise, CICS or IMS are good alternatives.

We arbitrarily define medium-volume transaction processing as 1 to 150 transactions per second. A transaction program receives input from a terminal or programmable workstation, does computation and database I/O, then generates an output message. Individual transaction programs usually don't carry on a conversation with the user. Such programs and transaction rates are not processed efficiently by TSO or CMS, and are best handled by a subsystem such as CICS or IMS.

High volume transaction processing exceeds 150 transactions per second and encompasses applications such as an airline reservation system or a nationwide banking network. CICS and IMS usually aren't suitable for such high volumes, so IBM offers a specialized operating system called TPF (Transaction Processing Facility). TPF requires highly skilled programmers and powerful dedicated hardware. It is used by a small number of sophisticated IBM customers.

SAA addresses low- to medium-volume transaction processing. IBM's strategy is to use a Common User Access (CUA) user interface on a programmable workstation, and to send formatted transactions to a host computer using SAA common communication support. The transactions are processed on the host by IMS or CICS, then they are sent back to the workstation and presented to the user. This scenario is called *cooperative processing*.

Alternatively, a host application running under TSO or CMS communicates with a non-programmable workstation using a CUA user interface. This user interface is not as powerful as the programmable workstation interface described above. This approach is best for low-volume applications, or circumstances where the cost of programmable workstations cannot be justified.

SAA does not address high-volume transaction processing because TPF is not included in the architecture. Customers may use the cooperative processing approach with TPF to provide an SAA-compatible user interface.

Database Management Systems

SAA includes a relational database that has a Structured Query Language (SQL) interface. Such databases are rapidly growing in popularity in the System/370 environment, but are not dominant today. Many databases used for commercial applications are based on 1970's technology, including the hierarchical, network, and inverted-list technology found in IBM's IMS, Cullinet's IDMS, and Software AG's ADABAS.

Typical applications run in a transaction processing subsystem and interact with a database system. Parts of the applications may also run in a time sharing or batch mode. In theory, any database that provides an SAA SQL interface (which is a subset of ANSI standard SQL) is considered to be compliant with the architecture. Third-party products, such as Oracle, may become prominent in SAA-compatible systems.

The IBM SAA database products for System/370 are DB2 (Data Base 2) for MVS and SQL/DS (Structured Query Language/Data System) for VM. The details of these products are discussed in Chapters 14 and 9, respectively. Customers are rapidly installing relational databases, especially DB2, but they are slowly moving their applications to relational database technology. The full migration to this new technology may require 10 to 20 years.

Office System Software

Most common office system software, including word processors, calendars, and spreadsheets, execute on PCs, PS/2s, and minicomputers. However, System/370 products play an important role in some office system networks. Sometimes System/370-based SNA networks connect the individual office systems. Furthermore, mainframes often are used for storage and distribution of electronic mail and documents.

Figure 6-9: Office System Software in SAA Environments

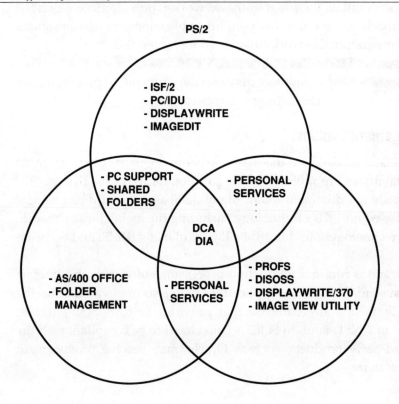

Under MVS, IBM provides document storage and distribution functions in DISOSS (Distributed Office Support System), which runs under CICS. This strategic product uses SAA Common Communication Support extensively, and works with SAA-compatible applications such as IBM's OfficeVision family. Although DISOSS is highly strategic and compatible with SAA, its low reliability, poor performance, and complexity have limited its popularity.

Under VM, electronic mail, document library, and calendar functions are provided by IBM's PROFS (Professional Office System), which runs under CMS. PROFS is very popular and is comparable to other computer-based mail systems, such as those found on non-IBM minicomputers. However, PROFS does not use SAA communication architectures, and its user interface is different from CUA. OfficeVision/VM is the SAA product that is functionally equivalent to PROFS.

Network Management

Systems Network Architecture uses System/370 computers as focal points for network management. This strategy has been controversial since the announcement of SNA in 1974, but IBM has steadily reinforced the mainframe's grip on network management. Nearly all control of a large SNA network is vested in two System/370 software products: VTAM (Virtual Telecommunications Access Method) and NetView.

In the 1970s, most customers were satisfied with VTAM's built-in network management functions. In the early 1980s, customers began using IBM network management tools, including NCCF, NPDA, and NLDM. Later, IBM combined these and other network management tools into a single product, NetView. Although it remains possible to manage a network without such tools, most large customers are now using NetView.

SAA includes the network management protocols that are used by NetView and VTAM. This further solidifies System/370's position as the central network manager. Chapter 17 covers the details of SAA-compatible network management and Chapter 19 describes NetView and VTAM.

Chapter 7

System/370 MVS TSO Environment

Large companies use IBM's Multiple Virtual Storage (MVS) operating system to run accounting, payroll, inventory management, billing, and other operational applications. The operating system has batch, time sharing, and transaction processing modes. MVS is the "Swiss army knife" of operating systems; it has every feature and can do almost anything a customer wants. But it isn't necessarily the best choice for every application.

As it evolved from OS/360, which IBM introduced in 1966, MVS contains a blend of new and old features. Many of the old features remain because customers demand upward compatibility. For example, MVS uses the same basic technique for storing executable programs as OS/360 did in 1966. (It also offers several newer techniques that perform better with modern computers.) To some people, the system seems complicated and outdated. Nevertheless, customers like the system because it provides the services they need.

IBM looked for a way to maintain MVS's momentum into the 1990s. SAA provides a partial blueprint for this. The architecture encourages cooperative processing between programs running under MVS and programs running in other SAA environments. Moreover, it positions the mainframe as a centralized database and transaction processor. This lets customers use the most cost-effective technology for new applications, while using the applications they have built over the past 25 years. SAA encourages customers to integrate their MVS applications with those running on VM, OS/2, and OS/400.

This chapter discusses the MVS operating system itself, including its time sharing subsystem, Time Sharing Option (TSO). TSO is a full participant in SAA. The IMS and CICS transaction processing subsystems run under MVS and participate partially in SAA. Hence, TSO is the most complete implementation of SAA within IBM's most important mainframe computer environment.

Multiple Virtual Storage Operating System

MVS is the premier IBM mainframe operating system. The company introduced it in 1974 to control the largest System/370 computers. Customers today mostly use MVS on 3090 and large 4381 systems. IBM customers with heavy batch data processing or moderate transaction processing requirements prefer MVS. They use the operating system's time sharing subsystem for program development and interactive computing.

MVS provides functions for customers to:

- Submit, execute, and control the output of batch jobs
- Write, debug, and execute programs
- Control computer resources and networks
- Use subsystems that provide database and transaction processing functions

Although MVS has transaction and time sharing modes, it is renowned for its excellent batch processing. The time sharing subsystem, TSO, has limitations that result from MVS's heritage as a batch operating system. The transaction processing functions provided by CICS (Customer Information Control System) and IMS (Information Management System) are important and will be discussed in Chapter 8.

IBM offers three versions of MVS:

- *Version 1 (MVS/370)* Allows multiple 16 megabyte address spaces
- *Version 2 (MVS/XA)* Provides multiple 2-gigabyte address spaces and an improved I/O subsystem
- *Version 3 (MVS/ESA)* Adds multiple 2-gigabyte data spaces to the MVS/XA design; provides fast access to data objects up to 16 terabytes (2^{40} or roughly 10^9 bytes)

All MVS versions include:

- *Virtual Storage Address Spaces*, which provide addressable memory to programs and isolate applications from each other

- *System/370 Multiprocessor Configurations* described in previous chapters
- *System Resource Manager (SRM)* for allocating processors, I/O devices, and memory to system users
- *Virtual Storage Access Method (VSAM)*, a high-performance B-tree file system that includes complete data indexing functions
- *Virtual I/O (VIO)*, which places temporary data in main storage and avoids physical disk I/O, if possible
- *Job Entry Subsystems (JES2 or JES3)* for scheduling job execution and spooling printed output
- *Functional Recovery Routines* that keep the operating system working after it encounters severe errors

MVS Structure and Design

The architecture and design objectives of MVS focus on integrity, data security, reliability, and performance. As with other major IBM products, MVS has many parameters that customers can tweak to suit their exact individual needs. Although customizing MVS is straightforward, customers usually have a large staff with strong technical skills to manage the system.

The next several sections discuss key technical features that have been part of the MVS design since its inception. Although all these features have counterparts in non-IBM operating systems, their MVS implementation is unique.

Virtual Storage Address Spaces

More than anything else, MVS's approach to memory management distinguishes it from other operating systems. The system uses multiple virtual address spaces to store programs executed by users. The term address space simply refers to a range of addresses (and associated data) that a program can access. The addresses begin with zero and end with the address space size. In MVS/370, the address space size is 16 megabytes, but in MVS/XA and MVS/ESA the address space size is 2 gigabytes.

Information can be shared among address spaces. MVS sometimes accomplishes this by using specific addresses for a particular piece of code or data. For example, the MVS nucleus, which contains low-level system functions, is part of all address spaces. It might be located between addresses 00000 and 0F1000 (hexadecimal) in every address space.

Nevertheless, most information in an address space is private. The *private area* of an address space can't be accessed by other address spaces, except by special arrangement. Shared access to a private area requires authorization by the operating system and coordination between two address spaces. With few exceptions, programs written by customers (and related data) reside in the private area.

A typical MVS system supports 10 to 1000 address spaces. Although the nominal address space size in MVS/XA is two gigabytes, a particular address space might contain only 500 kilobytes of programs and code. The rest of the address space is empty. If the total space required by the operating system and applications exceeds the computer's main memory capacity, MVS uses virtual storage paging and swapping. This moves information between main memory and auxiliary (disk) storage. Virtual storage works automatically; users and programmers need not be aware of it.

Figure 7-1: Evolution of MVS Address Space Concept

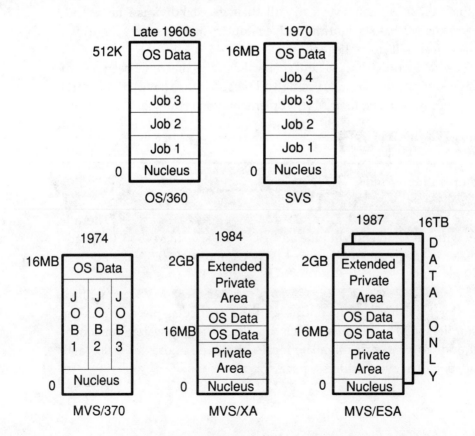

Address space size and structure are the biggest differences among the three MVS versions. MVS/370 (also called MVS/SP version 1) allows multiple 16-megabyte address spaces. The operating system occupies 8 to 12 megabytes of the address space, leaving 4 to 8 megabytes for user programs. In the 1980s, the limitations on program size became a major constraint on the growth of customer systems. Therefore, IBM expanded the address space.

MVS/XA (also called MVS/SP version 2) allows multiple 2-gigabyte address spaces. IBM accomplished this by introducing a new 31-bit addressing mode as the successor to the old 24-bit addressing mode. In MVS/XA, IBM arranged the first 16 megabytes of the address space almost identically to MVS/370. Most existing MVS/370 programs could run under MVS/XA without any changes.

It was easy for high-level language programs to use MVS/XA's 31-bit addressing mode; programmers simply had to recompile their programs. Converting assembly language programs to 31-bit mode required more effort because the new mode was incompatible with old coding styles. However, customers didn't need to change their programs because the 24-bit mode would still work. Hence, many programs still run in 24-bit mode.

MVS/ESA (also called MVS/SP version 3) adds multiple 2-gigabyte data spaces. Such spaces don't contain the operating system or its data areas; they contain only user data. Data spaces can be shared among multiple address spaces. This promotes efficient access and manipulation of huge data objects. IBM's intent is to provide high performance in accessing very large databases.

Multiprocessor Configurations

Since the 1970s, IBM has built its largest mainframes by connecting multiple CPUs to a shared memory and shared I/O subsystem. This type of architecture (discussed in Chapter 6) requires an operating system to be designed for multiprocessing. Compared with the other IBM mainframe operating systems, MVS has the most mature, complete, and efficient multiprocessor implementation.

An MVS system supports many address spaces, which execute concurrently, thanks to the system's multiprogramming functions. Within an address space, users can divide their applications into multiple tasks. Such tasks execute in parallel with each other. Hence, MVS offers two levels of parallelism, at the address space level and at the task level.

MVS lets any task run on any CPU. Because MVS systems usually have one to six CPUs to run hundreds of tasks, there is enough work to be distributed evenly among the CPUs. If one of the CPUs fails, the others continue operating without skipping a beat. This improves system reliability.

IBM's multiprocessor architecture has two disadvantages. First, performance doesn't increase in exact proportion to the number of processors. For example, a two-processor (dyadic) system usually offers about 1.7 to 1.9 times the capacity of a single-processor system. Second, the architecture can't apply the entire system's capacity to a single task; it relies upon having several tasks running concurrently to use the system's full capacity.

Nevertheless, MVS works better with multiprocessor systems than any other IBM System/370 operating system. IBM included multiprocessing in the first MVS system, but in VM, the company added the feature after the initial release. VSE doesn't support multiprocessing.

Virtual Storage Access Method

Perhaps the greatest strength of IBM mainframes is the potential for managing large data objects. Virtual Storage Access Method (VSAM) is the most prominent tool for storing and retrieving disk-based data in an MVS environment. VSAM provides sequential, random-access, and indexed methods for organizing data. Most major system software products, such as IMS, CICS, DB2, and MVS itself, use VSAM to access data.

VSAM is part of a product called Data Facility Product (DFP). DFP includes the entire MVS file system, and thus is inseparable from MVS. Although IBM packages DFP and MVS as separate products, together they provide a basis for the MVS SAA environment. Neither product can stand alone.

DFP contains *access methods*, which are application program interfaces (APIs) that control input/output (I/O) operations. Application programs call the access method by issuing a READ or WRITE request. The access method translates the request into low-level commands (called *channel programs*) for an I/O device, such as a disk or tape drive. MVS's input/output supervisor then schedules an I/O operation.

After an I/O operation completes, a hardware interrupt occurs. The input/output supervisor notifies the access method, and the access method passes the requested data back to the application program. Access methods insulate application programs from the details of the operation of I/O hardware.

The access method idea isn't new. Basic Sequential Access Method (BSAM) appeared in the 1960s. As its name suggests, it specializes in sequential files, such as those stored on magnetic tape (it also works with disk files). Queued Sequential Access Method (QSAM) provides an additional layer of functions beyond BSAM. It simplifies a programmer's access to sequential data, by handling the details of blocking, de-blocking, and buffering.

Indexed Sequential Access Method (ISAM) constructs indexes to speed up access to data. Each record in a file has a *key*, which identifies each record. For example, an "employee name and address" file might use "employee number" as a key. With the access method, programmers specify the key, rather than the physical location, of an employee's record.

Despite its usefulness, ISAM's technical design and performance were poor. In the early 1970s, IBM introduced VSAM as ISAM's successor. VSAM provides most of the functions of the access methods mentioned above, plus many other features. For example, VSAM allows great flexibility in constructing keys and allowing multiple indexes for a file. VSAM allows sequential, random, and indexed access to disk files.

VSAM is difficult for programmers to use because it has dozens of parameters. While this lets experts tune their systems to meet exact needs, not many programmers know how to tune VSAM. Many VSAM applications don't operate at top efficiency. Furthermore, IBM has made many changes to VSAM since introducing it in the early 1970s; the software occasionally has been unreliable.

MVS isn't the only environment that includes VSAM, but (as with multiprocessing) it offers the most robust and complete implementation. IBM also offers VSAM in VSE and CMS.

Despite its limitations, VSAM is the foundation for most database and transaction processing in IBM mainframes. Many customer applications and vendor software products rely on VSAM for storage and retrieval of important data. Although it isn't explicitly part of SAA, many SAA products (such as DB2, IMS, CICS, and MVS) require VSAM. Hence, VSAM is one of the underpinnings of cooperative processing in SAA.

Virtual I/O

In most operating systems, performance degrades as the system does more disk I/O. Virtual I/O (VIO) attempts to reduce this degradation by directing certain disk I/O operations to virtual memory. VIO's effects are analogous to those of "RAM disks" on personal computers, but VIO operates somewhat differently.

The MVS file system includes *temporary data sets*, which are files that disappear at the end of a job. Such files are useful for storing intermediate results; they often let the output of one program become the input to another program.

Normally the data sets reside on disks. Customers can selectively direct temporary data sets to VIO, which places the data sets in virtual memory. Under ideal conditions, this eliminates all I/O operations for such files.

Job Entry Subsystems

Within any MVS version, customers execute batch jobs and spool output using one of two Job Entry Subsystems (JES). A JES runs in its own address space. JES2, chosen by a vast majority of MVS customers, offers simple job scheduling. JES3 schedules complex sequences of jobs and efficiently handles large numbers of disk and tape mounts. JES3 has higher overhead than JES2, which makes it suitable for large computer complexes.

Figure 7-2: JES2 Multi-access Spool Complex

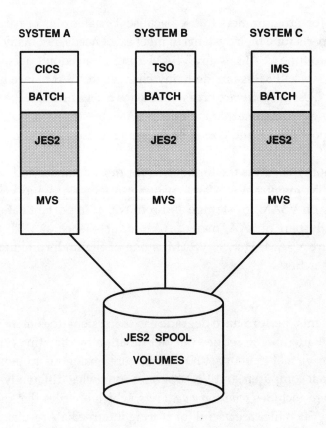

A customer can connect JES2, JES3, and VM's RSCS in a network. This lets users submit jobs for execution on any machine in the network. Similarly, users can route jobs to any machine for printing or output retrieval. The Job Entry Subsystems also include convenient protocols for file transfer.

Although batch processing is not explicitly part of SAA, it will at least be lurking in the shadows of every mainframe SAA application. Today, batch processing constitutes 30 to 60 percent of an average mainframe's workload. While batch processing undoubtedly will decline during the next 10 years, it is unlikely to disappear. Hence, the Job Entry Subsystems will remain an important part of the MVS environment.

Figure 7-3: JES3 Global and Local Processors

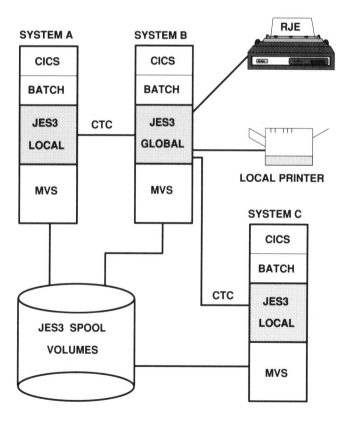

Reliability

Two error recovery philosophies prevail in IBM operating systems. Most common is the "crash and burn" theory: whenever anything major goes wrong, the system takes a memory dump, crashes, and restarts. This is the way it works in VM; on personal computers, MS-DOS omits the dump and restart features. This philosophy simplifies debugging at the expense of poorer reliability.

MVS employs the "hang on until the bitter end" approach. It attempts to recover from every error, and seldom gives up. Every operating system routine has a functional recovery routine (FRR), which tries to recover from any error. The FRR might retry the failing operation, refresh the failing code, execute a substitute program, or restore a corrupted data structure. Sometimes there are FRRs for an FRR.

Not surprisingly, this approach yields better reliability than the "crash and burn" approach. However, problem diagnosis is difficult in MVS. Therefore, the operating system has many diagnostic tools, intended for use by IBM or a highly trained systems programmer.

Enterprise Systems Architecture

Enterprise Systems Architecture (ESA) defines the third generation of System/370 architecture and it also refers to software features in MVS version 3. MVS/ESA expands the addressing limits beyond MVS/XA's 2-gigabyte limit. This positions the system to handle bigger databases and higher transaction rates than its predecessors.

MVS/ESA lays the foundation for future applications, such as image processing or knowledge-based systems, that will require substantial memory capacity. The operating system is highly compatible with MVS/XA. Most of the customers who have migrated to ESA have found that the conversion wasn't difficult.

IBM said that MVS/ESA provides the MVS SAA environment. It is likely that most SAA products will also operate under MVS/XA, but perhaps with fewer features or lower performance. The new features in MVS/ESA fall into three categories:

- Expanding addressing capacity
- Using the expanded capacity to improve performance
- Improving system management and reliability.

MVS/ESA allows data to be isolated from programs by storing it in *data spaces*. Like an address space, a data space is a map of virtual storage. However, it can store only data (or programs stored as data). Data spaces can be shared among multiple address spaces, if desired. MVS/ESA contains new services for programs to access the data spaces.

Hiperspaces allow fast access to data. Special new MVS services transfer data between an address space and a hiperspace. The system transfers data in 4-kilobyte blocks, and takes advantage of expanded storage.

Data window services enable programs written in high level languages (including the SAA languages) to access hiperspaces. Applications can access and scroll through large data objects, either permanent or temporary, without using an access method. Applications can treat such objects as addressable memory, rather than having to process them as collections of individual records. Objects stored in multiple hiperspaces can appear as a seamless single object by using data window services.

Virtual Lookaside Facility (VLF) lets privileged programs store data objects in ESA data spaces. This is a high-performance alternative to storing information in disk files. It is especially useful for frequently-used items, such as programs or command lists.

Library Lookaside (LLA) uses VLF to store frequently-used programs in a data space. It manages programs in MVS's "link list," which is a group of program libraries available to all system users. Previously, the "link list" was inefficient because the system had to load programs from the disk every time users requested them. LLA avoids re-loading the programs, so access is more efficient.

Hiperbatch stores VSAM or QSAM data sets in hiperspaces. This lets application programs access the data without physical I/O operations. Hiperbatch reduces contention for data shared by many batch jobs, and thereby improves system performance.

The latest features of MVS/ESA are not crucial for SAA, but they move MVS toward supporting large databases and efficient transaction processing. IBM's Data Base 2 (DB2) already takes advantage of some ESA services to improve its performance. It is likely the other IBM and third-party vendor products will also use unique ESA services to provide new functions or higher performance. Therefore, migration to ESA is inevitable for most large IBM customers.

TSO Programming Environment

Time Sharing Option (TSO) provides interactive access to MVS services. The product's name, for marketing purposes, is TSO/E (TSO Extended). Professional programmers are the most common TSO users, but people with limited computer skills sometimes use TSO. The product lets hundreds of terminal users share the system for:

- Editing programs and data
- Compiling programs written in C, COBOL, FORTRAN, PL/I, and other languages
- Writing programs in the SAA REXX procedures language
- Executing and debugging programs interactively
- Submitting batch jobs and retrieving job output at a terminal

TSO's programming environment is best for low-volume interactive tasks, such as database query, decision support, and professional programming. TSO does not handle high volume transaction processing or non-interactive processing efficiently. The system supports the following development tools:

- All SAA languages except RPG/400
- *Interactive System Productivity Facility (ISPF)*, including the SAA dialog manager, which simplifies developing CUA panels
- *Program Development Facility (PDF)*, ISPF's companion product, which provides program editing, library, and utility functions
- *Graphical Data Display Manager (GDDM)*, with a full set of SAA-compatible graphics functions

During the 1980s, TSO usage grew rapidly. The market for pre-packaged application and system software also expanded. Today, customers can choose from a wide range of high-quality products from IBM and many other vendors.

Office System Software

IBM's Distributed Office Support System (DISOSS) provides a comprehensive set of office system and support functions to a wide range of users. It stores and distributes office correspondence within a single system or across a network of many MVS systems. DISOSS runs as a CICS application under MVS. Using DisplayWrite/370, Personal Services, and Personal Manager, TSO users can access DISOSS to perform office functions, including:

- Document preparation
- Maintaining a library of documents
- Sending and receiving notes and documents
- Keeping a calendar of events
- Scheduling resources, such as conference rooms

DISOSS also works with OfficeVision/MVS. OfficeVision/MVS replaces the Personal Services and Personal Manager products. It uses an SAA user interface to help users perform routine office tasks.

Figure 7-4: Network with DISOSS and Related Products

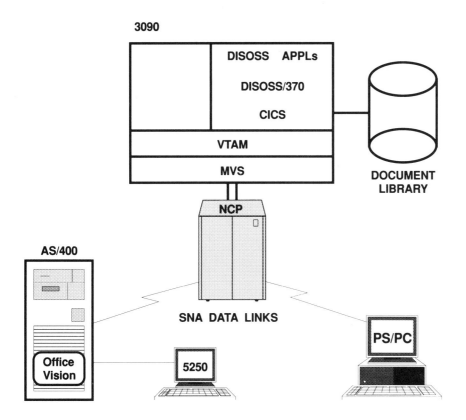

Chapter 8

System/370 Transaction Processing

From a business perspective, transaction processing is the most important form of mainframe computer workload today. For example, airlines process hundreds of reservations transactions per second. Transaction processing applications manage inventory, handle payroll, update account balances, and process stock trades. This technology is crucial to operations in modern companies; many business functions depend upon fast, reliable access to records stored in databases.

Partially for historical reasons, customers do most substantial transaction processing on mainframes. Transaction processing started in the 1960s, grew rapidly in the 1970s, and matured in the 1980s. SAA includes IBM's mainframe transaction processing subsystems, Customer Information Control System (CICS) and Information Management System (IMS). These subsystems provide an environment for running large, complex transaction processing applications.

SAA integrates applications running under IMS and CICS with applications running in other SAA environments, especially OS/2. Until the past decade, only mainframes had the capacity to do transaction processing. Now many inexpensive microprocessors and minicomputers have the power to process high volumes of transactions. They provide an alternative to the traditional mainframe-based approach.

Surprisingly, neither IMS nor CICS is a full member of SAA. IBM decided not to include SAA Common User Access functions in either product. However, applications could use the OS/2 Presentation Manager to provide a CUA user interface. SAA Common Communications Support connects programs running under

OS/2 to those running under CICS or IMS. Such cooperative processing is a key SAA feature.

Figure 8-1: Transaction Applications Under MVS

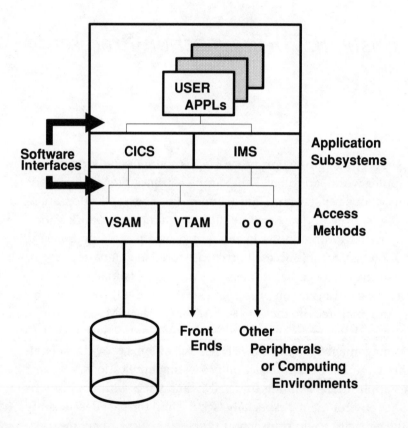

Cooperative Processing Transaction Applications

Cooperative processing divides an application's tasks among two or more machines. These machines may support different SAA environments such as OS/2 with Presentation Manager and MVS, CICS, and DB2. A developer could divide an application into two pieces: one handles the user interface, and the other does transaction processing and database access. A more sophisticated variation is to provide database access in both pieces of the application.

SAA addresses three facets of designing cooperative processing applications. SAA's Common User Access (CUA) component defines a consistent user interface that IBM, customers, and third parties will implement in their applications. The Common Programming Interface (CPI) conforms to recognized industry standards such as C, COBOL, and SQL, allowing portable applications across three major IBM computer families and four operating systems. Common Communications Support (CCS) connects nearly all IBM products using popular Systems Network Architecture (SNA) protocols.

Figure 8-2: Cooperative Transaction Processing

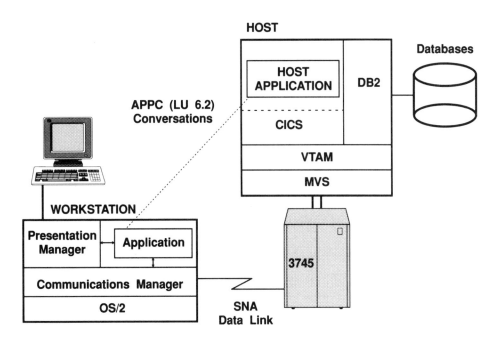

CICS and IMS provide two of the three legs of the SAA triangle. They provide important parts of CPI and CCS, but not CUA. The best implementation of

CUA is in OS/2. Nevertheless, the combination of CPI and CCS creates a sufficient foundation for the host-based part of cooperative processing applications. OS/2 can provide the "front end" user interface to the "back end" applications that run under IMS and CICS on the host computer. SAA provides the glue to hold these pieces together.

SAA protects a customer's investment in existing IMS and CICS software by maintaining an open architecture and by standardizing interfaces. This lets customers migrate existing applications from a host-based architecture to a cooperative processing arrangement without a complete redesign effort.

Customer Information Control System (CICS)

CICS is an application enabling subsystem that runs transaction programs written in COBOL, PL/I, or Assembler. The product has a *command level* programming interface that lets application programs request CICS services to send data to terminals and perform operating system functions. CICS supports many transaction application types such as inquiry, order entry, data entry, message switching, and database browsing. Although CICS provides comprehensive VSAM file access, many customers also use a database manager such as DB2.

Using the command level programming interface, programmers imbed special CICS EXEC statements into their application programs. These take the place of conventional I/O statements and enable the program to access databases, files, and communication devices. Before program compilation, a single-step translator converts the EXEC statements imbedded in the program into the source language. During execution, the EXEC statements result in API calls to CICS management routines.

CICS's terminal management functions communicate between terminals and user-written application programs. Basic Mapping Support (BMS) routes messages, provides terminal paging, and promotes device independence. Message routing allows application programs to send output messages to terminals that are not controlled by the transaction. Terminal paging lets programs create output without regard for the screen size of the terminal; users can retrieve the output in any order as individual pages.

Customers often run multiple connected CICS address spaces within an MVS system. This simplifies program testing, improves integrity, and raises system availability. CICS also handles communication between networked systems. Applications can access distributed files across multiple CICS systems.

Figure 8-3: CICS Applications Under MVS

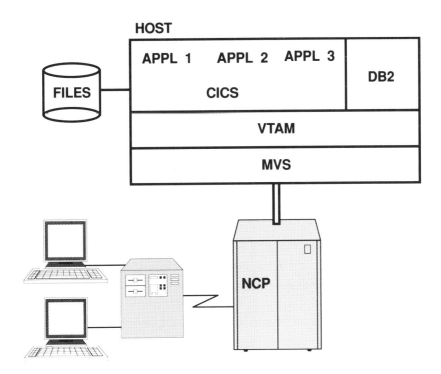

Transactions can communicate directly with CICS, IMS, or other systems supporting LU 6.2. *Distributed Transaction Processing* provides a mechanism for a transaction on a CICS system to converse with a transaction on a remote CICS system over an SNA network. This lets designers structure an application as two complementary transactions, one executing in a local system and the other in a remote system.

CICS security helps control access to information. Through a sign-on procedure, terminal users identify themselves to the system. CICS determines from each user's security code which functions the user may perform. The system notifies the master terminal operator of unauthorized access attempts and records such events in a log. CICS security facilities also work with IBM's Resource Access Control Facility (RACF).

The product also includes the following functions:

- *Task Management* provides a multitasking scheduler that allows concurrent processing of multiple transactions. It includes priority scheduling, transaction synchronization, and control of serially reusable resources.
- *Storage Management* controls virtual storage allocated to CICS. This includes storage acquisition, release, initialization, and request queueing.
- *Program Management* loads programs into virtual storage and allows simultaneous execution of multiple programs.
- *Time Management* tracks the time allocated to CICS tasks, detects stalled and runaway tasks, and allows tasks to be initiated at specified intervals or by time of day.
- *Temporary Storage Management* provides a *scratch pad* facility, letting an application program store data for a short time in memory or on disk.
- *Monitoring Facilities* gather system-wide performance data and provide accounting data for individual users.
- *Journal Management* creates, manages, and retrieves sequential data during CICS execution. Journals contain user-requested output and data logged by CICS management facilities. Applications often use such data for recovery purposes.
- *Dynamic Transaction Backout* reverses the effects of any transaction that fails. The rest of the CICS system continues to operate normally. This results in immediate recovery of databases after a transaction failure.
- *Emergency Restart* lets customers restart CICS at a predefined point if the entire system fails.

Using Databases with CICS

CICS lets programmers use several popular MVS file access methods, but it doesn't have a built-in database. Several vendors, including IBM, offer separate database management products that provide this function. Almost every database that runs in the System/370 environment lets CICS applications use its services.

IBM offers two major database systems to support CICS transaction applications: IMS and DB2. The IMS Database Manager provides a mature hierarchical database, which also works with the IMS Transaction Manager described shortly.

This approach was popular in the 1970s and early 1980s because it combined the simplicity of CICS transaction processing with the power of IMS databases. It also gave customers the flexibility to switch their applications from CICS to IMS transaction processing. However, IMS Database Manager is not part of SAA.

DB2 provides a more modern relational database with the Structured Query Language (SQL) interface. DB2 is described in detail in Chapter 14. Although DB2 is less efficient than IMS for some applications, it is easier to use. DB2's relational approach is consistent with computer industry trends and its SQL interface is compatible with SAA. Hence, DB2 is a good choice for entirely new SAA applications.

Third-party vendors offer additional choices. Relational database products, such as Oracle and Supra, offer nearly identical features to DB2. However, such products usually aren't 100 percent compatible with DB2. Other products, such as ADABAS, are not relational, but offer similar features including an SQL interface. Although some vendors claim that their products are compatible with SAA, prospective buyers should evaluate these claims carefully.

Information Management System Overview

Information Management System consists of two separate products: IMS Transaction Manager and IMS Database Manager. These products run multiple concurrent batch and interactive application programs. Unlike CICS, IMS's database and transaction processing functions are tightly integrated. The following sections describe the Transaction Manager and the IMS Database Manager.

IMS Transaction Manager

IMS Transaction Manager is an SAA environment that lets multiple applications share databases managed either by DB2 or IMS Database Manager. Application programs request IMS services through Data Language/I (DL/I). DL/I isn't a language, as its name implies. Rather, it is an Application Program Interface (API) that lets applications use IMS services such as terminal I/O. These services are mostly device independent; IMS applications are insensitive to the organization of physical data, changes in access methods, and the introduction of new I/O devices.

Figure 8-4: IMS Transaction Manager with Databases

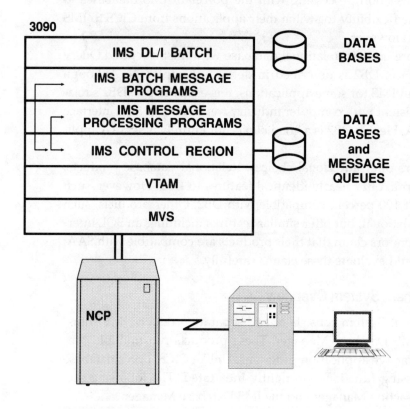

IMS provides management tools to improve the productivity of terminal usage and application programming. The transaction management services of IMS include:

- Transaction-initiated scheduling of applications
- Terminal management and message traffic handling
- Display terminal paging
- System command and control language
- Security
- Checkpoint, recovery, and restart services

Application programs use DL/I to send and receive messages. DL/I presents incoming transaction data to programs in the same format as information from databases. IMS transaction management services execute application programs concurrently with sending and receiving network data.

Most IMS transactions include the following steps:

- A terminal sends transactions via the network
- IMS places incoming transaction data into a queue
- IMS invokes the required application program
- The application receives the transaction data and generates an output message using DL/I
- IMS places the output message into a queue
- It sends the queued message to the terminal

Each terminal and each transaction program has at least one symbolic name. Messages begin with the symbolic name of the destination, which could be either an application or a terminal. IMS can provide *message switching*, which routes messages from one terminal to another. Nevertheless, application programs receive and process most incoming messages. IMS's Multiple Systems Coupling feature lets messages flow among multiple IMS systems, possibly running on different host computers. IMS has a fast path feature, which changes the application's view of IMS's message handling, thereby improving performance.

IMS schedules messages based on the class and priority of the application programs. Multiple programs can simultaneously update a database. When an application program updates a segment within an IMS database, IMS delays other programs from accessing the updated segment until the program has completed its entire update procedure. If the updating program fails, IMS rolls the database back to the last *synchronization point*.

Although IMS is transaction-driven, some applications must carry on conversations with users. The system stores the application's data areas between the interchanges of a conversation. A single conversation involves only one terminal user, but may take place with more than one application program.

IMS includes Message Format Services (MFS), which lets application programmers work with logical messages rather than device-specific data streams. Application programs can communicate with different terminals using a single set of editing logic. MFS lets designers tailor the presentation of data to suit the characteristics of each device, without changing application code. MFS also provides automatic paging for display devices.

Operators control IMS transaction management through a system command and control language. The commands display the status of system resources such as terminals, databases, message queues, and programs. They also let operations staff investigate problems and change the status of system resources.

IMS provides security through a combination of password, terminal, database, and program protection features. IMS works with standard security software, such as IBM's Resource Access Control Facility (RACF). Its security system notifies the master terminal operator and keeps a log of all attempts to violate security rules. IMS maintains system integrity through extensive checkpoint and restart functions, which it provides for both batch and interactive programs.

IMS Database Manager

The IMS Database Manager contains tools for users to:

- Define hierarchical database structures
- Create databases
- Access and maintain databases
- Reorganize databases
- Recover and reconstruct data

Using IBM's IMS database utilities, customers describe data structures from two viewpoints:

- Physical data structures seen by the system
- Logical data structures seen by the application

There is only one description of the physical data, but there might be multiple logical views of the data. The database descriptions are separate from applications programs. IMS treats the descriptions as data and uses them as it receives access requests from application programs.

Database descriptions use symbolic names to map collections of *fields* into *segments* and segments into databases. Applications use DL/I to access or modify data; they use symbolic names to identify the data to be processed. These names refer to the logical data structure, not the physical data structure. Through database descriptions, IMS maps the symbolic data names to corresponding physical data names, determines an access strategy, and accesses the physical data.

The database descriptions contain information about:

- Data organization
- Access strategy

- Physical attributes of the data
- Physical structure of the physical data segments
- Storage device characteristics

IMS databases have one of two general organizations: Hierarchical Sequential (HS) or Hierarchical Direct (HD). Application designers choose between sequential or indexed sequential access for HS data. Applications process HD data through either direct access or indexed direct access.

Within a database, IMS defines a hierarchical relationship among segments. Database administrators can establish logical relationships between segments in different hierarchical structures. Interrelating these data structures reduces redundancy and provides multiple data retrieval paths.

IMS offers a powerful and complete set of utilities to reorganize and recover physical databases. The IMS Database Manager's checkpoint and restart functions integrate well with the Transaction Manager and provide much higher integrity than CICS. However, the Database Manager is very different from IBM's relational database, DB2, and thus offers limited integration.

Database Migration Strategy

The computer industry's trend is toward transaction processing with relational database systems. IBM is following this trend by implementing relational databases in all SAA environments. IBM eventually will connect its various database products through the network. Application programs will not need to be aware of the network; the database system will automatically locate and process the data.

The IMS Database Manager is likely not to be included in this connectivity, but DB2 already has important connectivity features. In five years, it is likely that DB2 will be the primary IBM database product. Customers who use IMS databases will be persuaded to migrate to DB2.

IBM will provide migration paths from its major database products to DB2. Customers who are already using relational databases, such as those provided by OS/2 and AS/400, will find that migration isn't difficult. Migration from IMS database structures may prove difficult. IBM's strategic direction for databases, shown in Figure 8-5, advises customers to begin using relational databases in a single-user, non-networked environment. This could be on a workstation, mid-range computer, or mainframe.

Figure 8-5: IBM Relational Database Directions

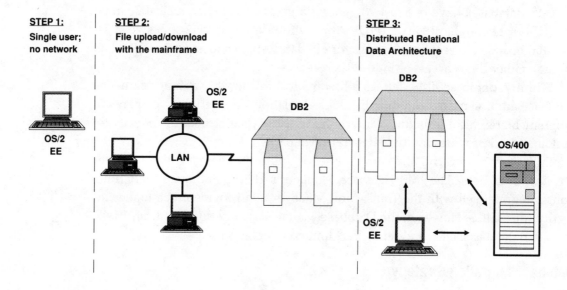

After successful single-user implementation, IBM recommends uploading and downloading from the mainframe. Using DB2 and related features, such as Enhanced Connectivity Facilities (ECF), this step is easy. Then the customer is prepared for implementing a full distributed relational database. This difficult step will require IBM's distributed relational database architecture, which is part of SAA.

Choosing Between IMS and CICS for Application Development

Some SAA developers must choose between IMS and CICS environments for their applications. Often, a company's current system configuration or development standards weigh heavily in favor of one environment or another. Under these circumstances, a decision is easy, but it may not be particularly pleasant.

CICS and IMS are more alike than they are different. Nevertheless, some differences are important to the SAA designer. These differences fall into the following categories:

- Message queueing
- LU 6.2 program-to-program communications
- Integrity and reliability
- Database integration

Message queueing is fundamental to the IMS design. Usually it stores incoming messages on a disk queue, and also queues outgoing messages. These queues not only provide long-term storage, they also help in scheduling and error recovery.

CICS's queues are not permanent, and they aren't a prominent part of the product's design. CICS transactions normally execute shortly after they enter the system, but IMS transactions may wait in a queue for seconds, minutes, or hours. IBM designed IMS to do batch processing of queued messages, but the company didn't include the feature in CICS.

Queueing isn't necessarily an advantage. It adds overhead and complicates the design of interactive applications. It complicates the use of LU 6.2, which is a primary tool for building cooperative processing applications.

CICS provides more complete communication services that work better in the "real world" than IMS. CICS has built-in LU 6.2 services that any programmer can use. IMS requires a separate adapter program for LU 6.2, which acts as a protocol converter. IMS applications can't use LU 6.2 verbs directly. This makes SAA compatibility difficult to achieve.

Although CICS and IMS integrity features seem comparable on paper, IMS's features usually work better in practice. Most CICS integrity controls are optional, while most IMS integrity controls are mandatory. IMS often is more reliable at the expense of higher overhead. IMS has been popular for very large databases running on large mainframes. Because CICS can operate "stripped down," it is popular for applications that don't need the highest integrity, or where low overhead is important.

IMS is tightly integrated with its Database Manager. Unfortunately, this database isn't compatible with SAA. Both CICS and IMS work with DB2, which is part of SAA. DB2's distributed relational database architecture will work with both CICS and IMS. Nevertheless, CICS offers slightly better DB2 integration. In comparing the database access features of the two subsystems, a customer should first consider access to existing data. This may determine which application enabling subsystem is the better choice.

CICS is the number one IBM transaction processing environment. It has over 40,000 installations, in contrast with IMS's 6,000 installations. CICS is more compatible with SAA features than IMS; this makes it a good choice for totally new applications. IMS manages many existing databases. It provides higher integrity and sometimes better performance than CICS, especially for large databases and high transaction rates. Both products fall short of full SAA compatibility.

Chapter 9

System/370 Virtual Machine Environment

VM is an interactive, multi-user operating system. This means that many users can concurrently carry on two-way dialogs with the system. IBM uses the name Virtual Machine/System Product (VM/SP), but most people call the product VM. Many VM customers have small System/370 configurations, using IBM 4381, 9370, or equivalent processors. Nevertheless, VM offers the widest capacity range of any IBM operating system—it operates on everything from the smallest to the largest System/370 computers.

VM has two major components, Control Program (CP) and Conversational Monitor System (CMS), that help users to do the following:

- Write, debug, and execute programs
- Create and edit files containing documents, programs, or data
- Run batch jobs
- Share and manage computer resources and networks
- Execute application programs and other operating systems

CP is a fundamental building block of VM that is needed to run any application. CP manages hardware resources and gives each user a separate working environment. CP lets individual users manage those resources, to some extent. For example, CP provides disk storage to each user, but the user specifies the contents of the disk. The system administrator tells CP how much control each user can have.

CP's multi-user structure enables shared system resources. CP creates the illusion that each person is the only user of the system. Within a user's virtual machine, CP provides the same functions that a real machine does. When a user logs onto VM, CP creates a virtual machine and starts an operating system in it. The operating system executes application programs and helps the user to do data processing tasks.

CMS is one of the many operating systems that can be used with CP. Every VM system contains CMS, which runs in more virtual machines than any other operating system. CMS executes only under CP—it can't run by itself on a real machine. The operating system supports only a single user running a single task. In many ways, CMS is similar in structure to the Disk Operating System (DOS) that runs on personal computers.

Figure 9-1: VM System with Local SNA Terminals

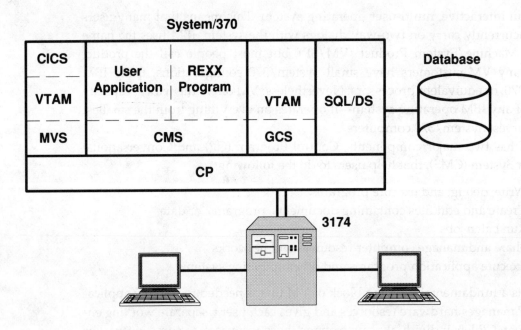

VM can be the operating system for a host computer in a Systems Network Architecture (SNA) network. SNA software subsystems, including VTAM and NetView, require a multitasking operating system. Because CMS only allows a single task, it is unsuitable for this purpose. VM includes the Group Control System (GCS), a multi-tasking virtual machine operating system, which manages SNA subsystems.

The VM operating system is first in a long list of software products that a customer will need. IBM and other vendors offer other VM-based software products for the following applications:

- Sending and receiving electronic mail
- Controlling batch job queues
- Manipulating information stored in databases
- Analyzing data and reporting results
- Managing routine office work
- Administering the VM system

Virtual Machine Concept

In the computer industry, the term *virtual* has many meanings. Usually it refers to something that is simulated, but doesn't exist physically. For example, a system's virtual storage (discussed in Chapter 6) may be larger than its physical memory. Programmers benefit from virtual storage because they don't need to divide their programs to fit into an arbitrarily small space. If virtual storage is a good idea, why not make other things virtual?

This led to the idea of virtual peripherals. By subdividing a disk into multiple minidisks, a system administrator creates *virtual DASD* that vary in size according to user needs. Virtual DASD users are unaware that they are sharing the physical disk with many other users. Virtual DASD is *not* the same as RAM disks, which simulate disks by placing information in memory.

When an application writes to a *virtual printer*, the system stores the output on a spooling disk. Such output remains on the spooling disk until a printer is ready. Meanwhile, the application can do another task or create more output.

A *virtual punch* also queues its output on a spooling disk. The system usually does *not* punch such output onto cards; rather, it transfers the output to another user's *virtual card reader*. When a recipient reads its virtual card reader, it receives an entire file of data. This is a popular way to transfer files between users. IBM uses the term *virtual unit record devices* to refer generically to virtual printers, punches, and card readers.

Not everything fits the virtual device model perfectly. Magnetic tape units, which can't be shared, must be dedicated to a particular user's exclusive use.

However, when a user has finished processing, the system operator can reallo-
cate the tape unit to another user.

A Central Processing Unit (CPU) is the ultimate virtual device. VM shares a
real CPU among many virtual CPUs through a technique called *time slicing*. A
real CPU executes instructions in a user's virtual machine for a short time, then
switches to another user's virtual machine to execute other instructions. This process repeats for each user, until it returns to the first user. The cycle then starts
over again. This creates the impression that all the virtual machines are running
concurrently on the real machine.

A *virtual machine* has a virtual CPU, a virtual console, virtual storage, virtual
DASD, and virtual unit record devices. VM lets the system administrator devise
a wide range of configurations for a user's virtual machine. A virtual machine
can have more devices, more memory, and different I/O addresses from the real
machine. A virtual machine can run any of the following operating systems:

- VSE and earlier DOS/370 operating systems
- MVS and earlier OS/360, OS/VS1, and SVS systems
- Remote Spooling Communications Subsystem (RSCS)
- Group Control System (GCS)
- CMS
- VM itself

Control Program (CP)

CP's role is to provide virtual machines, including virtual I/O devices, to all system users. The system must also communicate with terminals, programmable
workstations, mid-range computers, and other System/370 processors. CP includes
all the features that customers expect in a mainframe operating system, including
the following:

- A directory, which defines virtual machines and provides security
- Resource managers for processors, I/O, and memory
- Spooling, to handle input, file transfer, and output
- A command language that controls virtual machines and operates the
  hardware
- Features to simplify running operating systems under CP

Compared with other SAA operating systems, CP is very simple. Most users
need to know little about CP. An average CMS user learns a few CP commands,

however, the system operator must master many commands and options which are needed to control the system. From a user's perspective, most of VM's complexity is in CMS.

CP Directory

In many operating systems, a directory is a group of files. This is not true in CP. The CP directory defines the configuration of every virtual machine. It includes the following:

- User ID, which is the name of the virtual machine
- Password needed for entry into the system
- User priority, privilege level, and account number
- Size and architectural features of the virtual machine
- Types and addresses of virtual devices
- Disk space allocations and locations of minidisks

When a user logs on, CP searches the directory for the user's ID before starting a *session*. A user's directory entry specifies the initial configuration of a virtual machine. The user can change some of these specifications during a session by issuing CP commands. The directory limits the scope of changes, partially based on the user's privilege level. Some users seldom change their virtual machine configurations. Nevertheless, this feature is very useful, especially for operating systems other than CMS.

VM provides security by asking for a password when users log on. CP verifies this against the password in the directory. Individual minidisks may have passwords, and the system administrator may specify different passwords for reading or writing a minidisk.

The system administrator's duty of maintaining the CP directory takes considerable time and care. IBM sells a separate software product called VM/Directory Maintenance (DIRMAINT), which simplifies access to the directory. Furthermore, this product decentralizes the directory by allowing ordinary users to make limited changes to their own directory entries. This reduces the workload of the system administrator.

Processor, I/O, and Memory Management

The basic function of any operating system, including CP, is to share the CPUs, memory, and I/O devices among the system's users. CP's resource management strategy has familiar features such as virtual storage and demand paging, but it uses them in unusual ways within virtual machines. CP's I/O management strategies are unique.

CP operates on single processor and multiprocessor System/370 computers. Most VM systems operate in System/370 architecture mode, which allows virtual machines with up to 16 megabytes of virtual storage. IBM's VM/XA product enables virtual machines to have 2 gigabytes of virtual storage and operates in Extended Architecture (XA) mode. This lets users run MVS/XA under VM and also supports very large CMS applications.

CP's I/O subsystem manages real peripherals and creates virtual devices. Every virtual machine needs disk devices. CP creates minidisks, which are subdivisions of a real disk. Minidisks usually range from 1 to 100 megabytes, or more. The CP directory defines permanent minidisks and allows several virtual machines to share them. The system administrator controls a minidisk's size, location, and virtual address. The CP DEFINE command creates temporary minidisks, which are useful as application work space.

Virtual storage and demand paging allow CP to share the system's memory among many users. CP divides virtual storage into 4,096-byte blocks called *pages*. The number of virtual storage pages normally is greater than the amount of real storage on the system. CP keeps the excess pages in paging files on a disk. When a program needs one of the excess pages, CP moves it back to real storage. Page movement between disk and real storage is called *demand paging*. It works efficiently if the system needs the excess pages infrequently.

Spooling

Applications use CP's spooling subsystem in many imaginative ways. Besides its primary role in queuing and managing printed output, the spooling system is the foundation for file transfer and electronic mail delivery services. CP spool management functions, working with IBM's Remote Spooling Communication System (RSCS), use the SNA network to send output to other systems or remote printers.

Programs write data to the virtual printers that CP provides. Rather than sending such data directly to a real printer, CP stores it on a spooling disk. When the real printer is ready, CP transfers the data from the spooling disk to the printer. This maximizes the printer's productivity and avoids delaying the application's execution.

CP lets users and system operators control the priority of output. Users can show the relative importance of an output file by assigning it to a particular class.

CP determines the class from the directory or a CP command issued by the user. The system operator can override the user's assignment by using a privileged CP command.

Applications use CP spool storage to send files between virtual machines. The output from the punch of a virtual machine can be directed into another user's virtual card reader. Although this technique seems clumsy and inefficient, it is popular because it is easy to do. The sender and receiver don't have to be logged on concurrently. They can even be running on the different systems. IBM's PROFS electronic mail system uses this technique to send messages and notes between users.

Guest Operating Systems

CP's unique virtue is that any other System/370 operating system can run in a virtual machine as a *guest*. Under ideal circumstances, users are not aware that an operating system is running as a VM guest. Using an operating system in this manner is similar to using it in *native mode*. In native mode, an operating system runs alone on a machine, without CP.

This feature is useful to customers who need to run more than one operating system. Suppose a customer wants to convert from the VSE operating system to MVS. On an IBM 4381 processor, for example, the customer runs VM as the primary operating system, with one MVS guest virtual machine and one VSE guest virtual machine. Normal workload runs under VSE, but the customer can move programs one-by-one to MVS. Testing and conversion under MVS proceeds simultaneously with normal workload processing under VSE.

Many customers use CMS for their interactive (time sharing) workload and VSE for their batch processing. As discussed below, CMS's batch processing functions are mediocre. VSE, on the other hand, offers better batch processing, but has an inferior time sharing system. Through CP's guest operating system feature, customers can easily exploit the strengths of IBM's operating systems.

However, this feature entails significant overhead. Most operating systems operate less efficiently as VM guests than in native mode. Intuition suggests that two layers of operating system add to the system's overhead. Two operating systems are more expensive than one. The flexibility of running multiple operating systems sometimes makes up for these drawbacks. However, MVS has a reputation for operating inefficiently as a guest operating system. VSE performs better.

Conversational Monitor System (CMS)

CMS is a single-user interactive operating system that runs only under CP. It provides roughly the same services as the Disk Operating System (DOS) for Personal Computers. CMS manages the data, applications, and work flow in a user's virtual machine using the following tools:

- Command language integrated with a procedures language
- A file system that is simple and efficient
- Macros and subcommands that can be used within certain commands
- On-line help, with detailed information about any CP or CMS function
- Text editor, optimized for manipulating programs and data
- Limited batch processing facilities
- VSE and MVS compatibility features

File System

CMS's file system works best with small- to medium-sized minidisks. Like PC DOS, CMS assigns a letter (A–Z) designation to each of the virtual machine's minidisks. CMS files have a two-level name; each level is one to eight bytes long. The first level is the *filename*, which identifies the file. The second level, *filetype*, describes the contents of the file.

For example, file RANDOM LISTING C1 is the source program listing from an assembly language program called RANDOM ASSEMBLE C1. The names tell us that the user stored both files on the minidisk known to CMS as "C". The number "1" following the "C" says that there are no restrictions on access to the file.

CMS files have either fixed- or variable-length records. Its application program interfaces (APIs) for I/O follow the conventions established by other IBM System/370 operating systems. CMS emulates the access methods, including BSAM, QSAM, and VSAM, that are common to other System/370 operating systems. Users can easily adapt programs written for MVS or VSE file systems to CMS. However, the MVS or VSE operating systems can't directly read or write CMS files.

On-line Help

CMS is the most "user friendly" System/370 SAA environment. Its help facility displays full pages of text, that cover all the features of CP, CMS, and related products, including the following:

- CP and CMS commands, messages, and subcommands
- System editor, XEDIT
- Procedures languages: EXEC, EXEC2, and REXX
- Separate products, such the SQL/DS database

The pages displayed by the help facility are called panels. Their format is different from SAA Common User Access panels, but they serve the same purpose. Help includes three types of panels:

- Menu panels select the subject to be displayed
- Information panels display the subject matter
- Task panels select the task to be explained

Users select help topics by moving the display cursor under the name of the topic, and pressing ENTER. This approach is easy to use, but it diverges from SAA conventions.

Procedures Languages: EXEC, EXEC2, and REXX

CMS has three procedures languages. A program written in a procedures language contains CP and CMS commands combined with other logic statements, which are processed by an interpreter. CMS's three procedures languages are a result of evolution; the older EXEC and EXEC2 languages remain in the product for compatibility reasons. The syntax of the Restructured Extended Executor (REXX) language is more elegant, so most people prefer it. Furthermore, SAA includes REXX, but not EXEC or EXEC2.

Users create REXX programs by using the XEDIT text editor to put the program in a CMS file. A user executes the program by typing its file name. The REXX language is simple enough to be used by anyone who has an elementary knowledge of programming. Like BASIC, it has statements to do the following:

- Assign values to variables and compare them
- Perform conditional "If, then, else" logic
- Handle character strings
- Compute arithmetic formulas

REXX has a pleasant syntax, unlike procedures languages that require many dollar signs and ampersands. For example, a REXX programmer writes statements such as:

```
say 'Please enter your name'
randy = RANDOM(1,999)
If randy = 56 then say 'This is your lucky number'
```

Batch Job Processing

Work performed in a CMS batch job is almost the same as interactive work. The system operator starts a CMS batch virtual machine and it processes programs in first-in, first-out (FIFO) order. Normally users submit a REXX or EXEC program for batch processing. CP spools all output that would have appeared on the terminal. The user can receive such output in a virtual card reader, or print it on the system printer.

This approach is similar to that used by many minicomputer operating systems, such as UNIX, but is different from the approach used by MVS. MVS uses Job Control Language (JCL) to define batch jobs. IBM optimized JCL specifically for batch processing, so it is incompatible with TSO's interactive command language. Although JCL has a well-deserved reputation for being difficult and obscure, it works well for batch.

A few software vendors sell add-on software products, such as IBM's VM Batch Subsystem, that add the following improvements to CMS batch:

- Commands to submit, cancel, and check the status of a job
- Automatic job scheduling
- Monitoring, to ensure that a job doesn't stall or exceed time limits
- Concurrent execution of multiple jobs

Even with these improvements, the usefulness of CMS's batch processing falls short of both VSE and MVS. Nevertheless, it is adequate for a customer whose workload is mainly interactive.

Compatibility with MVS and VSE

The high-level language compilers for CMS closely resemble their MVS counterparts. Programs written in such languages usually are portable at the source code level between MVS and CMS. VSE-to-CMS conversion usually is more difficult than going from MVS to CMS.

CMS simulates the most popular MVS access methods, Basic and Queued Sequential Access methods (BSAM and QSAM), so many assembly language programs also can be moved easily to CMS. CMS has Virtual Storage Access Method

(VSAM), which includes indexed, sequential, and relative record access. CMS's VSAM is compatible with VSE VSAM, which is a subset of MVS VSAM.

Database Management System

IBM's Structured Query Language/Data System (SQL/DS) software product is a relational database that lets users access structured data stored on a VM system. The product maintains information in tables; application programs use Structured Query Language (SQL) to define, access, and manipulate the information. SQL/DS complies with the SAA Common Programming Interface SQL specification.

IBM says that people with little or no data processing experience can use SQL/DS. Indeed, the product is simpler than DB2, which operates under MVS. Nevertheless, SQL/DS is a complex product that requires planning and expert knowledge to produce top quality applications.

SQL/DS users access data only through SQL. Users enter SQL statements through one of the following methods:

- Issuing SQL statements from a terminal
- Embedding SQL statements in programs written in COBOL, PL/I, FORTRAN, or Assembler language
- Using a *front-end* program, such as IBM's Query Management Facility to generate SQL. This type of product improves the database query process by simplifying the user interface

SQL/DS includes Interactive SQL (ISQL), which lets users issue SQL statements directly from a terminal. It can reissue SQL statements previously entered, format query results before printing, and store SQL programs for future use.

SQL/DS has a precompiler that analyzes and processes *embedded SQL*. Users code programs in the third generation languages mentioned above. They insert SQL statements into the parts of the programs that need to access the database. The precompiler reads the source program, changes the SQL statements to comments, adds statements to call SQL/DS, and generates an access module. The precompiler stores the access module in the SQL/DS database. At execution time, SQL/DS uses the access module to process the SQL statements.

An embedded SQL program usually is more complex than its terminal-based counterparts: the program must specify the query, and it must also receive and process the result. Any SQL statements that can be used at a terminal are also valid in embedded SQL. However, embedded SQL requires extra statements that define an application's variables to the database. SQL/DS also allows *dynamic*

SQL, in which the application program builds a query at execution time. This provides extra flexibility in application design.

Programming Environment

VM's programming environment is best for low-volume interactive tasks, such as database query, decision support, end-user computing, and medium-sized scientific applications. CMS does not handle high volume transaction processing or batch processing efficiently. Most successful VM customers have avoided using the system for heavy production data processing.

The VM programming environment is easy for people with limited technical skills to use. The system supports the following development tools:

- *XEDIT* A robust editor for programs and data, which is included in the VM product
- All SAA languages except RPG/400
- *Interactive System Productivity Facility (ISPF)* Provides the SAA dialog manager function, which simplifies developing CUA panels
- *Program Development Facility (PDF)* Provides program editing, library, and utility functions; runs under ISPF
- *Display Management System (DMS/CMS)* Creates and manages display panels and generates simple application programs.
- *Graphical Data Display Manager (GDDM)* Provides a full set of SAA-compatible graphics functions.

During the 1980s, the installed base of VM customers grew rapidly. The market for pre-packaged application and system software also expanded. Today, customers can choose from a wide range of high-quality products.

Office System Software

IBM's Professional Office System (PROFS) provides a comprehensive set of office system and support functions to a wide range of users. It prepares, stores, and distributes office correspondence within a single system or across a network of many VM systems. PROFS helps users do many routine office tasks, including:

- Document preparation
- Proofreading, spelling checking, thesaurus, and reading comprehension analysis
- Maintaining a library of documents

- Sending and receiving notes and documents
- Keeping a calendar of events
- Scheduling conference rooms

Although PROFS has been popular with customers, it is not compatible with SAA. IBM's OfficeVision/VM product is compatible with SAA, and provides the same functions as PROFS.

Networking and Connectivity

A VM system can participate as a powerful host computer on an SNA network. A VM system, running VTAM and NetView, offers the same level of networking function as a similarly-equipped MVS system. VM's SNA networking capabilities are first-rate.

Figure 9-2: Integration Between VM and MVS Spooling

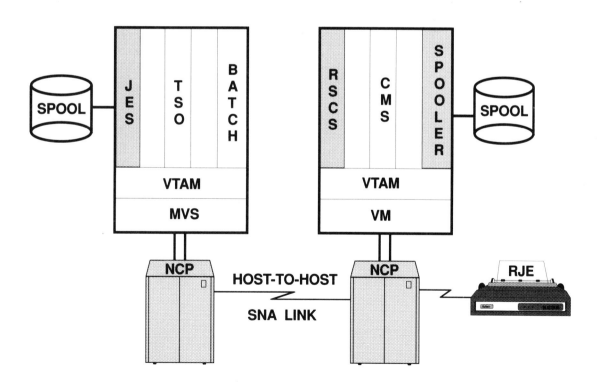

Although the communications products mentioned above are offered for all System/370 operating systems, Remote Spooling Communications Subsystem (RSCS) is unique to VM. It adds communication functions to CP's spooler. With RSCS, a customer can create a network of VM systems. Users can route files, jobs, printed output, and electronic mail to users on other VM and MVS systems. RSCS also sends output to printers attached to the network. The product integrates with the other networking products, including VTAM and NetView.

Another unique VM function is Group Control System (GCS), which provides a platform for running IBM's standard SNA networking software. GCS is a multitasking virtual machine supervisor. Virtual machines in a group under GCS can share common read/write storage and communicate with each other. IBM designed GCS specifically to run the networking products because the single-task CMS environment wasn't sufficient.

VTAM runs in one of GCS's virtual machines. VTAM provides the basic SNA network services for each host computer in the network. NetView also runs under GCS. It works with VTAM to automate network operations and management functions. Under VM, customers can use all the functions of IBM's SNA networking products. Chapter 19 describes these products in detail.

Chapter 10

Application System/400

In June, 1988 IBM announced the Application System/400 (AS/400) as its strategic line of mid-range business computers. Mid-range computers, which are bigger than Personal Computers but smaller than mainframes, range in price from $20,000 to $1 million. Small businesses and groups within large businesses use these machines for accounting, business management, manufacturing, and office applications.

The AS/400 is a multi-user system, in which users access the system via terminals. IBM designers combined the simplicity of System/36 and the advanced architecture of System/38 into the product. Applications written for the AS/400's predecessors, System/36 and System/38, can be moved to the AS/400 quickly and efficiently.

This compatibility is remarkable because System/36 and System/38 were dissimilar and represented opposing philosophies. Despite IBM's generic references to "System/3X," both systems had unique architectures and software bases. Conversion between the two architectures was difficult. Not surprisingly, System/36 and System/38 had somewhat different customers.

In positioning the AS/400 as the single successor to both System/36 and System/38, IBM wisely created only one mid-range SAA environment. By limiting the number of SAA environments, IBM will achieve SAA portability goals more easily. Software developers probably will upgrade the large base of System/3X application programs to be compatible with SAA. This may enlarge the market for both AS/400 and SAA.

The AS/400's compatibility with its ancestors detracts from its compliance with SAA. The AS/400 must work well with old applications, languages, terminals, and development tools—many of which are inconsistent with SAA. Furthermore, SAA has elements that don't fit well within the AS/400 design, for example, the graphical user interface.

System Architecture

AS/400 has a blend of architectural features, representing both mainstream and unconventional thinking. The system has a conventional bus structure, standard peripherals, and minicomputer-style packaging. Yet its addressing structure, microprogram organization, compatibility modes, and software packaging are unconventional. These architectural features, combined with IBM's marketing muscle, make the AS/400 unique and important in the marketplace.

Figure 10-1: AS/400 Functional Layers

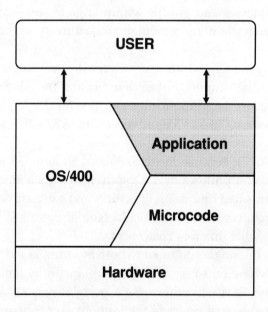

The main difference between the AS/400 and traditional computers (for example, the IBM 9370) is the structure of the software layers. A traditional system requires customers to purchase functions such as a database, communications, and security in separate packages. Customers must select, install, and maintain each package separately. Some companies hire highly skilled system programmers to do this.

IBM put many of the AS/400's database, security, and operating system functions into the microcode layer, which is called *Licensed Internal Code (LIC)*. Microcode provides a layer of functions positioned between the operating system and the hardware. Basic Input/Output Support (BIOS) of a Personal Computer is a well-known example of this idea. Microcode sometimes is called *firmware*, which reflects the fact that it isn't exactly hardware or software, even though it has the characteristics of both.

The AS/400's functional layers offer the possibility of excellent performance because the most important logic is close to the hardware. The OS/400 operating system and the microcode layer together provide all the basic system software functions, without requiring a customer to purchase and install several separate packages. The result is simplicity and good performance, but less flexibility than a traditional system.

The programmer's view of the AS/400 also is different. Programmers understand the internals of traditional systems and can, for example, add device drivers or modify the security system. In such *open systems*, system programmers have flexibility in customizing the system at the expense of more complexity.

The AS/400 is a *closed system*, which limits a programmer's access to system internals. System programmers cannot modify the database, for example, because it is built into the AS/400's microcode. Programmers cannot write programs in assembly language because IBM has not documented the machine's instruction set. Although this seems restrictive, it helps achieve SAA's portability goals.

System Processor

All current AS/400 models have one *system processor*, which internally connects to the system I/O buses, main storage, control storage, and the service processor. The main storage does not connect directly to an I/O bus. All peripherals connect to I/O processors which, in turn, connect to an I/O bus. IBM calls this multiprocessing, but it is different from the System/370 multiprocessing design described in Chapter 6.

The processor uses a 32-bit word, and the width of the system's internal data path is a full word. The hardware can do fixed point and binary arithmetic, but not floating point arithmetic. An address is 48 bits wide, which allows 256-terabyte (tera = 2^{40}, roughly 10^{12}) addressing. This exceeds all other IBM systems. The architecture also allows future products to expand to 64-bit addresses.

The *service processor* starts the system and continuously monitors the operation of the hardware. It communicates with the system operator through the control panel. The service processor performs fault isolation, error detection, and error reporting for the entire system.

Memory

Main storage stores instructions and data that are to be accessed directly by the system processor and I/O devices. It has 32-bit words, and it uses extra bits for error detection and error correction codes (ECCs). The system can correct any single-bit error or detect any two-bit error in any word. The main storage cycle time varies by AS/400 model, ranging from 120 to 600 nanoseconds (nano = 10^{-9}). Storage size can be from 8 megabytes to 192 megabytes.

Control storage provides a small, high-speed memory area that contains the most commonly-used LIC microcode. The system processor directly executes these simple instructions, but they are not seen by the programmer. User programs contain series of high-level instructions, which cause micro-instructions to be executed from control storage.

Control storage size is either 4,096 or 8,192 words, depending on the AS/400 model. Control storage is faster than main storage; it has a 60 to 120 nanosecond cycle time. Most LIC instructions execute in one control storage cycle. However, when LIC resides in main storage, the processor may be slowed due to the longer main storage cycle time.

Storage Management

The two main types of storage for user programs and data in the AS/400 are main storage and fixed disk storage. As in all modern computers, instructions and data must be in main storage before the processor can access them. The AS/400 uses virtual storage to create the illusion that the system has a large memory space and to move information efficiently between main memory and disk storage. The AS/400 processor architecture provides up to 256 terabytes of addressable memory. The practical limit to capacity is the amount of installed disk storage.

IBM and other vendors offer virtual storage on a wide range of systems. All strategic IBM operating systems, including OS/2, MVS, VM, VSE, and OS/400, implement virtual storage to some degree. However, the AS/400 uses an unusual approach, called *single-level storage*, in which the system makes no distinction between disk storage and main storage. It treats disk files as addressable memory. All storage appears as one seamless linear address space and the system accesses all data in the same way. There are no access methods or address space boundaries, as in MVS or VM.

Another unusual term is *object-oriented access*. The system stores programs, documents, databases, and other resources as objects, which are similar to files on other systems. Objects have a consistent architecture, including a description containing the name of the object and its location (volume ID) on the system; its size, in bytes; dates of creation or modification; and text describing the object.

When a user accesses an object, the AS/400 security system authorizes the access and makes sure that the usage is proper for the type of object. IBM calls this *capability-based addressing*. The AS/400's storage management system optimizes performance by spreading information across several disks.

Objects can be organized into groups called *libraries*. In non-IBM file systems, directories contain groups of files and perform the same function as libraries. Security can be applied to libraries, and thus an application that requires restricted access, such as financial reporting, can be placed in its own library.

Input/Output Subsystem

Input/Output Processors (IOPs) manage all devices connected to the AS/400. Each IOP independently manages one or more devices and coordinates its activity with the system processor. This allows overlap between I/O operations and computing. A system usually has at least three IOPs:

- *Storage IOP* Manages disk and tape units
- *Workstation IOP* Controls terminals and printers
- *Communication IOP* Connects communication networks

The I/O processors communicate with the system processor over an I/O bus, which forms the backbone of the system. Some AS/400 models have only one I/O bus, while others have several. Multiple buses have the advantage that several information transfers between IOPs and main storage can occur simultaneously. Hence, the multiple bus architecture contributes to the high performance of the largest AS/400 models.

The AS/400 product family has four fixed disk devices: an internal 315 megabyte drive, used in the smallest AS/400s; the 400 megabyte IBM 9332; the 856-megabyte IBM 9335; and the IBM 9336, which provides up to two 856-megabyte drives.

These products offer an average access time of about 20 milliseconds, with data transfer rates of 1.25 to 3.0 megabytes per second. Their performance is somewhat lower than the DASD products for System/370.

Although the AS/400 is a proprietary product, some of its hardware follows established industry standards. For example, the disk interface conforms to the EIA's peripheral interface standard, IPI-3. The I/O bus, IOPs, and I/O devices used with the AS/400 are similar to those built into the 9370. For example, the 9332, 9335, and some I/O adapters can be used with both the 9370 and the AS/400.

Hardware Packaging

IBM offers AS/400 hardware in three types of cabinets. The smallest AS/400s (models C04 and C06, for example) have IBM 9402 system units. Mid-level AS/400s (such as model C25) have IBM 9404 system units, which are available in several configurations and capacity levels. This 9404's compact enclosure resembles the packaging of the smallest System/36 computers. It is about 26" tall, 14" wide, and 30" deep; it can be plugged into a standard electrical outlet (90-140 volts, 50-60 Hertz). The smallest AS/400 models have less than 1 gigabyte of disk storage, and have limited main storage and processing capacity.

The largest AS/400s (model B30 and above) have IBM 9406 system units. System components plug into one or more IBM 9309 model 2 rack enclosures (the 9370 uses the same rack model). Each rack is about 62" tall, 26" wide, and 36" deep, and meets industry-standard EIA specifications. A rack contains the power supplies needed to operate the system; the rack requires 180-259 volt, 50-60 Hertz input power. I/O devices, such as DASD and tape units, slide into the rack as modular units. The 9406 systems easily expand as customer needs dictate.

The 9404, 9406, and some 9402 system units run the OS/400 operating system and applications. (The entry-level 9402 model Y10 runs the System/36 operating system.) Their architectures are identical; however, most peripherals and accessories are not interchangeable among all AS/400s. Furthermore, 9402 and 9404 system units cannot be upgraded to 9406 models.

Figure 10-2: IBM 9404 System Unit

Operating System/400

The OS/400 operating system includes all the standard features that customers expect on a mid-range system, plus other esoteric features. IBM highlights the following important features:

- Single integrated operating system
- Ease of use, installation, and maintenance
- On-line help and education
- Electronic Customer Support
- Comprehensive security for all system resources
- Multiple operating environments

The system has a menu-based user interface, which is similar to Common User Access for non-programmable terminals. Although the AS/400 has a command language (CL), the system can be set up and used by people who are not familiar with it. Menus use an object-oriented approach, consistent with the AS/400's storage management methods. A *fast path* technique gives expert users quick access to system functions.

OS/400 is "table driven"; it controls system functions through external tables of variables. Operating system installation consists of copying the software onto the fixed disk. No system generation is necessary. On a new AS/400, IBM preloads OS/400 onto the system disks. Each customer tailors the system by changing the values of variables in the system's tables.

On-line Help and Education

OS/400 has extensive on-line help facilities, which give context-sensitive information about either individual fields on the screen or entire system functions. Through an index search function, users can get the "big picture" of how to do a task. The index contains many synonyms, so users can ask for information in their own words, without knowing the system's terminology. OS/400 also includes Tutorial System Support, which covers basic AS/400 terminology, concepts, facilities, and operation.

Electronic Customer Support

Electronic Customer Support (ECS) provides tools to help customers service and support their systems and networks. ECS also provides remote access to IBM marketing information and IBM service facilities. Although sophisticated customers use this service extensively, people with limited data processing knowledge can also use it. ECS includes problem and change management, on-line and remote technical assistance, automatic hardware and software service, remote access to product specifications, and a menu-driven user interface.

Security

OS/400's security features let customers control access to their systems. The security administrator can specify who may access individual objects and libraries or restrict the functions that each user can perform. Users can have the authority to delete, manage, or use an object. OS/400 controls whether the usage is reading, updating, adding, or deleting. The system allows customers to select one of three levels of security:

- *Minimal* No passwords; any user can perform any function
- *Password* Passwords must be used for log-on, but any user can perform any function
- *Resource security* Passwords are required and the customer can control object usage, as described above

Multiple Operating Environments

OS/400's System/38 environment allows the execution of most programs written for the System/38. Customers can freely mix System/38 and AS/400 programs in the same job. OS/400 users can develop System/38 programs, however, they must be recompiled on a System/38 before execution. The similarity between the AS/400 and System/38 makes it easy for customers to convert to the AS/400.

The System/36 environment is more restrictive, but most System/36 applications operate on the AS/400. The system interprets System/36 Operations Control Language (OCL) and runs RPG II and COBOL programs after they have been compiled on the AS/400 system. Users will notice some operational differences, mainly due to changes in system menus. Some of these changes result from SAA user interface guidelines.

Applications running in the System/36 environment usually are at least 20 percent slower than their AS/400 or System/38 counterparts. Architectural differences, such as the AS/400's strict handling of invalid numeric data types, may also disrupt application execution. It is difficult to mix System/36 and AS/400 programs in the same job.

Database Management System

AS/400's built-in relational database diverges from computer industry database philosophies. First, IBM decided to imbed the database within the system architecture; the database depends on the AS/400's microcoded instruction set. Second, the database's native (i.e., built-in) application program interface is proprietary, and is *not* Structured Query Language (SQL). However, customers may buy a separate product that provides an SAA SQL interface. Third, most AS/400 application software on the market in 1990 uses the database's native interface and, therefore, is not compatible with SAA. This situation is likely to change.

The AS/400 database is a mature product because it evolved from the System/38 database, which IBM announced in October, 1978. The product is easy to use and has proven effective for application development. It offers the usual relational database features, such as:

- *Integrity*   Provides journaling, commitment control, and recovery
- *Data dictionary*   Controls data definition and includes a cross-reference facility
- *User views*   Allow separate definition of physical and logical databases
- *Application tools*   Help programmers write database applications

Although the AS/400 database has many conventional features, it is very different from the database products in MVS, VM, and OS/2. To provide compatibility with System/36, System/38, and SAA, IBM lets the user select from among three data definition methods: Data Description Specifications (DDS), Interactive Data Definition Utility (IDDU), and Structured Query Language (SQL).

Programming Environment

The AS/400 and SAA provide an environment that encourages customers to buy pre-packaged application software. Nevertheless, many businesses decide that writing their own custom applications is the best way to meet their needs. The AS/400's architecture and IBM's development tools strive to optimize application development productivity.

Programmers can choose from several third-generation languages, including the following:

- *RPG*   Most common System/36 and System/38 SAA language
- *COBOL*   Standard SAA language for business applications
- *PL/I*   Powerful SAA language, often used in System/370
- *REXX*   SAA procedures language
- *Pascal*   Not an SAA language, popular in academia
- *BASIC*   Simple, non-SAA language, common on PCs
- *FORTRAN*   Scientific SAA language, not ideally suited for the AS/400 environment

Besides these languages, OS/400 has a Command Language (CL) to do operating system tasks. CL is not part of SAA, but it has some of the same features as SAA's procedures language, REXX. CL programs can execute a single operating system command, or they can contain complex logic that displays menus and starts programs written in other languages.

IBM offers the AS/400 Application Development Tools (ADT) package at extra cost. ADT is not compatible with SAA, but software developers can use it to create SAA applications. It is a collection of tools previously offered with the System/3X computers, including:

- *Program Development Manager (PDM)* Displays lists of libraries and objects. PDM manipulates objects using standard operations, such as copy, delete, rename, run, and compile.
- *Source Entry Utility (SEU)* Provides full-screen editing and syntax checking of source programs. This editor evolved from the System/38, and has features derived from ISPF/PDF and the System/36 Development Support Utilities (DSU) editor.
- *Screen Design Aid (SDA)* Interactively designs, creates, and maintains application screens and menus.
- *Data File Utility (DFU)* Defines, creates, and maintains database applications for data entry, inquiry, or file maintenance. It is especially useful for generating test data.
- *Advanced Printer Function (APF)* Supports the advanced functions of IBM 5224 and 5225 printers, including forms generation, printing Optical Character Recognition (OCR) characters, creating logos, and generating bar codes.

Office System Software

Customers can purchase IBM's OfficeVision/400 (previously called AS/400 Office) software to provide office automation functions similar to those in PROFS or OfficeVision/VM. The product is easy to learn and use, requires no data processing skills, and can be used by large or small organizations. Its menus and screens are compatible with the SAA Common User Access non-programmable terminal standard.

OfficeVision/400 users mainly create and revise documents. The product includes useful spelling checking, hyphenation, proofreading, and reading comprehension analysis tools. Printed documents can contain graphs and images. The system electronically mails documents to anyone in a network by using a user ID or a predefined distribution list. Even if the local system doesn't know the location of an addressee, the network can locate that person quickly.

A calendar schedules daily activities, meetings, conference rooms, and equipment. The calendar also can start applications at specified dates and times. Application Program Interfaces (APIs) allow customers to write applications that work with their electronic mail system. For example, an application program can automatically generate mail, such as sales reports, and send the information throughout the organization.

OfficeVision/400 communicates with most other IBM office products, including DISOSS, PROFS, Personal Services/36, Personal Services/38, OfficeVision, Personal Services/PC, PS/TSO, and PS/CICS. The product uses SAA communication architectures, including Document Content Architecture (DCA), Document Interchange Architecture (DIA), and SNA Distribution Services (SNADS).

Connectivity

The AS/400 has nearly all the SAA connectivity features included in Common Communications Support (CCS). Nevertheless, the product deviates from SAA in one major respect: it uses the IBM 5250 terminal family as its main workstation. SAA CCS includes only the 3270 data stream, which is ubiquitous on System/370. Although it is possible to use 3270 terminals with the AS/400, the 5250 terminal family works better.

The AS/400 can communicate on the following SAA data links: IBM Token-Ring network, Synchronous Data Link Control (SDLC), and the SNA-X.25 packet data network interface.

The product extensively supports the following IBM network management facilities:

- Sending alerts to NetView, System/3X, and other AS/400s
- *Token-Ring network management* Reports errors on the ring
- *Distributed Host Command Facility (DHCF)* Lets System/370 terminals act as AS/400 terminals—in essence, this is reverse terminal emulation
- *Link Problem Determination Aid (LPDA)* Helps analyze problems involving analog communication lines by using special features of IBM modems.

OS/400 includes a wide variety of SAA network services, including the following:

- *Advanced Program-to-Program Communications (LU 6.2)* Provides the foundation for distributed transaction processing, including many SAA network services

- *Low Entry Networking (PU 2.1)* Allows peer-to-peer networking of small systems and mainframes
- *SNA Distribution Services (SNADS)* Transfers files and documents asynchronously through a network
- *3270 Data Stream* Emulates a 3270 cluster controller for connectivity to System/370 host computers
- *Distributed Data Management (DDM)* Allows remote access to files residing on other AS/400s or CICS on System/370.

The AS/400 also supports many other non-SAA IBM communications protocols, including Binary Synchronous (bisync), asynchronous (async), PC file transfer, and Remote Job Entry (RJE). No other IBM mid-range computer supports more communication protocols than the AS/400.

Chapter 11

The SAA User Interface

The user interface defines how a computer application interacts with the people who use it. Common User Access (CUA) specifies the parts of the user interface that must be consistent for all SAA applications. CUA embraces many standard design principles, but it has a few novel features. To develop the architecture, IBM surveyed the academic literature on the psychology of computer interaction, examined current application designs, and researched the latest technology. The company tried to make CUA easy to use, interesting to learn, and consistent.

This chapter describes the ideas behind the SAA user interface. The next chapter covers application design considerations. This book doesn't discuss the user interface at the "nuts and bolts" level (for example, what the Alt+F4 key sequence does). Such information appears in tabular form in IBM's *SAA CUA Advanced Interface Design Guide*.

The main idea in CUA is to have consistent structures, formats, and interaction techniques across many applications. The goal is for users to quickly develop a clear understanding of application behavior. IBM calls this a *conceptual model*. After users learn an application that uses the conceptual model, they can apply some of their skills to other applications. This cuts the time needed to learn new applications.

The kind of consistency embodied in CUA isn't new. Over the past 30 years, designers have used generally-accepted user interface principles in building their applications. For example, most CICS applications are somewhat similar in "look and feel." Applications written for Apple Macintosh computers must follow a detailed set of rules for user interaction. Although CUA is different from these examples, it follows computer industry trends by formalizing the user interface.

Common User Access Evolution

IBM plans for SAA to have a life span of 20 years or more. The entire architecture will develop further through evolution. This approach isn't unusual for IBM products and architectures; SAA follows other successful offerings such as SNA and System/370. Customers and competitors expect IBM products to evolve.

CUA is the part of SAA that is likely to change the fastest. It is the most original part of the architecture, and the art and science of user interfaces are changing quickly in the computer industry. Also, IBM didn't fill in all the details of CUA in 1987 when first announcing SAA. The details took time to work out, and it was clear that not every feature would be successful.

The first step in CUA's evolution happened in 1989. CUA was divided into two separate models because IBM hadn't clearly stated the differences between programmable and non-programmable workstation versions in 1987. CUA 1989 also gave more details about the graphical user interface, and added several new features, such as the workplace environment. CUA will evolve further as the technology for user interaction matures. CUA's future, however, partially depends on whether OS/2 is successful in the marketplace.

IBM has noted that several areas of CUA need more definition:

- Mouse interaction techniques and the functions to tailor them
- Keyboard interactions for people who don't use a mouse
- New input techniques, such as touch screens or voice
- Context menus, which pop up next to objects on the screen
- Icon glossary, which explains objects on the screen
- Additional text editing techniques

Entry Versus Graphical User Interfaces

IBM had to make CUA work in all three SAA hardware environments. System/370 and AS/400 computers mostly have non-programmable terminals that display character-based menus. Such terminals don't handle graphics efficiently. PS/2 computers work well with both character and graphical displays. Many computer professionals believe that graphical user interfaces are easier to use, but they aren't practical for all SAA computer environments. Therefore, IBM developed two CUA user interfaces: the limited *entry model*, and the advanced *graphical model*.

The character-based entry model operates in all SAA hardware environments. It works best for applications that have panels with menus, such as data-entry applications. It lacks the impressive appearance of the graphical model, but it has most of the basic features. The entry model is the first choice for CUA applications on the AS/400 and System/370. It also may be the best choice for some PS/2 applications.

Figure 11-1: CUA Entry Model Example

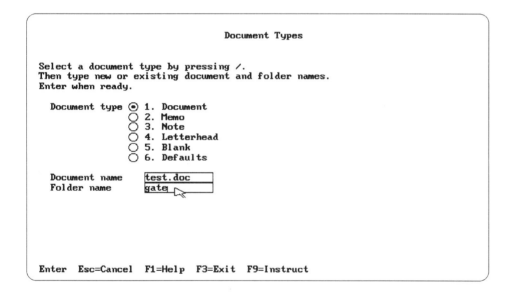

IBM called it the entry model because it is the "entry level" to CUA for many customers. It is similar to, but less powerful than, the graphical model. IBM's *SAA CUA: Basic Interface Design Guide* manual discusses the entry model in detail. The graphical model is more interesting because it is closer to the state-of-the-art in user interfaces. Therefore, it is the main topic of this chapter.

OS/2 Extended Edition is the main environment for the graphical model. This operating system has features derived from PC DOS, Microsoft Windows, and IBM GDDM graphics. CUA uses the window management functions of the operating system extensively, including action bars, pull-down menus, dialog boxes, and pushbuttons. IBM wants all SAA workstation applications to use the graphical model.

Figure 11-2: CUA Graphical Model Example

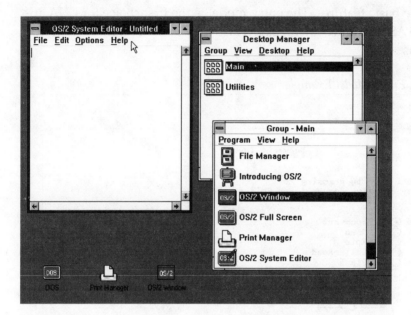

IBM also offers the *text subset* of the graphical model, which works on non-programmable terminals. It is slightly different from the graphical model, but also includes action bars, pull-down menus, and windows. The subset provides graphics for complex mainframe applications that don't require fast response time.

The *workplace environment* is a recent extension of the graphical model. It contains icons, objects, and actions that are common in offices. The workplace has pictures of telephones, file cabinets, calendars, folders, and in-baskets. For example, users can move icons representing documents between folders by dragging them with a mouse. IBM's OfficeVision/2 product provides the workplace environment.

Principles

Knowing that CUA is likely to change, designers must structure their applications to take advantage of future enhancements. One way to prepare for the future is to be consistent with IBM design principles. IBM's tradition of upward compatibility insures that software will keep working as long as it follows architectural structures and rules.

The two main design principles of CUA are:

- The application must develop the user's conceptual model
- Users must control the application, but not vice versa

A user's assumptions about what a computer interface is, what it does, and how it works should be consistent for all CUA applications. Well-designed applications use every opportunity to reinforce the user's conceptual model by working in the expected way. CUA often defines the outcome of a user's action, but sometimes user expectations should define the outcome. Hence, the designer's role is crucial.

CUA applications are *user driven*. Users must be in complete control of the sequence of events in an application. The application doesn't drag users through an arbitrary series of actions to accomplish a task; it lets users do the actions in any reasonable order. Although many traditional applications don't follow this philosophy, CUA applications do things the user's way.

User's Conceptual Model

Several techniques help to develop and reinforce the user's conceptual model:

- Using metaphors
- Being consistent
- Using modes sparingly
- Making the interface transparent

A metaphor links two unrelated ideas. It is useful for relating an abstract computer interface to a familiar idea. For example, graphically moving a document icon to a wastebasket icon can represent deleting a file. Or an application might have a computer-based panel that looks like a standard business form. CUA encourages using metaphors, and the workplace environment uses them extensively.

Consistency

A CUA application must be consistent with the hardware and system software environment. For example, it must use keys that are available on the workstation keyboard. Also, it cannot use any keys that might conflict with the operating system's key usage. CUA applications must integrate well with the system, even though parts of the system may not comply with SAA rules.

CUA applications must be consistent in:

- *Presentation* The appearance of items on the screen
- *Interaction* How users work with the user interface
- *Actions* How users ask the application to do a function
- *Dialog Sequence* The dialog between the person and the machine

CUA has rules that promote consistent presentation. Some rules dictate the exact placement of objects. For example, scroll bars are at the bottom and right edges of a window, and they have a specific appearance and color. They are visual cues that the information displayed might extend beyond the window. CUA defines the appearance, but not all the contents of a window. Sometimes applications themselves choose the placement of objects. For example, CUA doesn't dictate the location of dialog boxes (also called pop-up windows). An application designer must decide their placement and make them consistent within the application.

CUA defines *actions* that regularly occur in applications. For example, the Move action repositions a window on the screen. Other actions involve file operations, editing, option selection, help, and window management. CUA has pushbuttons for important actions including OK, reset, cancel, help, yes, no, retry, and stop.

The CUA *object-action principle* links actions to objects. First, users select an object in the body of a window. Then they select an item on the action bar, and a pull-down menu appears. If any of the actions listed on the pull-down menu are invalid for this object, they appear in gray and can't be selected. This approach lets users know which actions are valid for particular objects, and thus builds their conceptual models.

Modes

Inside a *mode*, users can execute actions that may be different from those used outside the mode. Users enter the mode before doing the actions, and exit the mode after they have finished. For example, an Edit mode in an application lets users modify documents. The application's editing commands are valid only in the Edit mode. Modes complicate learning because they may require users to know a lot about application structure.

CUA applications use modes sparingly. Sometimes modes are unavoidable; if so, designers must limit their scope. Inside any mode, applications give visual cues that show the mode. The methods for ending the mode must be obvious. Knowing how to exit a mode without doing damage is especially important.

The CUA user interface has three built-in types of modes:

- *Modal Dialogs* Use dialog boxes to ask for information that the application needs to continue.
- *Spring-loaded Modes* Need a continuous effort, such as pressing the shift key, to keep the dialog in the mode.
- *Tool-driven Modes* Let users select a tool, such as a paint brush, which makes the mouse pointer look like the tool.

Transparency

An application should let users focus on the substance of the tasks at hand, not on the internal workings of a computer program. Many users think of the computer as a means of getting things done, and they don't want to learn any more than necessary. They need to "see through" the application, hence the term *transparency*. Designers must structure the user interface to the natural flow of the application. Although CUA offers tools for developing a user interface, it relies on designers to make the interface transparent.

The user interface must be visual, so users see, rather than memorize, what to do. Users should see a list of items from which they may choose. The user interface must provide visual or audible feedback for every choice, action, or key press. In CUA, applications use the cursor, color, emphasis, and selection indicators to show users what they have done.

With users in control of the application, errors are inevitable. The user interface must be forgiving by letting users undo their actions easily. Actions that could cause damage require confirmation. Users appreciate applications that don't punish them for their mistakes.

User Interface Components

The rest of this chapter outlines the major pieces of the CUA graphical user interface. IBM uses the vague term *user interface components* to refer to these pieces. Chapter 12 discusses them in greater detail. IBM divides the components into three categories, each contained in every application: presentation, interaction, and actions.

Presentation

Presentation defines what appears on the screen. Applications display objects and actions. *Objects* include anything that users focus on and manipulate as a single item. Applications might also define *sub-objects*, which are parts of objects. For example, if file folders are objects, documents are sub-objects. *Actions* are operations that users execute on objects; they create, destroy, modify, or manipulate the objects. Actions may change the properties of objects, such as size or type style.

The main visual components (called WIMPS) of the graphical user interface are:

- Windows
- Icons
- Mouse Pointer
- Screen

Multiple overlapping windows cover the screen background. Applications define themselves as icons, which users can temporarily move aside to suspend applications. Applications present objects in windows for users to manipulate by moving the mouse pointer to specify their next interaction. All CUA graphical applications support these components of the user interface.

Windows

An application uses a window to present objects and actions to users. Graphic CUA has two types of windows: primary and supplemental. Every application has a movable and sizable primary window, which presents the main dialog of an application. Applications present objects in the *client area* and actions in the action bar.

In many applications, the client area is like a piece of paper. In word processors, for example, the client area initially is blank. In an accounting application, it might look like an invoice form. IBM calls this type of form an *application object*.

There are two objects in the invoice example: the form, which is an application object, and the information, which is a *user object*. The user object has sub-objects, such as quantity, description, and unit price. The objects may appear as they do in paper-based systems, and users mainly manipulate them directly in the client area, without using the action bar.

Any *supplemental windows* created by an application are subordinate to the primary window. They are either secondary windows or dialog boxes. A *second-*

ary window behaves like a primary window, but it lets a dialog take place concurrently with the one in the primary window. For example, a Help dialog runs in a secondary window. Because secondary windows are movable, scrollable, and resizable, they can handle information that won't fit in a dialog box.

Figure 11-3: Primary and Secondary Windows

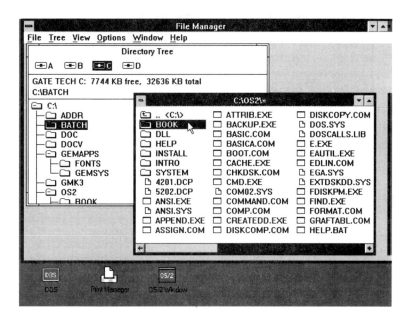

A *dialog box* asks for information needed by an action. A *modal dialog box* temporarily halts the dialogs in the application's other windows; users must finish interacting with it before doing anything else. For example, users select the name of an input file in a modal dialog box. A *message box* also is a modal dialog.

A *mode-less dialog box* works in parallel with the associated window and lets users switch between it and the application's other windows. For example, users might control printing of a file through a mode-less dialog box. After printing starts, the focus of the dialog returns to the primary window. It is possible to switch back to the dialog box to cancel printing.

Figure 11-4: Modal Dialog Box

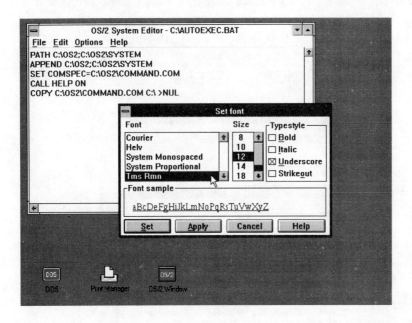

Figure 11-5: Mode-less Dialog Box

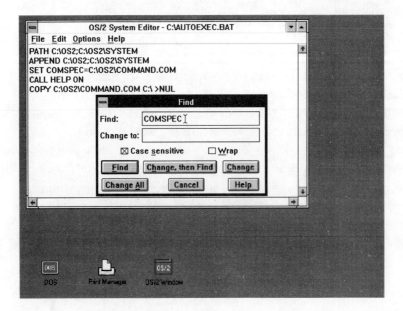

Window Components

Windows have areas called *window components,* such as a title bar, window border, action bar, client area, pushbuttons, and scroll bars. Not all windows have all these components; a message box, for example, never has scroll bars.

The *title bar* contains a system menu icon, the window title, and two window-sizing icons. Users select the system menu icon to display a pull-down menu that controls the window. The pull-down menu includes the restore, move, size, minimize, maximize, and close actions. The title tells users the name of the application. If the application is working on a particular file, its name also appears. The window-sizing icons provide a fast way to move the window, and achieve the same result as the minimize, maximize, and restore actions.

Each type of window has a different *window border.* Sizable windows have a color boundary with eight segments. Fixed-size windows have borders that aren't segmented. Modal dialog boxes have different borders from mode-less dialog boxes.

Figure 11-6: Window Components

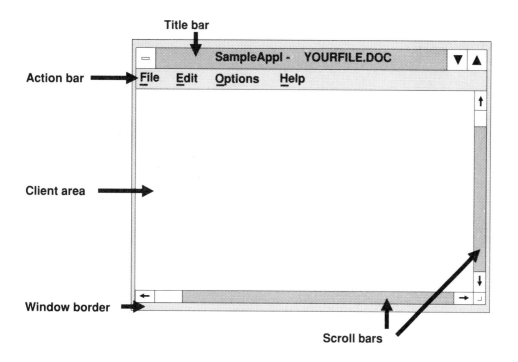

The *action bar* is below the title bar and lists the major categories of actions within the application. The application defines the action bar, but CUA has the standard actions File, Edit, View, Options, and Help. Action bar items have an underlined character, which shows its abbreviation (called a *mnemonic*).

Pushbuttons let users select actions in windows that don't have action bars, such as dialog boxes. Pushbuttons usually select simple actions. For example, they let users acknowledge an error message by selecting the OK action or exit from a dialog by selecting the Cancel action.

The *client area* is where applications display objects and users access them. It is the largest and most important part of a window. *Scroll bars* give a visual cue that more information is available for display. They let users view information above, below, to the left or to the right of the displayed information.

Interaction

Interaction specifies the way users work with the user interface components. The main approach is *point-and-select*: users point at things and then select them. A mouse can point at anything on the screen, but the keyboard only can point at the active window.

Selecting Objects and Actions

There is a big difference between selecting objects and actions: selecting an object only identifies it. The application highlights the selection, but does nothing with it. Selecting an object doesn't imply a commitment to do an action. Applications must provide a simple way to deselect an earlier selection. Users must be able to back out of a wrong selection without causing any damage.

Selecting an action causes immediate execution, and gives visual feedback. For example, selecting "File" on the action bar displays a pull-down menu (this isn't an action). Selecting "Print" on the pull-down menu starts an action that places a report on the output queue. A dialog box tells the user that the report is on the queue.

The selected action doesn't necessarily operate on the selected object. Some actions don't require an object, such as Exit, which ends an application. Objects normally remain selected after an action is finished. This lets users do a series of actions on the same object. If an action deletes or otherwise mutilates objects, it must deselect them.

Inside a window's client area, CUA has *selection fields* and entry fields. A selection field is a group of related choices from which users can select. *Entry fields* are for data entry, requiring input from the keyboard. Applications must provide enough visual cues to let users know which fields can be entered by either the keyboard or mouse.

Single selection allows only one choice per selection field. *Extended selection* lets users apply an action to several selected objects. It uses a spring-loaded mode to collect the choices by pressing the shift key and using the mouse to select multiple objects. With the keyboard, CUA uses the Shift+F8 key to enter *add mode*, which lets users select several choices.

CUA allows a combination of mouse and keyboard input. Data entry is practically impossible with a mouse, but some other tasks are difficult with a keyboard. Hence, users must be able to switch between the mouse and keyboard at virtually any point in the dialog.

Visual Cues

The keyboard and mouse provide different visual cues. The keyboard uses a *selection cursor* and the mouse has a *mouse pointer*. The mouse pointer moves anywhere on the screen, but the selection cursor stays inside a window.

The keyboard selection cursor shows the current position of keyboard input. The type of selection cursor depends on the type of field. The cursor is a dotted outline box for selection fields. It becomes a text cursor for entry fields.

The mouse pointer usually is an arrow, but it changes shape depending on the current action. In a drawing package, for example, it might become a paintbrush. The mouse pointer changes to an hourglass shape while the system is doing routine calculations.

Users need to know where to enter their input, which choices have been selected, and which choices aren't available to them. CUA has five types of *emphasis* to make these distinctions:

- *Cursored* Selection cursor (dotted box) showing a choice
- *Selected* Reverse video
- *Cursored and selected* Reverse video inside a dotted box
- *Unavailable* Reduced contrast (gray)
- *Current state* A check mark showing that a specific choice is now active, usually in a pull-down menu

Figure 11-7: Pull-down Menu with Unavailable Choices

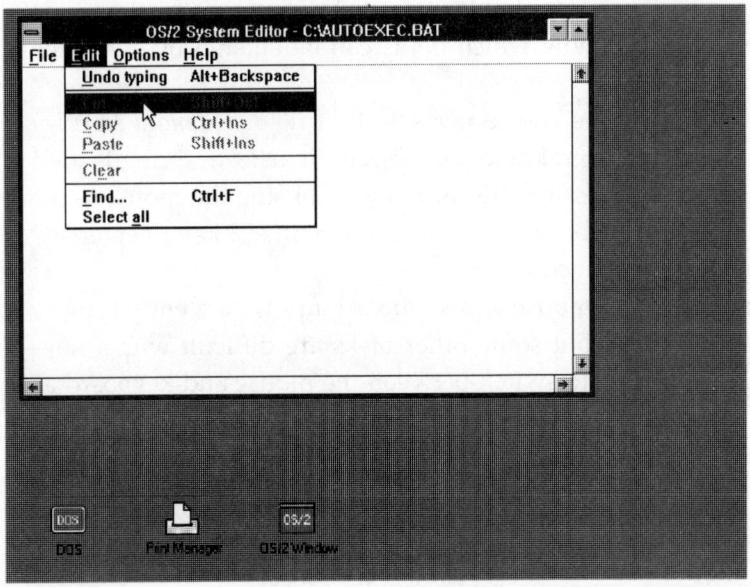

Using the Keyboard

Keyboard interaction means either typing data or moving the selection cursor to a choice and selecting it. Pressing the directional arrow keys, the tab keys, or a mnemonic, moves the selection cursor among the selection or entry fields. A mnemonic is a single character within a selection, defined by the application, but usually is the first character. The letter for the mnemonic is always underlined.

CUA has three types of keyboard selection:

- *Explicit* Users move the selection cursor to a choice and press the space bar to select it.
- *Implicit* Users move the selection cursor to a choice and it is selected automatically.
- *Mnemonic* Users type the single character corresponding to the choice, and it is selected or deselected automatically.

Using the Mouse

Mouse interaction means moving the mouse pointer anywhere on the screen and selecting a choice. CUA has four mouse operations:

- *Click* Pressing and releasing a mouse button on a choice. This selects objects and actions.
- *Double Click* Two clicks within a user-defined interval. After double-clicking objects that have an implied action, the application executes the action.
- *Drag select* Pressing a mouse button and holding it while moving the mouse pointer to another location. The application selects all items in the mouse pointer's path.
- *Direct manipulation* Same as drag select, except that the mouse changes the size or location of an item.

CUA allows up to three mouse buttons. The first button is for click, double-click, and drag select. The second button supports direct manipulation. The application can define the third button. Note that IBM's PS/2 mouse has only two buttons. Direct manipulation also is possible with a one-button mouse.

Actions

There are quite a few functions that most applications have in common. For example, applications usually read an input file, save an output file, and edit data. Hence, CUA defines several common actions to handle some of the generic functions that every application does. It isn't necessary to use all the common actions in every application. CUA contains guidelines to help designers decide when to use them.

Users execute common actions through action bar pull-down menus and dialog boxes. CUA defines common actions and pull-down menus for File, Edit, and Help. The architecture also provides guidance for developing View and Options menus.

File and Edit, if present, must be first on the action bar. Help must be the last choice. Some actions on the pull-down menus first display a dialog box. An ellipsis following the name of an action (for example, Open...) is a visual cue that it will use a dialog box to ask for more information.

The following sections discuss the most complex action bar pull-down menus and their associated dialog boxes.

File Pull-Down Menu

The File menu works with entire files. Every application that handles files as single objects must provide this menu. Some actions, such as New, Open, and Exit, have the potential to wipe out changes that the user made. Therefore, such actions must determine whether a user made changes, and if so, prompt the user to save the files.

The File pull-down menu includes the following standard actions:

- *New* Clears all information from the client area, letting users create new files. Usually it puts the name "Untitled" in the window title bar.
- *Open...* Reads an existing file and puts it in the client area. It uses a standard dialog box to prompt for the filename.
- *Save* Writes the file in the client area to the disk (or other storage device). If the Open... action read the file, this action overwrites it. If the file was Untitled, this action prompts for a name, and thus is the same as Save as...
- *Save as...* Writes the file into a new file. A dialog box asks for the name of the new file. The action doesn't change the original input file.
- *Print* Schedules a file for printing, and may use a dialog box to ask for printing options.
- *Exit* Ends an application and removes its windows from the screen. Exit is optional because it is the same function as the Close action in the system pull-down menu.

Edit Pull-Down Menu

The standard Edit pull-down menu supports a simple text editor. It uses the familiar editing metaphors, including Cut, Copy, and Paste. The editor also incorporates the idea of a clipboard, which simplifies moving information between applications. IBM grouped the Edit actions by task: undo actions, clipboard actions, and non-clipboard actions. Application designers may add their own actions to the following list:

- *Undo* Reverses the most recent user action.
- *Cut* Copies the selection to the clipboard and deletes it from the object being edited.
- *Copy* Duplicates the selection onto the clipboard, without disturbing the selection itself.
- *Paste* Copies the contents of the clipboard into the object being edited at a specified location.
- *Clear* and *Delete* Both remove the selection from the object without copying it to the clipboard.

Figure 11-8: The File Pull-Down Menu

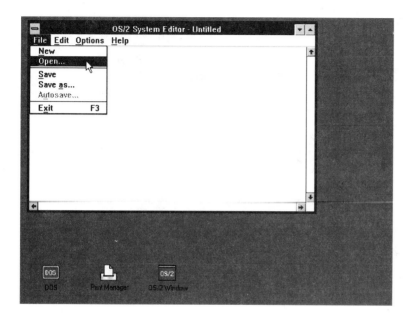

Standard Dialog Boxes

CUA defines two standard dialog boxes: Open... and Save as... Actions in the File pull-down menu use these dialog boxes to ask for further information about files to be read or written. These dialog boxes depend on the OS/2 file system's naming conventions, but designers could adapt them to other naming conventions, if necessary.

The main purpose of the Open dialog box is to determine which file to read. This dialog box works best when the selection list of files is short, for example, fewer than 50 files.

At the top of the client area, users may type the name of the desired file. Below the filename, the box shows the current directory. In the middle left part of the client area is a selectable list of files in the current directory. To the right of that list is a list of directories, containing selectable alternatives to the current directory. This allows users to change the directory.

Double-clicking on a file attempts to open that file. Pressing the enter key or selecting the OK pushbutton also starts the Open action. Applications may add their own options to this dialog box.

Figure 11-9: The Open Dialog Box

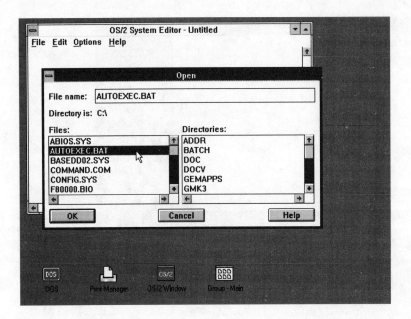

The Save as... dialog box is nearly identical to the Open dialog box, except that it has no selectable list of files. Because the dialog assumes that the filename doesn't already exist, there is no need to display the names of the existing files in the directory.

Chapter 12

Designing a User Interface

This chapter describes in more detail the architectural features of the CUA graphical model. It elaborates on the components of the user interface from the designer's point of view, and introduces programming for the OS/2 Presentation Manager and Dialog Manager. More details on programming are discussed in later chapters.

User Interface Component Descriptions

The components of the SAA user interface provide for presentation, interaction, and user actions. The architecture uses action bars and pull-down menus to offer users a list of possible actions. Scroll bars let users see information that isn't displayed on the screen. Controls, including radio buttons and entry fields, enable choices to be selected and data to be entered. Dialog boxes solicit information, such as file names, needed to complete an action.

An application gives feedback to users through several mechanisms, including an hourglass pointer, progress indicators, and messages. By asking for help at any point in the dialog, users easily recall how to use an application. SAA has window techniques that allow viewing several objects concurrently or several views of one object.

Action Bars and Pull-Down Menus

Applications determine the contents of the action bar and the Presentation Manager displays it. To perform actions, users press the Switch-to-Action-Bar key (usually F10) and then press the Enter key after selecting a choice from the action bar using the cursor keys. They can also click on an action bar item with a mouse. The Presentation Manager then displays a pull-down menu, which contains a list of choices. After users make a selection, the Presentation Manager runs the application code of the selected action. Either the action executes immediately or it displays a dialog box that asks for more information.

Note that the Presentation Manager does nearly all the user interaction in the scenario described above. The application's main role is to provide the items on the action bar and associated pull-down menus. The application also must have routines to perform each action listed on the pull-down menus.

Each item on an action bar is a single word, including a unique one-character mnemonic. The first character of each action bar item is a capital letter. The action bar choices are in the following order:

- File
- Edit
- Application-specific choices, the most popular are first
- Help

Figure 12-1: Pull-down Menu

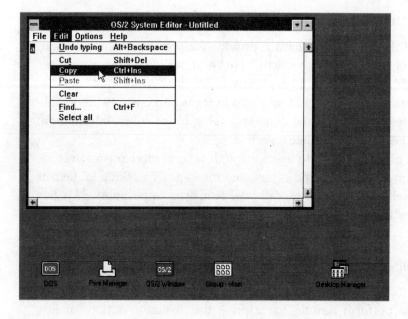

Choices on pull-down menus can be more than one word long. Application designers arrange the choices in descending frequency of use. Horizontal solid lines separate groups of related choices. For example, the File pull-down menu might contain New, Open..., line, Save, Save as..., line, Print, line, Exit. Choices that lead to a dialog box, such as Open..., contain an ellipsis.

Pull-down menus can contain icons or bit maps, as an alternative to text descriptions. This approach is useful in a graphics application, for example, to specify shading patterns for objects. If it isn't practical to assign mnemonics to the choices in a pull-down menu, designers can use numbers as mnemonics.

Frequently-used pull-down menu choices have *accelerator keys* listed directly to the right of their descriptions. Users can type such keys anywhere in an active window to start an action immediately without using the action bar or selecting from a pull-down menu. Applications use notations such as "Alt+Ins" to depict a two-key accelerator.

Pull-down menus usually don't change. However, choices on the menus aren't always applicable to the objects at hand. The Presentation Manager displays such choices in reduced contrast ("grayed out"). Pull-down menus also may contain several choices; a check mark shows the current selection. It moves whenever the user makes a different selection.

CUA applications limit the number of choices presented to users at any point in the dialog. This reduces confusion and raises user productivity. With *cascading pull-downs* one pull-down menu invokes another pull-down menu. Choices in the subsidiary pull-down menu can do an action or display a dialog box. Designers use cascading pull-downs:

- When a pull-down menu must specify many actions, and some of these can be grouped into related sets
- When an action requires a choice among a short list of attributes, which would otherwise be displayed in a dialog box (for example, landscape versus portrait orientation)
- To simplify or eliminate a dialog box that contains several sets of related options

A right-pointing triangle to the right of a choice on a pull-down menu is a cue that there is a cascading pull-down menu. After users select the choice, the cascading pull-down menu appears to the right of the triangle.

Figure 12-2: Cascading Pull-down Menu

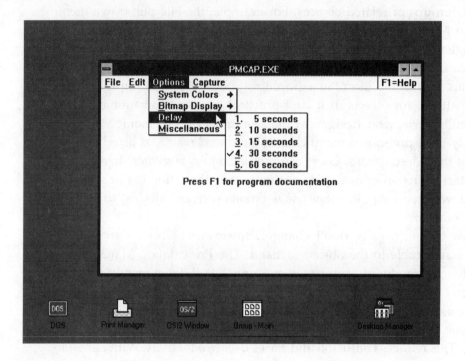

Scroll bars

Applications often must display objects that are too long or too wide to fit on the screen. Users determine the number of windows on the screen and the size of each window. Hence, CUA has scroll bars to scroll the information in a small window.

A scroll bar appears in a window as a thin, shaded rectangular area that contains a *slider box*. It has an arrow in a square box at each end. A window may have either a vertical or horizontal scroll bar, both, or neither. A vertical scroll bar is on the right side of a window and spans the entire height of the scrollable client area. A horizontal scroll bar is at the bottom of the window and spans at least half the width of the scrollable client area. Applications use the space next to the horizontal scroll bar for icons, page numbers, or other similar items.

The slider box shows the visible window's position within the scrolled information. For example, at the halfway point of viewing a document, the slider box is at the midpoint of the scroll bar. The size of the slider box shows the proportion of the information that is visible. For example, if a user is viewing an entire document in one window, the slider box covers the whole scroll bar. On the first page of a 100-page document, a tiny slider box appears at the top of the vertical scroll bar.

The arrows show the possible directions for scrolling. When it isn't possible to scroll further in a direction, the Presentation Manager "grays out" an arrow. Whenever the size of the window changes, or the information changes, the scroll bar also changes. Scroll bars always show the current state of the viewable information.

The mouse is the most comprehensive way to control scrolling. It offers three types of scrolling:

- *Incremental* By clicking on an arrow, the display scrolls one increment of information. Applications define the increment. Often the vertical increment is one line of text, and the horizontal increment is one character.
- *Page* Clicking above or below the slider box scrolls up or down one page. A page is slightly less than the size of the visible window; some information from the previous page always remains on the screen as a reference point.
- *Direct Positioning* Dragging the slider box on the scroll bar moves to a point proportional to the box's location.

The keyboard also controls scrolling. When the cursor is at an edge of the scrollable area, an arrow key scrolls incrementally. This achieves the same result as incremental scrolling with the mouse. The PgUp and PgDn keys request vertical page scrolling, and the Ctrl+PgUp and Ctrl+PgDn keys request horizontal scrolling.

Controls

Controls let users select choices or enter data. For the most part designers put controls in dialog boxes to ask for information to complete an action. Nevertheless, they are valid in any window. Presentation Manager provides most CUA controls, including radio buttons, check boxes, and entry fields. Presentation Manager doesn't provide value set or spin button controls (described below), so applications that need these functions must provide them in their own code.

A designer may use controls alone or in combination to achieve a desired effect. Often it is desirable to give users several ways of completing a dialog. For example, a designer might want to present a list of files to be selected, but also let users type a file name directly. This requires combining list boxes and entry fields within a single dialog box. CUA gives designers the freedom to mix and match the controls described below.

Radio buttons give a fixed set of binary choices that are mutually exclusive. A radio button consists of a circle and text. A radio button field contains two or more choices, but users can select only one choice in a field. A dot appears in the circle of a radio button after a user selects it. For example, a radio button field sets the orientation for printed output: one button for Landscape and one button for Portrait.

Figure 12-3: Radio Buttons

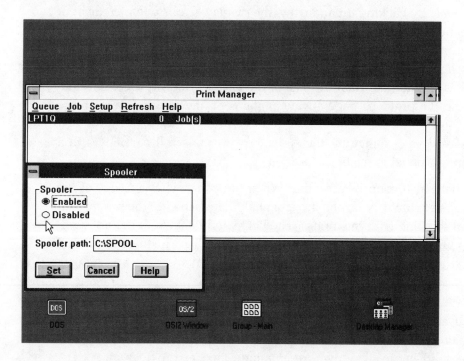

Check boxes give one or more binary choices that aren't mutually exclusive. Each box shows whether the choice is in effect. A check box consists of a square box and text. The Presentation Manager fills in the box with an X after a user selects it.

Figure 12-4: Check Boxes

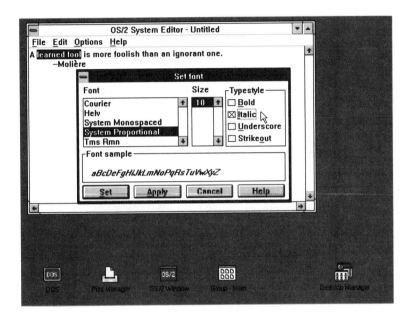

List boxes are rectangular boxes with scroll bars that let users choose one item from a scrollable list. Designers use list boxes to display a list with a variable number of items, such as file or directory names.

Pushbuttons show users the actions that are offered in dialog boxes, secondary windows, and message boxes. Dialog boxes and message boxes almost always have pushbuttons; secondary windows may have action bars instead. A pushbutton is a rectangle with round corners that encloses a text description, such as OK, Cancel, or Help. Users can select pushbuttons with the mouse, an accelerator key (such as Esc, which means Cancel), or a mnemonic.

Single-line entry fields let users type information that is shorter than one line. This control consists of descriptive text and a rectangular box for typing values. Users can scroll within entry fields, but short items, such as telephone numbers or dates, must have boxes large enough to hold the entire item. The *auto tab* option moves the text cursor to the next entry field after filling an entry field; this is useful for high-volume data entry applications.

Multiple-line entry fields consist of a rectangular box with typed data that can be more than one line long. For example, this control is useful as the text area of a word processor. Scroll bars show whether the text extends beyond the boundary of the window. Within multiple-line entry fields, the Enter, Tab, and Insert keys operate in a similar manner to word processing software.

Figure 12-5: Pushbuttons

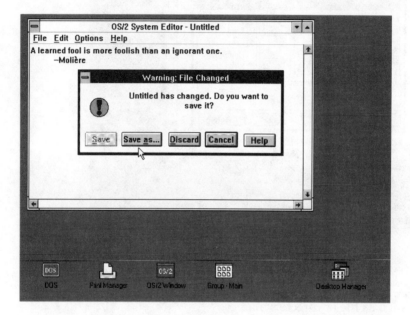

Combination boxes integrate the functions of entry fields and list boxes. Designers use this control to let users either type information or select items from a list provided by the application. *Drop-down combination boxes* are similar, but the list box doesn't appear until users ask for it. The entry field contains a down-arrow as a visual cue that the list box is available.

Drop-down lists are similar to drop-down combination boxes, but they don't have an entry field for typing text. Instead there is a single selection field with one choice displayed as a default value. Designers use drop-down lists, rather than list boxes, when they don't expect a choice to be changed often.

Value sets are selection fields that behave like radio buttons. The screen doesn't show a radio button; instead, users select an item by clicking with the mouse or moving the selection cursor. Items in a value set are either text or graphics. The main advantage of this control is that it requires less space on the screen than radio buttons.

Figure 12-6: Single-Line Entry Fields

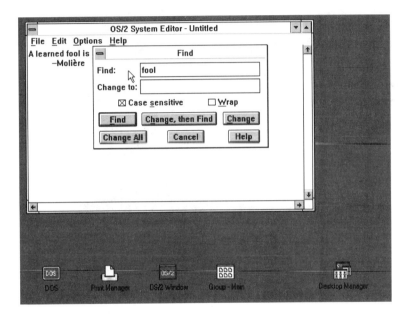

Spin buttons let users specify an entry field by scrolling through a circular list of choices. The field can contain characters or numbers, but the list of choices should be in consecutive order, so users can anticipate the next choice. For example, a spin button asks users to enter the day of the week from a list of the seven days.

A *field identifier* describes the purpose of a selection or entry field. A *group identifier* describes a related set of fields. The controls are necessary to let users know what information the application expects to be entered. CUA defines four such identifiers:

- *Field Prompt* Static text that describes a selection or entry field. It is above or to the left of every field
- *Column Heading* Identifies an entry or selection field that has similar items arranged in a column, such as a list box
- *Group Heading* Indicates a related set of fields. This identifier usually appears in combination with field prompts

■ *Group Box* A rectangular frame with a title, which groups related choices that work together

Figure 12-7: Group Box

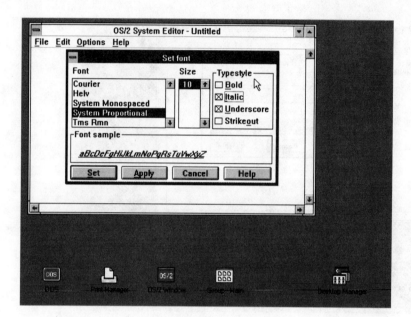

Dialog Boxes

A *dialog box* is a window that pops up when users initiate an action. It asks for information needed by an application to continue a request. Modal dialog boxes require users to complete the dialog box before proceeding with the application. Modal dialogs are essential for many purposes, such as opening files. Mode-less dialog boxes let users interact with the application's other windows without completing the dialog box. Mode-less dialogs are useful when users might want to switch between the dialog box and the application's main window repeatedly.

Modal dialog boxes disappear when users select the OK action or any other action that completes the dialog box. Mode-less dialog boxes disappear when the user closes their parent window. On any dialog box, either the Close action from the system menu of the dialog box or the Cancel pushbutton will end the dialog box.

The application decides the initial location of a dialog box, based on the following CUA guidelines. The dialog box should avoid obscuring any pertinent information in the underlying window. When the application stacks multiple dialog boxes, it should vertically offset the top dialog box below the title in the underlying dialog box. Users can move the dialog box, but they can't change its size and shape.

Pushbuttons in dialog boxes initiate actions immediately. Designers should place them in a horizontal line at the bottom of dialog boxes. All such pushbuttons must be the same height. When a dialog box has several pushbuttons, the application highlights one of them as the default action by using a bold border. Usually the default action responds positively to the dialog, such as by using the OK action. However, if the OK action could destroy data, then Cancel should be the default action.

CUA specifies standard pushbutton names for dialog boxes, as follows:

- *OK* Accepts any changed information in the dialog box, executes the action, and closes the box
- *Apply* Accepts any of the user's changes of properties. Leaves the dialog box open to allow further changes
- *Reset* Cancels any changes made by the user, and redisplays the dialog box
- *Cancel* Closes the dialog box without doing any of the requested changes. This doesn't affect previously committed changes
- *Help* Displays context-sensitive help for the item to which the cursor is pointing

Feedback

An application uses *graphical feedback* to inform users when it will take a long time to complete a request. Users need to know that they temporarily can't use the keyboard or mouse while the application processes a lengthy request. CUA defines two ways to do this: an hourglass pointer and progress indicators, but IBM recognizes that these may not handle all application scenarios. Hence, designers can invent their own methods of graphical feedback.

Applications change the shape of the mouse pointer to an hourglass when the application is doing major operations such as file opening, saving, and initialization. This tells users that the application is doing the requested operation, and won't accept more requests until it completes. Longer operations, including disk formatting or disk backup, require different strategies.

A *progress indicator* is useful for many types of complex requests. It is a dialog box, with a graph showing progress toward completion as its most prominent element. The graph is a partially shaded (or filled with inverse color) horizontal rectangle that shows the progress. Under the rectangle, the application displays scale markings from 0 to 100 percent. Below the scale markings, a timer shows the elapsed time in minutes and seconds. Above the rectangle, the application reserves space for messages alerting the user to errors that might occur. A Stop pushbutton, located at the bottom of the dialog box, lets users end the process prematurely. In stopping the process, the application maintains as much of the data as possible.

Complex processes should take as much advantage of the operating system's multiprogramming features as possible. This lets users continue normal work while a lengthy operation is running. For example, a spreadsheet could let users type input while recalculating undisplayed cells. However, it isn't always practical to let users work while an operation is in progress. For example, saving a file during a disk backup might impair the backup's integrity.

Applications often provide feedback in the form of *messages*. Messages are modal, and they appear in message boxes or dialog boxes. A *message box* contains an icon, message text, and pushbuttons. The icon depicts the message's urgency: information, warning, or action. The text is either a statement or question, which conveys the needed information. Pushbuttons let users interact with the message box. Often the box contains a Help pushbutton.

Information messages tell users about events that the application considers to be normal. The OK pushbutton lets users acknowledge the message and removes the message. The system doesn't beep when it displays an information message.

Warning messages tell users about possible trouble. For example, an application issues a warning message when users try to destroy important data. The message gives users the opportunity to confirm an action, or cancel it before damage occurs. Warning messages may have the following pushbuttons:

- *OK* Causes the application to remove the message and continue
- *Cancel* Causes the application to remove the message and take no action; it is the alternative to OK
- *Yes* Provides an answer, if the message is a question
- *No* Always paired with Yes

Action messages tell about error conditions that require user actions. Such errors range in severity from minor to severe, and may affect only the application or the entire system. The stop-sign icon marks an action message, and the text describes the error. The message box can contain the Retry, Cancel, and Help pushbuttons. The Retry pushbutton lets users correct I/O device errors. The Cancel pushbutton removes the message and takes no action.

Figure 12-8: Message Box

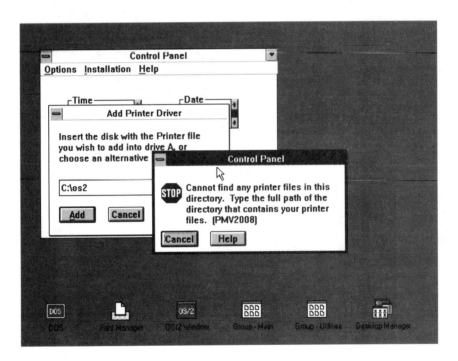

Audible feedback is a beep from the computer that notifies users of errors. Applications shouldn't beep if the user has told the Presentation Manager not to beep. Applications should beep when:

- Displaying warning and error messages
- Users type incorrect mnemonics
- Users try to select an unavailable choice

Help

Help gives information about choices, fields, or how to proceed with an application. It isn't a tutorial, but it is an immediate reference for an experienced user. It helps users recall how to use an application.

Figure 12-9: CUA Help Panel

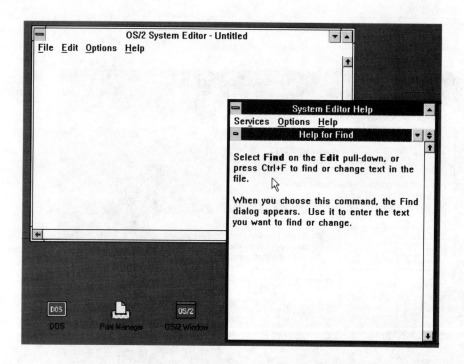

Help displays a window that contains requested information. Whenever the window is active, users interact with it by accessing its Help action bar pull-down menu. Users initially request help in the following ways:

- Pressing the F1 key
- Selecting the Help pushbutton
- Using the Help pull-down menu on the action bar

CUA defines several types of help information. Designers must decide which of the following types of help to include in an application:

- *Contextual* (or field-level) Specific information about the item that the selection cursor is pointing to
- *Help for help* Information about using the help facility
- *Extended help* General information about the window from which users requested help
- *Keys help* Lists of the application's key assignments
- *Help index* Alphabetic list of all help information
- *Tutorial* Access to the application's tutorial, if offered
- *Reference phrase help* Explanation of unusual words or phrases used by an application.

If possible, an application displays the help window where it is completely visible on the screen and it doesn't obstruct the view of the application's windows. Ideally the designer locates it to the right of the associated application window. If it must cover the application's window, the help window should cover the minimum information possible. Users may change its size and position.

Figure 12-10: Help Pull-down Menu

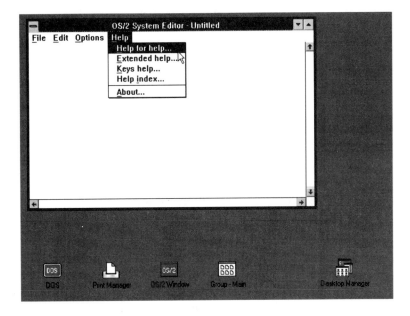

CUA defines a standard action bar pull-down menu for help, which designers must consistently use. The architecture also defines the order of the items in the pull-down menu. The last entry is About..., which displays the application's logo panel. The logo panel contains the application name, version, part number, copyrights, and trademarks. If the application is an IBM product, the panel also contains the familiar IBM logo.

Specialized Window Techniques

The *multiple document interface* lets users view many objects concurrently, or the same object many times. *Split window* gives multiple views of one object in a single window. These techniques are useful for word processing and office applications.

Figure 12-11: Multiple Document Interface Application

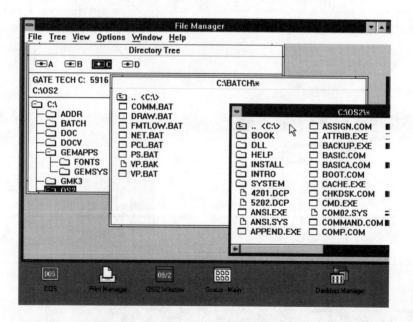

With the multiple document interface, the application puts each document in a secondary window. The secondary window is unusual because it can be minimized (to become an icon) and it doesn't have an action bar. The actions of the primary window can apply to the secondary windows. The choices on the action bar can be context-sensitive, and apply only to the selected secondary window.

For example, when one secondary window contains a graphic and another contains a document, the application's drawing functions wouldn't be offered in the document window.

Split window lets users view several parts of an object at a time. Users can split the window vertically, horizontally, or both. Split bars separate the two or four panes in the window. Users can request the split from the system pull-down menu, or by clicking on the black split box, which is above the up-arrow on the vertical scroll bar.

CUA Workplace Environment

The workplace environment is an extension of the graphical model that simulates a real workplace. The most obvious workplace is the office, but this idea could be generalized to include other workplaces such as the factory, farm, school, or laboratory. The workplace environment is different from the graphical model because it:

- Provides for more direct manipulation of objects
- Adds icons to handle common functions such as printing and deleting objects
- Offers more features for applications to share information
- More closely makes the system an extension of reality

Objects found in the workplace, such as telephones, file cabinets, folders, printers, and documents appear on the screen as icons. Users manipulate these objects with a mouse. The method of manipulating these objects parallels the methods used in an office. For example, users open the file cabinet, find the correct folder, and drop a document into the folder.

The workplace environment structures objects in ways that reflect the real world. For example, file cabinets contain folders; folders contain documents; documents contain words, charts, and graphs. The architecture divides objects into three categories: *container*, *data*, or *device*. Container objects, such as file cabinets, hold other objects. Data objects, such as documents, contain information. Telephones and printers are examples of device objects.

The categories subdivide further by object class. Examples of object classes are: spreadsheet, printer, and chart. All objects in a class have common properties.

Properties define objects. *Common properties*, such as creation date, apply to all objects. *Class properties* describe an entire class of objects. For example, a chart object class would have properties like type (bar, line, or pie), size, and color.

When users create a chart, they assign specific values to properties, and can change those values later.

The workplace environment is *object-oriented*, which means that users work with visible items, and select the ones they want to work on. *Object handlers* are programs that manipulate and manage objects. The system's *list handler* displays the contents of container objects in icon or text form, and lets users operate on objects in the container. Its functions are similar to the OS/2 File Manager or the MS-DOS Executive in Microsoft Windows.

Correspondingly, the workplace has three types of primary windows:

- Workplace window
- Object handler windows
- List handler windows

The workplace window displays user and system objects, such as folders, documents, printers, and telephones. It is the first window that appears, and it is the window from which users start all activities. Objects in the window appear as icons, but they can have text associated with them.

When users open objects, the system displays them in windows. For example, opening a document invokes the object handler for documents. The object handler lets users view, create, and change the properties of an object. When users open container objects, the system invokes the list handler. The list handler then displays the contents of the container object, and lets users operate on *whole objects* within the container. The operations include: open, move, copy, and delete.

Although the workplace encourages direct manipulation of objects, it also lets users manipulate objects through action bar pull-down menus. IBM added the Properties... action to the File pull-down, which lets users access the common properties of objects. A new Send... action supports an electronic mail facility. In the list handler, IBM also added the File actions Move..., Copy..., Rename..., and Discard. The View pull-down menu lets users display objects in various formats.

Users open objects by double-clicking the mouse on an icon. Most direct manipulation operations use dragging techniques involving source and destination objects. The user drags the source object to the destination object. This provides a simple way to move and copy objects. The rules for direct manipulation are:

- Dragging to a container represents a move operation
- Dragging to a device is a copy operation
- Dragging to an entry field copies the data appropriate for the object

- Moving or copying a container works on its entire contents
- Pressing the Ctrl key while dragging changes the operation to a copy; pressing the Alt key changes the operation to a move

IBM's OfficeVision/2 product implements many of the services of the workplace environment, but IBM plans to have the operating system support such services directly. This means that application developers won't have to support the services in their own code.

Implementing the User Interface Components

Under OS/2, IBM provides two vehicles for implementing the user interface components described in this chapter. Presentation Manager lets programmers develop applications using any interface component. However, the Presentation Manager requires a large coding effort and high programmer skill.

The Dialog Manager lets programmers use a subset of the CUA graphical interface and requires much less programming effort than the Presentation Manager. Dialog Manager uses the Presentation Manager, and thus appears similar to users. It is suitable for applications that require only action bars, pull-down menus, scroll bars, radio buttons, check boxes, list boxes, pushbuttons, and entry fields.

IBM and other vendors may offer additional tools that simplify developing CUA applications. It is likely that UNIX, DOS, and other operating system environments will run applications that have CUA-compliant user interfaces. This will give designers additional options beyond the ones discussed in this book.

Presentation Manager Implementation

The Presentation Manager component of OS/2 automatically handles some of the interface components. For example, it contains the logic to select from the action bar, display the pull-down menus, and let users select items on the menus. Presentation Manager also handles dialog boxes, and provides nearly all the controls defined by CUA. Application code mainly handles the client area and manages any objects in the application's windows.

Highly interactive applications, which respond directly to each keystroke or mouse movement, work best with the Presentation Manager. However, Presentation Manager programming is complex and difficult. Many programmers are unprepared for the complexity of its Application Programming Interface (API). Successful developers point out that the Presentation Manager has a one-year "learning curve." Nevertheless, it lets programmers use the full range of CUA graphical services discussed in this chapter.

Dialog Manager Implementation

Not all applications are highly interactive. Applications that consist mainly of fill-in-the-blanks operations are prime candidates for the Dialog Manager. It uses technology developed on IBM mainframe systems, notably Interactive System Productivity Facility (ISPF). Designers will consider using Dialog Manager for porting certain types of mainframe applications.

Dialog Manager uses a procedural programming technique that is familiar to most application programmers. Presentation Manager, on the other hand, uses an event-driven technique. Dialog Manager handles all user interaction, and doesn't return control to the application until users have completed interaction with a panel. Hence, Dialog Manager applications don't receive individual keystrokes or mouse movements as they occur.

Programmers define Dialog Manager application *panels* using the Dialog Tag language, which is part of the SAA Common Programming Interface. Panel definitions determine the contents of the client area, action bar and pull-down menus. Applications request, via an API, that the Dialog Manager display a particular panel, after which, the Dialog Manager handles all navigation, selection, and text entry. Applications retrieve the results of these operations from a pool of variables.

Dialog Manager provides the following services that the Presentation Manager doesn't:

- Validating and translating fields
- Designing panel layouts
- Sizing windows
- Establishing defaults

Dialog Manager has three types of windows: primary, modal dialog boxes, and help. Based on the window type, it provides the correct window border, title bar, and system menu contents. As directed by the tag language, it provides the following controls:

- Radio buttons
- Check boxes

- List boxes
- Entry fields

Dialog Manager fully supports the action bar and associated pull-down menus. It provides scroll bars and lets users change the size of windows. The tag language defines messages, but it doesn't use message icons. The Dialog Manager provides an extensive Help function. It doesn't, however, support the multiple document interface or split window techniques.

Chapter 13

Application Design and Programming

The SAA Common Programming Interface (CPI) contains specifications for languages and services to help programmers develop applications. Knowledge of CPI lets programmers write code that can be moved from one SAA environment to another. Although most of CPI's ingredients are familiar and proven, in practice they don't guarantee 100 percent portability. Many real applications need functions (for example, Job Control Language or equivalent) that aren't part of SAA.

IBM published specifications for the languages and services included in CPI. Many of these elements conform to standards developed by official standards groups such as ANSI and ISO. Others are specific to IBM product lines.

Each CPI element has an IBM reference manual that describes the syntax and semantics of each of its features. This chapter describes each CPI element generally. Readers who want to know the details of particular features should refer to the IBM volumes listed in the bibliography.

CPI provides two technical strategies for application development. One strategy emphasizes traditional tools:

- Third generation languages
- Procedures languages
- Database interface
- Dialog interface
- Presentation interface

The alternative strategy uses fewer, but higher-level tools:

- Application generator
- Query interface

IBM's AD/Cycle includes tools developed by IBM and other vendors to execute both strategies. The tools apply to each phase of an application's life cycle. AD/Cycle tools themselves use cooperative processing between a PS/2 workstation (which provides the user interface), and a central repository running on a System/370 mainframe.

The AD/Cycle strategy, unveiled in 1989, has been under development for many years. It is an essential part of IBM's effort to improve the application development process by:

- Providing a single place for information to control the development process
- Handling the entire application life cycle with one integrated approach
- Offering an "open" framework of development tools, useful to both vendors and customers
- Protecting customer investments in existing application development tools, skills, and data
- Letting customers adopt new application development technologies

Languages and Services

Programmers write SAA applications using three standard third generation languages: FORTRAN 77, COBOL 85, and C. The SAA versions of these languages conform to ANSI and ISO standards. Report Program Generator (RPG) and PL/I are popular within the IBM customer base; thus they were included in SAA.

An application generator can automatically code any of the languages listed above. Alternatively, customers can select IBM's application generator, Cross System Product (CSP). This approach also works with AD/Cycle, as described later in this chapter.

A procedures language, based on VM's Restructured Extended Executor (REXX), provides a command and macro language. This interesting language lets users write entire small applications or glues pieces of large applications together. Functionally, it is a substitute for Job Control Language.

CPI includes several other important services for application programming, including:

- *Structured Query Language (SQL)* Provides access by programs to relational database services.
- *Query Manager* Provides access to databases and report writing for end-users.
- *Presentation Manager* Handles the keyboard, graphics, and windows.
- *Dialog Manager* Offers a simple interface between applications and the Presentation Manager.

Application Generator

IBM derived the CPI application generator specification from Cross System Product (CSP). This product has been available for many years and, as its name suggests, was designed with portability in mind.

Advertised as a fourth generation language (4GL) for professional programmers, the application generator is an alternative to standard high level languages. Programmers create applications interactively, using a dialog-oriented, fill-in-the-blanks approach. CSP works with other parts of CPI, including the SQL database and the dialog manager.

CSP has prompting, tutorial, and interactive syntax checking functions. It eliminates some of the tedious steps required by traditional development methods. Programmers perform several phases of the development process under its guidance:

- Developing screen panels
- Designing files and logic
- Debugging code
- Testing the finished application

CSP has two parts: application development (AD) and application execution (AE). The AD function generates an application that is independent of the operating system and hardware. When the application runs, the AE function automatically adapts the code to the specific system in which it is running. Thus, customers can develop applications on one SAA system and execute them on another. The latest CSP version also generates COBOL code.

Procedures Language

REXX, the SAA procedures language, allows both operating system commands and conventional programming statements. The procedures language is similar to batch files in DOS, but is much more powerful. REXX is popular in the mainframe environment; programmers and end users both have found it easy to master. REXX features include:

- Execution of system commands
- Dynamic interpretation of statements
- Internal and external program calls
- Structured programming statements, including DO, IF-THEN-ELSE, and SELECT
- Expressions that operate on either numbers or character strings
- Extensive string parsing facilities

Database Interface

SQL provides services to define, retrieve, insert, delete, and update information in a relational database. With the relational data model, users view the database as a set of tables. The tables have rows and columns, similar to records and fields.

Applications access data through operations on tables. The applications are unaware of the physical structure of the database. Storage and management of data can be optimized independently, without affecting the portability of the application.

In SQL, users specify what is to be done by the database system, but not how it is done. SQL syntax resembles conventional programming languages. It performs arithmetic on retrieved values and has built-in functions for summation, grouping, ordering, and simple statistics such as means, minima, and maxima. Queries can retrieve selectively from several tables and sort the results.

Users enter SQL statements interactively or imbed them into the source code of an application program. A precompiler processes the imbedded SQL statements and translates them into subroutine calls. Then users compile, link, and execute their programs.

The following is a simple query embedded in a FORTRAN program:

```
    EXEC SQL BEGIN DECLARE SECTION
         CHARACTER * 20 XX
         INTEGER        YY, ZZ
    EXEC SQL END DECLARE SECTION

    EXEC SQL DECLARE C1 CURSOR FOR
X        SELECT LOCATION, QTY
X        FROM INVENTORY
X        WHERE PARTNO = :ZZ
```

```
EXEC SQL OPEN C1
EXEC SQL FETCH C1 INTO :XX, :YY
EXEC SQL CLOSE C1
```

SQL is an integral part of IBM Data Base 2 (DB2), SQL/DS, and the OS/2 Database Manager. The AS/400 database requires an extra product to support SQL. SAA SQL is consistent with the ANSI SQL standard X3.135-1986. It is compatible with current DB2, SQL/DS, and OS/2 Database Manager products.

Query Interface

The query interface composes interactive queries of a relational database and creates reports containing the answers. The first SAA-compliant query product was the OS/2 Query Manager. Later IBM enhanced the Query Management Facility (QMF) for MVS and VM to comply with the SAA query specification.

Using a series of menus, users access and summarize information, then report the results. On-line HELP guides users in making their requests. The product executes SQL statements or it prompts users to enter all necessary information to complete a query. Applications can build and manipulate queries, procedures, and report specifications through a subroutine call interface. QMF can store the results for access by other applications.

Presentation Interface

The presentation interface contains a complete set of functions for displaying and printing information. It includes an Application Programming Interface (API) that supports a window system, interaction via the keyboard and mouse, and comprehensive graphics. It also handles fonts and images. Only OS/2 Presentation Manager provides the full presentation interface.

Graphics functions are nearly identical to the System/370 Graphical Data Display Manager (GDDM). SAA window functions are similar to those provided by Microsoft Windows. GDDM is part of the MVS and VM SAA environments, but IBM has no plans to offer SAA windows under these operating systems. Hence, mainframe applications may use graphics, but the system software doesn't provide windows.

Dialog Interface

The dialog interface promotes interaction between the user and the application by formatting the screen and by passing data from the keyboard or mouse to the program. It is similar in concept to *forms packages* used on minicomputers, or Basic Mapping Support (BMS) in mainframe CICS systems.

The dialog manager displays panels on the screen. They contain menu selections, HELP information, data requests, and messages. The dialog manager also performs input field validation, issues error messages, and navigates through the hierarchy of panels. It manages pools of variables, which contain information supplied or used by applications.

Programmers define dialog manager panels using the dialog tag language, which is part of CPI. Panel definitions determine the contents of the screen's client area, action bar, and pull-down menus. Applications request, via an API, that the dialog manager display a particular panel. After displaying the panel, the dialog manager handles all navigation, selection, and text entry. Applications retrieve the results of these operations from a pool of variables.

AD/Cycle – SAA Application Development Strategy

IBM's AD/Cycle strategy provides a framework for programmers and business professionals to develop and maintain applications. This framework provides tools to develop high quality applications. IBM's strategy fosters development of SAA applications while continuing to support existing approaches.

AD/Cycle provides tools to support the entire application life cycle. The life cycle consists of the following phases:

- Requirements definition
- Analysis and design
- Coding
- Building and testing
- Maintenance

Each tool focuses on a specific part of the life cycle. AD/Cycle lets application developers enter the application development life cycle at any stage and select an appropriate tool. The framework also provides a smooth transition from tool to tool. All AD/Cycle tools conform to CUA, which presents a consistent look and feel across the life cycle.

Figure 13-1: AD/Cycle Phases

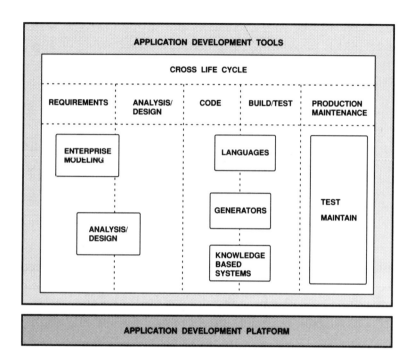

IBM couldn't solve the entire application development problem itself. AD/Cycle is a combination of IBM and third-party tools. IBM initially included products of the following vendors:

- Index Technology Corporation
- KnowledgeWare, Inc.
- Bachman Information Systems

To promote AD/Cycle tools written by users and vendors, IBM provides an open framework. This consists of interfaces and common support functions, which let AD/Cycle adapt to many application development needs. Software vendors participate in AD/Cycle by integrating their tools with this framework. SAA CPI includes some of the rules and guidelines for such integration.

AD/Cycle is IBM's SAA solution for application development. AD/Cycle lets customers develop, maintain, and execute SAA applications in any of the strategic IBM operating system environments.

The strategy is evolutionary. Over the next 10 years, IBM and its business partners will gradually release the AD/Cycle tools and support services across all SAA environments. IBM is persuading customers to start following its application development strategy now. The recommended steps are:

- Establishing structured development methods and techniques
- Taking inventory of application development assets
- Modeling the enterprise
- Installing the foundation products such as DB2, SQL/DS, AS/400 database, ISPF, and OS/2 Extended Edition, which implement the SAA CPI
- Standardizing the process of application development throughout the enterprise

Using CPI with structured development methods and a formal life cycle process will require cultural and organizational changes that must be introduced carefully. It will take several years until everyone in an enterprise accepts these changes, so early preparation is essential.

The following sections describe the main features of AD/Cycle.

The AD/Cycle Model

The application development life cycle consists of the phases mentioned above. The AD/Cycle model conceptually groups tools into sets that concentrate on specific activities within the life cycle. The tool sets are:

- *Enterprise Modeling* Defining and validating a business model of data and processes
- *Analysis and Design* Performing requirements analysis and application design, including database design
- *Languages* Producing and debugging application programs using third-generation languages
- *Application Generators* Writing high-level specifications, rather than detailed procedural code
- *Knowledge-Based Systems* Producing expert systems
- *Testing and Maintenance* Building, testing, and maintaining applications
- *Cross Life Cycle* Supporting activities that span life cycle phases

The SAA application development tools and platforms are part of the AD/Cycle model. Future IBM products will also conform to the model.

An *application development platform* integrates tools through a consistent user interface, an application development information model, tool services, and a repository manager. The *application development information model* lets the tools share information throughout the life cycle. The *repository manager* is the single, central source and control point for application development information. CPI includes the programming interface to the repository; this provides a consistent interface within each SAA host environment.

Enterprise Modeling

IBM believes that enterprise-wide models of data and processes should drive application design. Customers need tools to develop an enterprise model and validate it through prototyping. Prototyping is useful for understanding user requirements early in the development cycle. The enterprise model becomes the base for designing applications.

AD/Cycle tools for enterprise modeling are:

- *Information Engineering Workbench (IEW)* (KnowledgeWare) Captures, models, and analyzes an organization's use of information.
- *PC PRISM* (Index Technology) Helps organizations develop and analyze enterprise models that align their business and systems objectives.
- *DevelopMate* (IBM) Refines and validates an enterprise business model through prototyping. The repository manager controls all modeling information, which other tools can share.

Analysis and Design

In the analysis and design phase, analysts use business requirements to develop application designs. AD/Cycle includes standard tools that produce standard analysis and design documentation, including:

- Decomposition diagrams
- Data-flow diagrams
- Entity/relationship diagrams
- Data structure diagrams

AD/Cycle techniques are consistent with software engineering and information engineering principles. The tools for analysis and design are:

- *IEW Analysis Workstation* (KnowledgeWare)   Refines user requirements and creates specifications that are logically complete, consistent, and correct.
- *IEW Design Workstation* (KnowledgeWare)   Designs information systems specified in the Analysis Workstation and creates physical specifications for both data and processes. The product then passes this information to application generators.
- *Excelerator* (Index Technology)   Helps systems professionals to develop data and process models, validate and cross-reference design information, and design prototype screens or reports. It automatically generates system documentation. Customized versions of Excelerator work with IBM's DB2 and CSP.
- *The Bachman Re-Engineering Product Set*   Includes tools for data modeling and knowledge-based DB2 database design. The product fully integrates with the DB2 catalog; thus its designs are available to the CSP application generator.

Languages

C, COBOL, FORTRAN, and the REXX procedures language provide the foundation for third-generation language programming in SAA. IBM added RPG and PL/I to the architecture to meet particular needs within its customer base. AD/Cycle supports all SAA languages.

Future IBM third-generation language products will provide more tightly integrated compilers, editors, and dynamic debuggers. The company also plans to improve the integration of code produced by application generators.

IBM envisions that information captured from the front-end analysis and design tools will be used to generate third-generation language programs. Programmers can tap this information within debugging tools to simplify testing. Eventually AD/Cycle will let programmers edit, compile, and debug their applications on PS/2 workstations. (Several third-party vendors already provide this function.)

Application Generator

Application generators use high-level specifications, rather than detailed procedural code, to create applications. Programmers achieve higher productivity because less detailed application specifications are necessary. Such specifications are portable to various execution environments. Furthermore, this tool works well for development staff with low technical skill levels.

Cross System Product (CSP) is IBM's SAA application generator. In the first release of AD/Cycle, IBM added several features to the product. CSP now automatically develops cooperative processing applications. The applications include a CUA user interface on the PS/2. The CSP workstation front end runs on the PS/2 and connects via SAA communications to the application running on an SAA host computer.

CSP application development and execution can take place on different SAA hardware platforms. CSP accomplishes this by generating machine-independent code that is interpreted during execution. CSP also generates COBOL source code, which uses CSP run-time services. IBM initially offered COBOL source code generation in IMS environments, and plans to extend the feature to other SAA environments.

IBM integrated CSP into AD/Cycle by having the application development platform and the repository control the information needed to develop an application. The product includes an *external source format facility*, which uses the information supplied during enterprise modeling, analysis, and design phases.

Expert Systems

Tools to develop expert systems, based on artificial intelligence technology, are part of the AD/Cycle framework. IBM calls these *knowledge-based systems*. Knowledge-based systems use graphical PS/2 workstations to define rules, facts, and other information needed by expert systems.

Code produced by knowledge-based systems may be combined with high-level language code or application generator code. Knowledge-based system modules can call and be called by high-level language modules. As with the other languages, programmers may use an integrated edit, compile, and debug cycle.

AD/Cycle uses the application development platform to store information about objects in knowledge-based systems. This allows sharing of knowledge-based application development information with other AD/Cycle tools.

Testing and Maintenance

Testing is a key part of the application life cycle. A comprehensive testing program requires tools for test data creation, management, and analysis. IBM also provides tools for software maintenance, re-engineering, distribution, and packaging.

AD/Cycle includes two tools for testing and maintaining applications. Software Analysis Test Tool provides a CUA graphical interface for interactive browsing, query, and reporting of test coverage information. The product provides an animated display of test execution, replayed on a structure chart of the application.

Workstation Interactive Test Tool does regression testing of SAA interactive applications. This product automatically records and re-executes interactive application test sessions. A CUA interface displays test results and analyzes test case discrepancies.

The AD/Cycle Application Development Platform

AD/Cycle will result in a development platform that includes five application development technologies:

- User Interface
- Workstation Services
- Application Development Information Model
- Tool Services
- Repository

User Interface

Products within AD/Cycle that run on PS/2 workstations use the graphical CUA user interface. All IBM tools are compatible with CUA and IBM is encouraging users and third parties to follow CUA guidelines. IBM anticipates that many applications developed using AD/Cycle will include a CUA user interface.

Workstation Services

AD/Cycle uses a cooperative processing approach in which the PS/2 workstation is the primary window into the AD/Cycle environment. This combines the advantages of an interactive graphical workstation with the capacity and information sharing capabilities of host systems. Although the main AD/Cycle user interface runs on a PS/2 workstation connected to a host, non-programmable terminals can still access existing tools and some new functions.

Workstation software may be delivered on diskettes or downloaded from the host. A simplified download procedure allows for management of software distribution in a network configuration.

Interactive System Productivity Facility/Program Development Facility (ISPF/PDF) works with a Workstation Platform for OS/2. This feature lets PS/2 workstations use the host application library. ISPF/PDF runs on the System/370 and communicates with the Workstation Platform running on the PS/2. This is the first step of a strategy to provide an integrated application development platform.

Application Development Information Model

The Application Development Information Model defines the structure and format of information in the repository. It also lets application development tools share the repository. IBM developed the model, but users and software vendors may extend it to integrate future tools into the AD/Cycle framework. IBM provides guidelines for extension of the model.

The information model provides the data architecture to share information between tools. For example, the information model includes these objects:

- Source code
- Panel text
- DB2 data definitions
- COBOL data structures
- Data-flow diagrams

Tool Services

AD/Cycle provides *tool services* that manipulate and validate data within the information model. These services make it easy for tools to use the information. Standard operations such as copy, delete, and store simplify tool design by reducing data manipulation. Other tool services, such as version and configuration control, help with application building and integration.

Repository Manager

AD/Cycle has a repository manager, which controls access to application development information throughout the application life cycle. The repository curtails redundant information during the development process and thus improves the consistency and integrity of application design.

The SAA CPI repository interface gives tool builders access to the repository and lets them extend the tool services and information model supplied by IBM. Repository Manager/MVS provides the interface for MVS/ESA and MVS/XA using TSO. Repository Manager/MVS uses DB2 for storing and retrieving repository information. IBM plans to implement the repository CPI under VM and OS/400, providing remote access from OS/2 Extended Edition.

IBM's Dictionary Model Transformer helps in the transition from existing IBM information bases (such as dictionaries and libraries) to the repository. This product, working with Repository Manager/MVS, moves information controlled by IBM's DB/DC Data Dictionary to the repository.

Cross Life Cycle Tools

Although most application development tools focus on one phase of the application life cycle, some apply to several life cycle phases. These manage access to information by people involved in the development process, or process data shared by multiple members of a development team. The cross-life-cycle activities include:

- Process management
- Project management
- Impact analysis
- Documentation
- Reuse

Process management controls the approach for application development; it sets the tools, sequence of tasks, and checkpoints for the developing applications. Defining standard development procedures is a part of process management. By automating process management, customers can precisely control the development process, improve quality, and cut development time.

Project management ties closely with process management. It tracks the development process and collects historical data for future project estimates. Project management also uses completion checkpoints identified by process management to produce progress reports.

Impact analysis evaluates the effect of specific changes to applications before the changes actually occur. For example, impact analysis determines which panels and code modules would be affected by a change to a given data element. *Documentation* is an integral part of developing applications. It starts with gathering data at the requirements phase and extends through writing operator procedures and training materials. *Reuse strategy* provides an inventory of items that can be used in multiple applications, such as include files, subroutines, and documentation. This improves productivity by avoiding redundant design and programming efforts.

IBM's initial AD/Cycle framework didn't include specific tools to handle any of the functions mentioned in this section. Some of the non-IBM tools previously listed contain a few of these functions. As SAA matures, IBM is likely to introduce several cross life cycle tools, perhaps as part of the SAA Common Applications component. Eventually, this might become the most important part of the CPI.

Chapter 14

Application Enablers

Application enablers manage program execution, user interaction, and database access, and thus are important foundations of the Common Programming Interface. Not every CPI product falls into the application enabler category. Compilers and language products are not application enablers even though they are included in SAA and mentioned in earlier chapters.

Application enablers support cooperative processing. Early cooperative processing applications, such as AD/Cycle and OfficeVision, operate between PS/2 and System/370 computers. These computers will probably provide the main cooperative processing environments in the early 1990s. In theory, cooperative processing also encompasses the AS/400, but its CPI products were not fully developed at the time of writing. Hence, this chapter focuses on key application enablers for PS/2 and System/370.

The key application enablers, discussed in this chapter, are:

- *OS/2 Presentation Manager* Gives programmers the greatest control of the user interface on PS/2 workstations
- *Interactive System Productivity Facility (ISPF)* Offers a user interface for MVS TSO and VM CMS that is a character-oriented subset of CUA
- *OS/2 Dialog Manager* Provides an easy-to-program subset of the CUA user interface, mainly suitable for data processing applications on PS/2s
- *Database 2 (DB2)* Provides IBM's most complete relational database, intended for MVS systems

- *Query Management Facility (QMF)* Helps end-users and programmers access databases and prepare reports

Other IBM products, covered in previous chapters, comply with CPI and are equivalent to the products listed above:

- *SQL Data System (SQL/DS)* Provides relational database services under VM, which are equivalent to those provided by DB2
- *OS/2 Database Manager* Manages relational databases within OS/2 Extended Edition.
- *SQL/400* Works with the AS/400 database to provide SAA SQL services to RPG, COBOL, and PL/I programs
- *OS/2 Query Manager* Offers a query and report generation function for the OS/2 Database Manager

Two application enabling subsystems are not fully compatible with SAA, but allow execution of CPI programs:

- *Customer Information Control System (CICS)* Supports medium-volume transaction processing under MVS
- *Information Management System/Transaction Manager (IMS)* Provides high-performance transaction processing under MVS

SAA applications running under these subsystems must provide their user interface on a workstation because neither subsystem includes a CUA user interface. Chapter 8 describes application development under IMS and CICS. Another approach, discussed below, is to use ISPF for user interaction and program execution on the System/370 mainframe.

OS/2 Presentation Manager

OS/2 Presentation Manager provides a window-based graphical user interface. It introduces a new style of API for advanced graphics and user interaction. The Presentation Manager lets users run applications by selecting them from menus and icons with a mouse or keyboard. The product meets the following design goals:

- Display multiple windows on the screen, each containing an application
- Integrate advanced graphics into the operating system
- Provide a standard interface for device independent graphics
- Manage applications, files, and system operation easily

User Interface

The graphical user interface provides an intuitive, consistent way for users to specify actions to be taken, finish tasks, get task-related help, and scroll a window's contents. Users control the size and position of windows on the screen. Applications can change to icons, conserving screen space; selecting an icon makes an application reappear.

Application developers directly control the product's user interface functions. Nevertheless, the Presentation Manager API promotes consistency among application user interfaces. The Presentation Manager's user interface complies, with some exceptions, to CUA. Ultimately, IBM intends to provide full CUA compliance. Thus, OS/2 applications will be consistent with a wide range of IBM products.

The Presentation Manager API lets software developers use the graphics, user interface and window management functions in their application programs. This API is part of the CPI Presentation Interface. Applications are device independent; Presentation Manager drivers route device output requests to the appropriate OS/2 device driver.

Application programmers can choose options that simplify developing CUA features, thereby eliminating the tedium of window and user interface management. The Presentation Manager user interface includes dialog boxes, action bars, pull-downs, scroll bars, specialized pointers, and selection icons. The system font is a proportional font, which is attractive and readable. Programmers can create their own fonts using the OS/2 Programming Tools product.

Windows

Presentation Manager applications run in one or more windows, which have a hierarchical parent-child relationship. Inside a window, applications typically use graphics functions, which are an integral part of the Presentation Interface. A clipboard lets users transfer text and graphics between Presentation Manager windows.

Many character-based OS/2 applications will run in a window without modification. Applications that don't run in a window must run outside the Presentation Manager's screen group. They can operate concurrently with Presentation Manager applications, but they occupy the entire screen while running. Presentation Manager runs up to 43 applications concurrently, subject to limits imposed by applications and hardware configuration.

Presentation Manager comes with an application that accesses and manages files on disk. Rather than requiring line-oriented commands, the *file manager* application displays the structure and contents of the directories in a graphical tree format. The product uses icons to identify the contents of the directories, including data files, executable programs, and subdirectories. Many routine tasks, such as selecting files and moving them, are easy to accomplish with simple mouse movements or a few keystrokes. OS/2 automatically executes a program whenever the user selects an associated file. For example, selecting a document can start a word processing program.

Figure 14-1: OS/2 File Manager

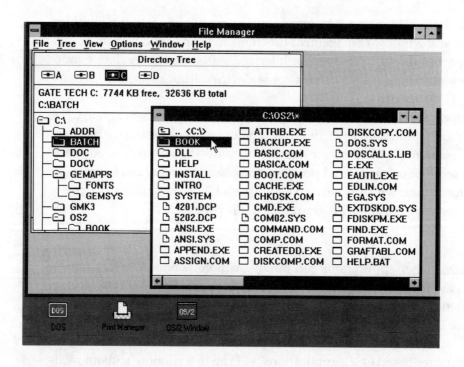

Graphics

The product supports a wide range of graphics primitives, attributes, and processing, including transformation, clipping, correlation, and bounds.

Graphical data may be vector or bitmap. Vector graphics contain geometric elements, such as lines, boxes, or ellipses. They are preferred for transferring graphics to other systems or for operations such as rotation or transformation. A bitmap is a matrix of bits that digitally represents a graphic as individual dots. Bitmaps provide higher efficiency for some applications. OS/2 can keep graphics in memory for later manipulation or refresh.

Applications store and retrieve graphics pictures using *metafiles* stored on disk. Metafiles contain editable, revisable vectors that applications can exchange. They also allow complex graphics to be combined, edited, and used with other applications.

Programmer Tools

The OS/2 Programmer Tools product contains tools for developing text and graphics applications for the Presentation Manager. These tools include:

- *Font Editor* Defines each character of a font, and stores the definitions in a disk file
- *Dialog Editor* Creates pop-up windows. It defines user interface controls and positions them. The editor saves the definition for inclusion in the application
- *Bitmap and Cursor Editor* Creates a bitmap, icon, cursor, or pointer. The editor stores the shapes in a matrix; the resource compiler then creates a resource file
- *Resource Compiler* Produces resource files for use by applications
- *Header Files* Define API functions and data structures needed by applications
- *Sample Programs* Illustrate the Presentation Manager API, including user interface, windowing, and graphics features

Interactive System Productivity Facility

Interactive System Productivity Facility (ISPF) is the dialog manager for interactive applications on System/370 host computers. It provides a subset of the SAA CPI dialog interface for MVS and VM environments. It implements a subset of CUA, mainly intended for data processing applications. An ISPF dialog consists of:

- Selection panels that show processing choices to users
- Programs that perform the requested processing

- Data entry panels that prompt users to enter information
- Display panels that supply information to users

Dialog Applications

Programmers write dialog applications in SAA languages including REXX, C, PL/I, COBOL, and FORTRAN. One way to create ISPF applications is through the companion Program Development Facility (PDF) product. PDF provides tools, such as a text editor, to simplify the development of dialogs. ISPF contains a dialog test facility to help programmers in debugging.

When an application invokes a dialog, ISPF:

- Displays a hierarchy of panels based on user selections
- Invokes programs from panels
- Communicates with users through data entry panels, display panels, and messages
- Provides Help and tutorials
- Generates output to be passed as input to another process; for example, input to a batch job
- Maintains a pool of variables, shared among ISPF applications
- Provides split-screen displays, letting users partition the screen into two or four areas
- Formats and displays graphics screens using GDDM

Using CUA's object-action interaction style, ISPF keeps objects in view and takes actions against them. The action bar or a selection field on a panel may choose the actions. The main panel remains visible and pop-up windows obtain data for the application. The command, message, and function key areas conform to CUA standards. ISPF also gives users the option of retaining the old-style ISPF panels rather than using CUA.

Dialog Tag Language

Developed many years ago, ISPF's own panel language isn't compatible with SAA. ISPF now lets programmers develop dialog elements (panels, command tables, and messages) using the CPI Dialog Tag Language (DTL). The ISPF Conversion Utility converts these DTL dialog elements to the ISPF internal panel format. After conversion, users can run dialog applications on IBM 3270 display terminals.

ISPF's dialect of DTL is similar to that of the OS/2 Dialog Manager. ISPF implements CUA elements such as pop-up windows, action bars, and action bar pull-downs on IBM 3270 terminals. Programmers can port ISPF DTL code to the OS/2 Dialog Manager. Although ISPF checks the syntax of all DTL tags, it doesn't handle all features supported by OS/2. ISPF issues warning messages for tags and attributes that it doesn't support.

CUA Features

ISPF automatically provides CUA-compatible Help. It includes support for contextual help on action bar choices, pull-down choices, and list columns. It provides extended help after contextual help and lets users display a panel with a brief description of each valid key.

The product includes National Language Support and Double-Byte Character Set (DBCS). IBM has translated ISPF's panels and messages to eight languages including Danish, German, Japanese, Chinese, and Spanish.

OS/2 Dialog Manager

The OS/2 Dialog Manager helps developers manage the interaction between their applications and end users. The Dialog Manager API is part of the OS/2 Programming Tools product. For OS/2, the product provides essentially the same functions that ISPF does for System/370. Therefore, the Dialog Manager provides significant elements of the SAA CPI dialog interface.

With the product, application developers can easily take advantage of Presentation Manager facilities. Dialog Manager resides in a layer between the application program and the Presentation Manager. It provides APIs for display-related dialog services, dialog variable handling, and dialog session control. As mentioned in previous chapters, programming the dialog manager is easier, but less flexible, than programming the Presentation Manager.

The Dialog Tag Language (DTL) defines dialog elements other than application program logic, including: application panels, help panels, application command tables, and messages. The compiler for DTL is part of the OS/2 Programming Tools.

Programmers write SAA Dialog Manager programs in C, FORTRAN, or COBOL. OS/2 Dialog Manager's structure is similar to the other dialog managers, ISPF and EZ-VU. This will simplify migration of applications to the OS/2 environment.

Data Base 2

IBM Data Base 2 (DB2) provides the relational data model for MVS through the SQL data language. The product offers many functions for both transaction processing and decision support applications. DB2 is IBM's strategic database product for its largest systems, which support IBM's biggest and most influential customers. It is a cornerstone of the IBM database and cooperative processing strategies in SAA.

Relational Data Model Implementation

The relational data model uses tables as basic units of information. A table is a matrix with columns and rows. At the intersection of every column and row is a specific data item, called a *value*. A database may contain many tables; the tabular data format insulates users from the details of accessing the physical data structure. With tables, programs don't navigate through data as they do in IMS.

A *view* is an alternative representation of the data in one or more tables. A view may contain a subset of the columns in a table, or it may consist of multiple joined tables. After defining a view, users access it as a table. Views offer two important advantages: they protect secret data and reduce complexity.

Database administrators create an *index* to speed access to data in a table. The index key consists of one or more columns. Users who access data never explicitly mention indexes in their SQL code. DB2 uses an index if it decides that the index will provide fast access to the data. DB2 creates two types of indexes:

- *Unique Index*   Ensures that the keys are unique for each row in a table. For example, this could guarantee that users enter no duplicate employee numbers into a payroll table
- *Clustering Index*   Puts rows in a particular physical sequence. A clustering index may store data the way an application usually will access it, for example, alphabetically by name

The DB2 *system catalog* consists of tables that contain information about the data and objects that DB2 manages. Authorized programs use SQL to retrieve data from these tables. The system catalog contains information about tables, columns, indexes, and authorization.

SQL Implementation

Structured Query Language (SQL) is a high-level database access language that simplifies programming. SQL statements reference data by name and value, but not by data access paths, data placement, or order. SQL, in a single statement, will access:

- Several columns from one row of a table
- Multiple columns from multiple rows of a single table
- One or more columns from multiple rows of multiple tables
- Columns calculated from other columns

Based on the data names and values coded in SQL statements, DB2 accesses or changes the specified data.

Figure 14-2: SQL's Relationship to Applications

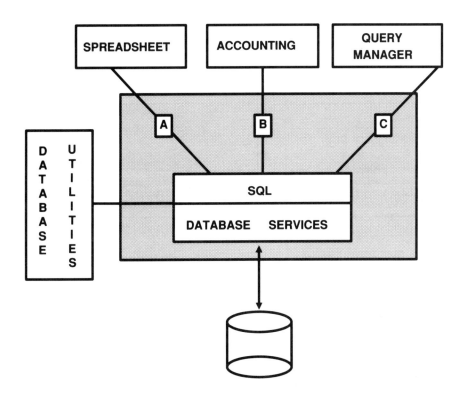

SQL does operations on mathematical sets. DB2 returns, updates, or deletes an entire set of data that meets the conditions specified in an SQL program. SQL controls the commitment of updates, defines data structures, and provides access controls. The language is consistent; it uses the same syntax and produces the same output whether invoked interactively or from within a program. Programmers can test most SQL statements interactively before including them in a program.

Application programs must declare the data items they process. The declaration generator uses information in the DB2 catalog to construct declaration statements for COBOL or PL/I programs. Application programmers invoke the declaration generator from TSO or as a batch job. It produces an SQL description of the table and a corresponding PL/I or COBOL structure.

DB2 maintains indexes and other information to locate data requested by SQL programs. To retrieve data, SQL programmers don't need to know its physical structure. Furthermore, users can process queries in remote DB2 systems. In contrast, IMS database programmers and administrators must know the data structure and decide whether to process data sequentially or use an index. DB2 makes these decisions automatically.

Figure 14-3: Distributed Database Architecture

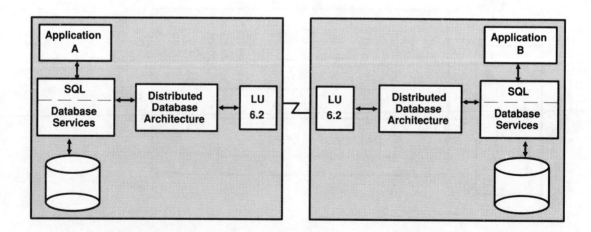

SQL programs never contain references to indexes. First, programmers precompile and bind their programs. During the bind procedure, DB2 selects an access path to the data. DB2 considers all available indexes when choosing the access path. Therefore, programs are unaware of additions and deletions of indexes.

DB2's automatic access path selection reduces program maintenance. For example, an administrator may delete a seldom-used index. When a program tries to use the deleted index, DB2 automatically establishes a new access path. It isn't necessary to change the application program. DB2 also allows limited distributed database functions, which let applications retrieve and update information in remote systems. Application programs need not know the location of data; DB2 automatically distributes the query through the network as shown in Figure 14-3.

Application Programming Tools

TSO, IMS transaction manager, and CICS subsystems may concurrently access DB2 data. IMS or CICS programs can access DB2 databases, IMS databases, or both. Users execute SQL through applications written in COBOL, FORTRAN, C, PL/I, and assembler language. DB2 Interactive (DB2I) runs under ISPF, which runs under TSO. Using DB2I, users:

- Enter SQL statements and view the results
- Execute DB2 commands
- Perform database development functions such as precompilation
- Run TSO database applications
- Invoke DB2 database utilities

Using DB2I, programmers can create and edit SQL statements they plan to include in their programs, execute those statements, and review the results. They can also create, load, and delete test tables and can use DB2I to check the contents of tables. DB2I is a useful tool for application programmers, database administrators, and system administrators.

DB2I provides Help information. By pressing a function key, users can view up to 500 panels that explain DB2 functions in detail. DB2 also adds text to TSO's help facility. This helps application programmers and database administrators to enter DB2 commands, precompile programs, or run utilities.

DB2I and QMF complement each other. Professional programmers use DB2I in the application development process. QMF users don't write application programs; the product is useful to people with limited programming skills.

The Application Programming Process

DB2 programmers write source programs that contain imbedded SQL statements. Preparing the programs for execution requires four steps:

- *Precompilation* Checks SQL syntax, produces a modified source program, and generates a Data Base Request Module (DBRM)
- *Compilation* Translates the modified source program to machine language
- *Binding* Uses DBRMs to produce an application plan, and stores it in the database. At execution time, DB2 uses the application plan to control access to data
- *Linkage Editing* Generates the executable module

The compilation and linkage editing steps are the same with DB2 as with conventional programming. The precompilation and binding are unique, as discussed below.

Before programmers compile a DB2 program, the precompiler processes it to extract the SQL statements. The precompiler also checks the syntax of the statements and copies them into the DBRM, which is input to the bind process. As the precompiler executes separately from DB2, program development doesn't disrupt normal database operation.

Binding converts the DBRM, a set of syntax-checked SQL statements, into a set of instructions to DB2. These instructions, called an *application plan*, tell DB2 where data is, how to get to it, and what to do with it. Binding includes four functions:

- Validating the SQL statements
- Determining whether the user doing the bind is authorized to access the resources named in the SQL statements
- Selecting the access path to the data
- Building the control blocks to let DB2 access the data at execution time

The advantage of the precompilation and bind process is better performance. With this approach, part of the database processing is finished before execution. When applications run, they only process data. DB2 also offers the option of handling SQL dynamically, without precompilation or binding.

Capacity, Reliability, and Recovery

DB2 operates efficiently under MVS/ESA by taking advantage of IBM's latest hardware and software architectures. It also works under MVS/XA. DB2 operates with IMS and CICS, so existing customers need not install a new transaction processing subsystem.

The database handles large tables, up to 64 gigabytes (64 x 10^9). Customers can partition large tables into smaller pieces; they reorganize and recover the pieces individually. DB2's recovery mechanism includes disk logging, automatic log archiving, and automatic recovery on restart.

DB2 operates continuously. Many system administration tasks that require IMS to shut down don't stop DB2. The product is a separate MVS subsystem, which stays up when IMS, CICS, or TSO is down. Through SQL, customers may add, delete, or change data definitions without stopping the subsystem.

Figure 14-4: DB2 Product Relationships

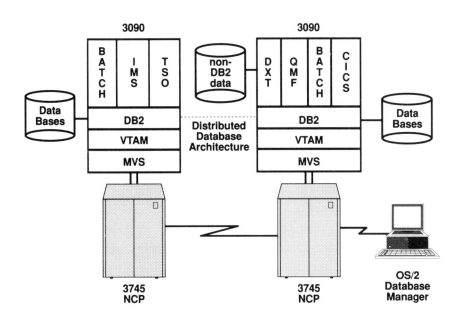

DB2 protects data from system, storage media, and program failures. An application may operate under several subsystems (such as batch, TSO, CICS, and

IMS); DB2 coordinates recovery across subsystem boundaries. DB2 synchronizes commitment of changes to the database, which allows for recovery regardless of when errors occur. DB2 coordinates its recovery with IMS and CICS to resolve potential inconsistencies without loss of data.

When restarting after a system failure, DB2 automatically restores data to a consistent state. It backs out of uncommitted changes and completes the processing of committed changes. Recovery of the most important databases can proceed first; this lets critical applications start running quickly. Customers can optionally delay recovery of less important databases. When an application fails, DB2 isolates the work associated with the failing program. Then it backs out of all uncommitted data changes without interfering with other system activities.

DB2 recovers from media failures by using system backups (called image copies) and the system log. To simplify media recovery, DB2 keeps track of logs and image copies. A DB2 recovery utility restores the data from the image copy and applies the changes recorded in the system log. An incremental image copy speeds the backup process by copying only blocks that changed since the last image copy.

Utilities

DB2 provides several on-line database utility programs. Users initiate these utilities by JCL, TSO CLISTs, or ISPF panels supplied with DB2. The major utilities provided are:

- *Load*   Reads data from disk or tape, data unloaded from SQL/DS, or data acquired by the Data Extract (DXT) product
- *Image Copy*   Creates a sequential backup
- *Recovery*   Uses image copy and log records
- *Reorganize*   Unloads and reloads a table space or partition
- *Statistics*   Updates the DB2 catalog with binding and reorganization statistics

DB2 utilities don't limit activity on other databases. Under the right conditions, DB2 allows concurrent application and utility execution on the same database. These functions provide for database administration without disturbing on-going processes and data.

Security

DB2 has comprehensive security. SQL can authorize a user to retrieve data from a particular table, but prohibit that user from changing any data in the table. Customers can centralize or decentralize control of security. They may delegate control of particular databases to individual users or groups within an organization.

DB2 provides two security mechanisms: authorization statements and views. In SQL, authorization statements grant and revoke authority for all data and program access. These statements let people who administer or define databases specify which data other users may access. They also limit access to DB2 commands and database utility programs. Views can present a subset of the rows or columns in a table. Users or programs see only the data defined in the view; other data in the table isn't accessible.

Query Management Facility

Query Management Facility (QMF) provides interactive query and report writing from relational databases for people with limited programming skills. The product produces customized reports and charts. QMF works with DB2 under MVS and SQL/DS under VM. Applications written in third generation languages can call QMF directly and have reports returned to the application. The product integrates with many other IBM products including ISPF and Graphical Data Display Manager (GDDM). QMF includes:

- Both SQL and Query By Example (QBE) styles of database query
- Data definition through SQL
- Interactive report generation
- Simple commands for queries, report forms, and procedures

The query and report writing functions usually work together. However, the query function can be used independently from the reporting function. Novices can produce useful results with a small subset of QMF's features and commands. The system includes helpful sample queries. Users display output in tabular, matrix, graphical, and free format. Users create a query using one of three methods:

- *Prompted query* Guides users step by step
- *SQL* Provides the line-oriented SQL syntax
- *Query By Example (QBE)* Defines a tabular language that uses a pattern technique

Prompted query is the simplest way to access relational data. Users don't need to know any query language; QMF prompts them to build a retrieval query step by step through a window-based interactive dialog. This implementation is consistent with the OS/2 Query Manager.

Either SQL or QBE retrieves and formats information for display at a terminal. Users then scroll through the data. QMF also displays the original query and lets users modify it to obtain different results. Users may save the results, print them, save the query, or start another task.

QMF normally displays query results as a simple table. It uses a standard *form*, which defines the format for presenting the results. Customers develop their own forms and maintain a library of forms. Users supply specifications for a report, such as headings, footings, and column headings, by filling in and changing the values in the form. After developing a form, users can specify a query and have QMF display it at a terminal. With only a few specifications, QMF produces many types of reports.

The *table editor* is an easy way to update a database without having to write a query. It searches tables for specific rows of data, then it changes or deletes one row at a time. The table editor also adds rows of data to a table.

Queries can access tables or views at a remote DB2 location. Users do this by adding a location qualifier to the table name. The table editor and many QMF commands (such as DISPLAY and EXPORT) work with remote tables.

Interactive Chart Utility (ICU) graphically presents data retrieved by QMF. ICU is part of the Presentation Graphics feature of GDDM. Host Data Base View (HDBV) lets users download QMF reports to the personal computer for use by a variety of personal computer products.

To simplify repetitive reporting tasks, a *procedure* executes a series of commands. Using a single command, users can execute both SQL- and QBE-style queries. Thanks to QMF's integration with ISPF, it is easy for users to create and modify queries and procedures. Users easily correct and insert data by typing over incorrect information or into blank spaces. Deletion is also easy. The product includes prompts and Help panels to guide users in performing tasks.

QMF queries and reports on entity-relationship information in the AD/Cycle repository. It uses the prompted query feature to retrieve from the Repository Manager. Users can tailor the query output into customized reports. QMF also provides an interactive bridge to the repository's specification dialogs.

QMF provides a subset of the CPI Query Interface plus many extensions. QMF can export SQL queries and QMF forms to other SAA-compatible query and report generators, such as the OS/2 Query Manager. Application programs written in C or COBOL use QMF's query and report writing facilities through the SAA callable interface. This provides portability among SAA computer environments.

Chapter 15

Network Architecture

SAA Common Communications Support (CCS) connects applications, systems, networks, and terminals. It relies on strategic communication architectures including Systems Network Architecture (SNA) and Open Systems Interconnection (OSI). CCS lets customers develop and run distributed applications on a network of IBM computers and provides internetworking with non-IBM computers.

Nearly all SAA communication features are part of SNA, which defines distributed communication functions, including the formats and protocols that relate these functions to each other. SNA sets the rules for interconnecting IBM computers, terminals, and applications. It is a big architecture, with many possible subsets, some of which are now obsolete. SAA includes mostly modern SNA features and omits the obsolete ones.

The OSI seven-layer model provides the foundation for the structure of most modern computer networks, including SNA. However, SNA isn't compatible with, and doesn't directly communicate with OSI. Although IBM included both architectures in SAA, SNA is more important than OSI for practical reasons. Every SAA computer environment offers a complete and proven SNA implementation. But IBM's OSI products are new and don't cover all SAA environments completely. Therefore, most customers in the United States probably will use SNA in implementing CCS.

Figure 15-1: OSI Versus SNA Layers

	OSI	SNA
7	Application	NAU Services Manager
6	Presentation	Presentation Services
5	Session	Data Flow Control
4	Transport	Transmission Control
3	Network	Path Control
2	Data Link	Data Link Control
1	Physical	Physical

This chapter introduces the basic ideas and terminology needed to understand SAA networks. We focus on SNA, rather than OSI, for the reasons mentioned above. The discussion covers the architectural components, network configurations, physical paths through the network, and sessions.

Network Structure

Users access SNA networks to exchange information. A user is either a person or an application program that uses network services. People interact directly with the network through terminals. The combination of a person and a terminal thus constitutes a network user.

Increasingly, people interact with SNA networks through application programs. Such programs also are users of the network. The programs execute in host computers (such as System/370 or AS/400), personal computers, terminal cluster controllers, or other devices. The programs may reside in software or firmware. Programs, in turn, provide services to people or to other application programs. Although programs and people are users, they aren't part of formal SNA architecture. Nevertheless, programs participate in SAA.

SNA network functions divide broadly into two categories:

- Services that exchange information between pairs of users

- Network management, which includes startup, termination, error recovery, and statistics reporting

SNA provides these functions through protocols that interconnect multiple SNA nodes. The next sections discuss node architecture and node components.

SNA Nodes

SNA nodes are the physical building blocks of SNA networks. They are machines that generate and handle SNA protocols. Each node provides functions that correspond to all seven layers of the OSI model. There are two major categories of functions within a node:

- *Transmission Subsystem*   Transports information from one node to another.
- *Network Addressable Units*   Represent users in the network, and provide network management services.

Each SNA node has a transmission subsystem, which routes messages through the node and connects to adjacent nodes. It does the low-level network functions covered by OSI layers 1, 2, and 3. Nodes also have Network Addressable Units (NAUs), which can be Physical Units, Logical Units, or System Services Control Points. NAUs are responsible for high-level network functions corresponding to OSI layers 4 through 7.

Every node contains one *Physical Unit* (PU), which represents the physical device in the network. The PU is software (or firmware) that manages the SNA node. Nodes may also have a *Physical Unit Control Point* (PUCP), which activates and deactivates the node; otherwise they have a *System Services Control Point*, which directs network management at a high level.

SNA nodes may contain *Logical Units*, (LU) which represent users in the network. LUs provide network services to their users. They translate user requests (for example, to send or receive data) into formatted SNA protocols. Not all SNA nodes have LUs. For example, a communication controller, such as an IBM 3745, usually doesn't have users, and therefore has no LUs.

There are two major categories of SNA nodes: peripheral nodes and subarea nodes. Figure 15-2 shows these node categories.

Peripheral Nodes

Peripheral nodes are endpoints for routing in an SNA network. They connect directly to subarea nodes. Some peripheral nodes can connect to other peripheral nodes as peers, but older peripheral nodes connect only to a subarea node. Peripheral nodes can connect several terminals to a communication line. The IBM 3270, 5250, and 4700 terminal product families and most micro- and mini-computer products, including PS/2 and AS/400, operate as peripheral nodes.

Three of SNA's node types are for peripheral nodes:

- *Cluster Controllers* (type 2) can support many users and may be programmed by customers. Many popular products, including IBM 3270 and 3770, provide this node type.
- *Enhanced Cluster Controllers* (type 2.1) are intelligent devices with peer-to-peer networking functions. As their name and number suggests, they evolved from node type 2.
- *Terminal Nodes* (type 1) often support only one user and usually cannot be programmed by customers. Though popular in the late 1970s, they are seldom seen today.

Figure 15-2: Node Categories

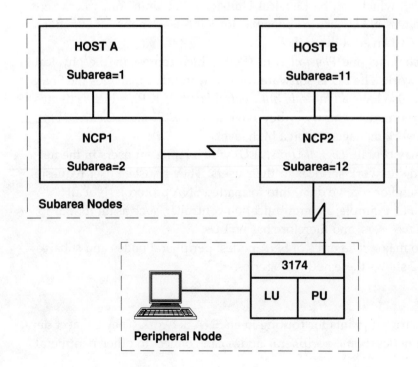

Subarea Nodes

Subarea nodes communicate with peripheral nodes and other subarea nodes concurrently. Subarea nodes provide more sophisticated routing functions, requiring more powerful processors than peripheral nodes. They serve three main purposes: running applications, serving as a focal point for network management, and routing large amounts of information.

SNA provides two subarea node types:

- *Host Computers* (type 5) contain a System Services Control Point (SSCP), which provides high-level network management. A type 5 node is a general-purpose computer, such as a System/370 or AS/400, which runs a customer's applications.
- *Communication Controllers* (type 4) mainly control data links and provide network routing services. Normally they don't have an SSCP. An IBM 3745 (or equivalent) front-end processor and IBM's Network Control Program (NCP) software provide SNA node type 4 functions.

Physical Units

Physical Units (PU) represent hardware devices to the network. Usually the node itself (or something directly attached to it) is the device represented by the PU. There is exactly one PU per node. Hence, the PU provides a foundation for network management within each SNA node.

PU functions for network hardware are analogous to LU functions for network users. As users aren't part of the SNA architecture, neither are hardware devices. The PU gives hardware devices a port through which they can communicate with SNA's centralized network management. This is useful for reporting hardware failures and reacting to changes in the network configuration.

A PU provides services to manage a node and any of its physical resources, such as data links, control panels, or terminals. Such management services usually are part of the software or firmware that constitutes the PU. They work with the SSCP using a distributed technique to:

- Activate and deactivate data links
- Help recover from failures
- Provide control functions for node operators
- Report network management statistics
- Manage and control the node's local stations

There is a one-to-one correspondence between node types and *PU types*, which means the terms are almost interchangeable. Note, however, the theoretical distinction: PU type refers only to PU functions, which are a subset of node functions. Node type refers to the functions of the entire node. In practice, most experts use the term PU type. The PU types are:

- Host computers (type 5)
- Communication Controllers (type 4)
- Low Entry Nodes (type 2.1), for peer-to-peer networking
- Cluster controllers (type 2)
- Terminal nodes (type 1)

IBM hasn't announced PU type 3. The company often skips numbers in its product lines and architectures. This provides full employment for consultants, authors, and industry pundits, who can then speculate why IBM didn't offer particular imaginary features. It keeps customers puzzled, too.

Logical Units

The main purpose of SNA is to provide for information exchange between users across the network. The *Logical Unit* (LU) is the port through which users get access to network services. *Sessions*, controlled by LUs, provide logical connections between users. The term *logical* means that the connections aren't directly wired; data may traverse several intermediate nodes as it passes through the network. Users need not know about physical paths through the network or details of SNA routing.

Most SNA nodes support either applications or terminals. The Logical Unit (LU) function translates requests by programs or terminals into SNA protocols, so that they can have sessions with other LUs. LU-LU (pronounced LU-to-LU) sessions provide temporary logical connections between pairs of LUs for an exchange of messages. Within these sessions, LUs are responsible for:

- Providing an interface to the user
- Requesting sessions with other LUs
- Starting and ending LU-LU sessions
- Defining units of work
- Deciding when to send or receive data
- Correlating requests and responses

SNA has eight types of LU-LU sessions:

- Application to printer/keyboard (type 1)
- Application to 3270 display (type 2)
- Application to 3270 printer (type 3)
- Application to office printer (type 4)
- Application to application (types 6.1 and 6.2)
- Application to 5250 display (type 7)
- Nonstandard implementations (type 0)

IBM didn't include all these session types in SAA because some are now obsolete. LU 6.2, which provides for program-to-program communications, is part of SAA. SAA also includes the 3270 data stream, therefore LU 2 is important. Though excluded from SAA, some of the other session types (such as LU 0, 1, and 7) remain useful and popular.

Experts use the terms *LU-LU session type* and *LU type* interchangeably, for example: "My PS/2 is an LU type 2." Given that many LUs concurrently support several session types, the term LU type isn't strictly accurate. Nevertheless, most people use the term anyway.

System Services Control Points

System Services Control Points (SSCPs) provide focal points for services to manage an SNA network. The SSCP coordinates the efforts of multiple LUs and PUs. Considering this broad role, the SSCP runs on an SNA host computer; it doesn't exist within small computers such as PS/2s. Furthermore, big networks divide management duties among multiple SSCPs, usually running on different hosts.

SSCPs provide the following functions:

- Directing network startup and shutdown
- Helping to establish LU-LU sessions
- Scheduling error recovery
- Interacting with operators and executing their commands
- Collecting measurement data on network usage
- Keeping track of network resource status

Figure 15-3: SNA Architectural Components

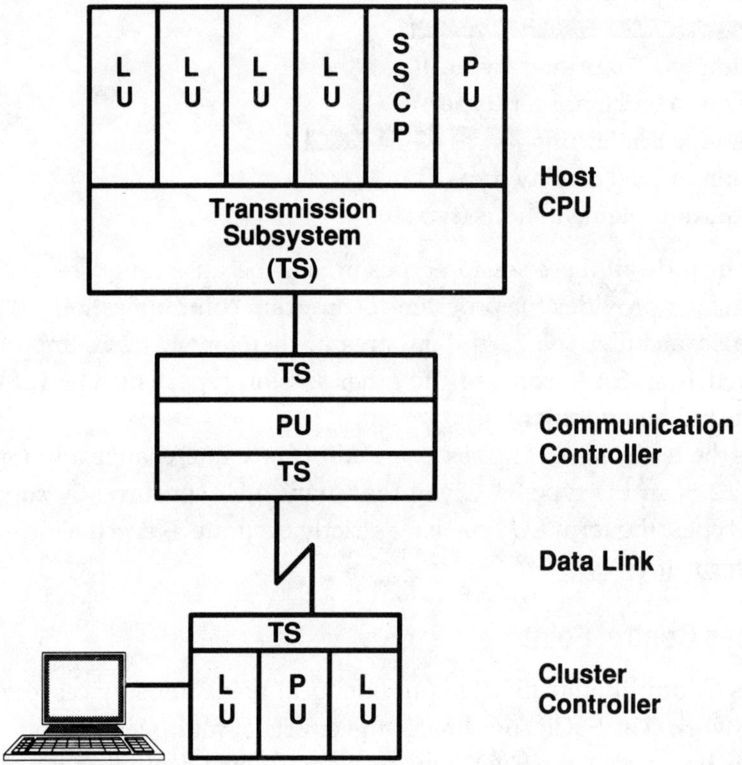

Sessions

Whenever two network addressable units want to communicate, SNA requires that they establish a *session*. A session is a temporary logical connection between two NAUs for an exchange of messages governed by negotiated rules. The most important kind of session takes place between pairs of LUs. Nevertheless, sessions involving PUs and SSCPs are crucial to the network's operation.

SNA provides only connection-oriented services. This is in stark contrast to other network architectures, such as OSI, which also provide connection-less services. With such services, communication partners need not establish a session. They can exchange individual packets of information without the formality of setting up a connection.

Although connection-less services offer obvious advantages in efficiency, they provide fewer features and lower integrity. Often applications must provide the features or integrity that the network omits. SNA doesn't offer this trade off; its transmission subsystem assures sequenced message delivery and requires connections between NAUs.

Figure 15-4: Network Addressable Units and Sessions

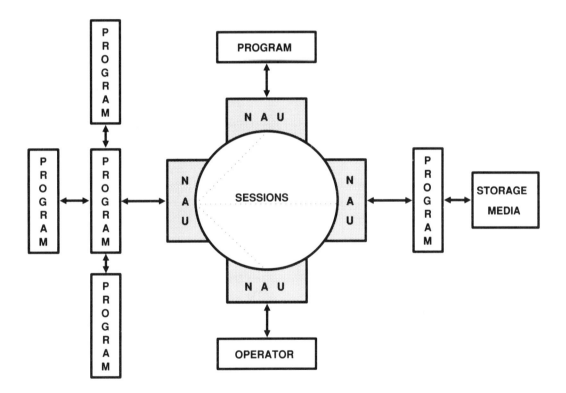

Session Classes

SNA offers five session classes:

- *LU-LU sessions* Carry the conversations between network users. The network starts and stops such sessions upon request
- *SSCP-SSCP sessions* Provide services to establish LU-LU sessions between LUs controlled by different host computers

- *SSCP-PU sessions* Manage nodes in hierarchical SNA networks. SNA uses them to activate data links, send alerts, and monitor response time
- *SSCP-LU sessions* Assist in starting and ending LU-LU sessions in hierarchical SNA networks
- *PU-PU sessions* Provide notifications of path interruptions in hierarchical networks, using an implicit session

SNA defines protocols for starting and stopping sessions. Many sessions begin at network startup and end at network shutdown. Such sessions usually involve the SSCP (SSCP-SSCP, SSCP-PU, and SSCP-LU). The network establishes LU-LU sessions when users want to communicate. When the users finish communicating, the network terminates the LU-LU session. Although sessions are temporary, they often continue for several hours; few sessions are less than one minute long.

Figure 15-5: Hierarchical Tree Topology

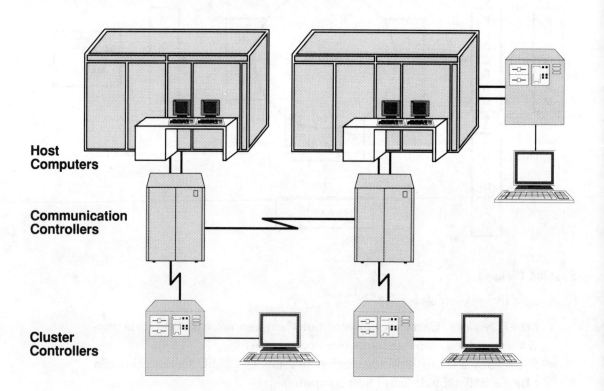

LU-LU Sessions

An LU-LU session is like a telephone call. Communication takes place between two users in a conversational manner. One party places the call. The caller starts the conversation; the parties then take turns talking while the other listens. Information flows in either direction in real time. When the conversation is over, the parties agree to end the call.

The telephone network routes the call automatically, but the parties to the conversation don't need to know how the telephone network operates. The LU's function is analogous to the telephone handset. The handset translates sound waves into electrical signals; it also translates electrical signals into sound waves. The LU translates user requests into formatted network protocols and vice versa.

Network Topology

SNA provides two styles of network topology. Since 1974, the architecture has offered the hierarchical approach shown in Figure 15-5. About 10 years later, IBM started offering a peer-to-peer networking style, illustrated in Figure 15-7. Recently, IBM has been integrating both styles into a single network. The hierarchical style offers important benefits for large networks, and the peer-to-peer style is simple to set up and easy to maintain. It works well with small networks.

The earliest SNA networks used a tree topology, shown in Figure 15-5, which was purely hierarchical. Later the architecture evolved to the hierarchical mesh topology shown in Figure 15-6. This provides up to 16 virtual routes between any pair of host computers or communication controllers. Thanks to its high reliability and capacity, mesh topology is common today.

Peer-to-peer topology first appeared in networks of System/36 and System/38 computers. AS/400 combines the peer-oriented features of its System/36 and System/38 predecessors. OS/2 Communications Manager operates as a cluster controller in a hierarchical SNA network. It also connects PS/2s peer-to-peer across either wide area network or local area network links. Peer-to-peer topology is especially useful on a Token-Ring local area network because it efficiently handles direct communication across the ring. It doesn't require the participation of a host application or an SSCP.

Figure 15-6: Hierarchical Mesh Topology

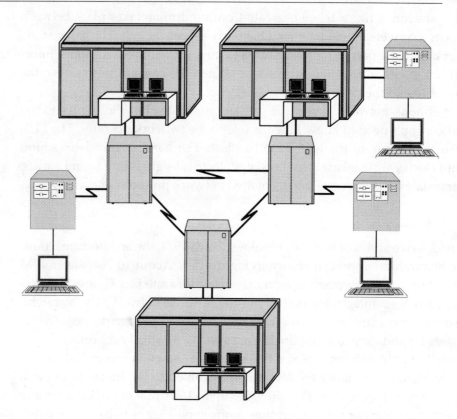

Domains

Figure 15-8 shows a hierarchical SNA network with one host computer, two communication controllers, and four cluster controllers. The host and its connected SNA nodes constitute a *domain*. Domains provide a mechanism for concentrating and dividing network management responsibility. Each domain has one SSCP, which manages all nodes, PUs, and LUs included in the domain. In a single-domain network, the host computer is the central point for network management.

A multiple-domain network contains more than one host computer. Each host controls specific network resources, including applications, communication controllers, cluster controllers, and terminals. Network designers and operators decide which hosts manage which resources. This approach works well in big networks because it lets customers distribute network management tasks among several locations.

Figure 15-7: Peer-to-Peer Topology with Token-Ring

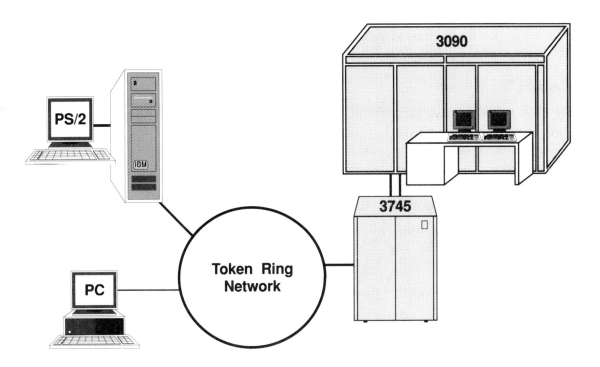

Most System/370-based SNA networks have multiple domains. The basic SNA products, such as Virtual Telecommunications Access Method (VTAM) and Network Control Program (NCP), include multiple domain networking as a standard feature. Another name for this feature is *Multiple Systems Networking Facility* (MSNF). MSNF lets LUs in one domain communicate with LUs in a different domain. Even though different SSCPs manage the LUs, they can communicate directly with each other.

To manage communication between LUs in different domains, an SSCP has a *Cross-Domain Resource Manager* (CDRM). Each host's CDRM communicates with other CDRMs in the network. A CDRM helps establish and terminate sessions between a host's LUs and those managed by other CDRMs. The CDRMs, in effect, work as agents that introduce the LUs to each other.

In contrast, SNA networks hosted by AS/400 and other IBM mid-range systems operate as single domains. SNA provides the services for applications to communicate with terminals. The host may use peer-to-peer SNA to connect to other mid-range computers. It may also act as a cluster controller in a hierarchical SNA network. However, most mid-range computers cannot be a host in a multiple-domain SNA network.

Subareas

Big SNA networks have hierarchical addressing similar to the numbering plan used in the telephone network, which has 3-digit area codes and 7-digit telephone numbers. An SNA network has up to 255 *subareas* and 32,767 elements within each subarea. A subarea is either a host computer, including all applications and directly attached terminals, or a communication controller and all connected lines, cluster controllers, terminals, and NAUs.

Figure 15-8: Network with One domain and Three Subareas

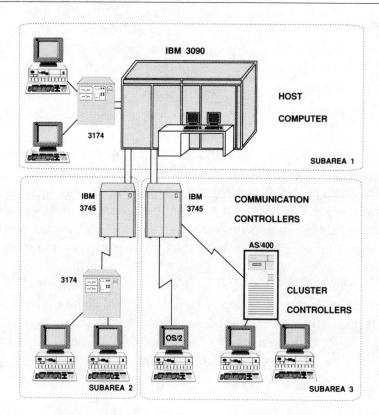

An *element* is a network resource within a subarea. All NAUs are elements. Other kinds of network resources, including data links and I/O channels, are also elements. The combination of the subarea number and element number is the *network address*.

The number of host computers plus the number of communication controllers determines the subarea count. The total size of the network, from an addressing perspective, is the sum of the element counts of all subareas. Today SNA theoretically allows up to 8 million elements per network. However, customers can interconnect multiple SNA networks, so this is not a severe limitation. Furthermore, it is possible for IBM to expand SNA to 48-bit addressing, which would allow networks with 281 trillion elements.

Routing

The SNA transmission subsystem provides a *path* between two LUs so they can communicate. Data flows over the path, which consists of a series of nodes and data links connecting the LUs. SNA network configurations can provide up to 16 paths between a particular pair of LUs; this improves reliability and lets customers control the quality of service.

Although SNA users refer to LUs by name, the network uses numerical addresses. Each SSCP provides a domain-wide directory, which translates names into addresses. The SSCPs provide a distributed directory by communicating with each other. This insulates users from changes in the physical network.

All messages routed by SNA contain an *origin address* and a *destination address*. A full address consists of a subarea number and element number; however, sometimes SNA uses an abbreviated address to reduce network overhead. SNA routes messages based on their destinations.

Each subarea node contains a *path table*, which lists the nodes that are adjacent to it. The path table also lists the communication links available to each adjacent node. SNA looks up the destination's subarea address in its path table, and decides where to send the message next. The path table determines the next subarea node in the message's path, and which link will carry the message to the next node.

A *virtual route* (VR) is the entire path between the subarea nodes serving an origin LU and a destination LU. Think of it as a pipeline that connects two subareas. The path table structure allows up to 16 virtual routes per pair of subareas. However, a session between two LUs must take place entirely on one virtual route. SNA is different from most network architectures because all messages in a session follow the same path.

Figure 15-9: SNA Subareas and Path Tables

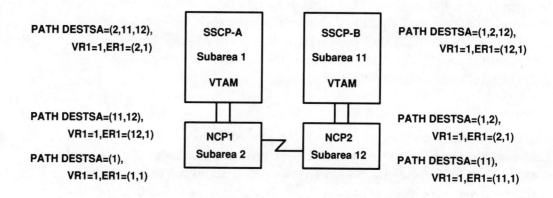

When a message reaches its destination subarea, SNA then examines the element number in the destination address. Each subarea contains a table of element addresses for its network resources. If the subarea node is the message's final destination, software passes it to the user. Otherwise, the node must determine which peripheral node will receive the message.

The subarea converts element addresses to local addresses within the destination node. Peripheral nodes don't handle full network addresses; they use an abbreviated address structure. SNA's *boundary function* converts element addresses into the local addresses used by peripheral nodes. This simplifies configuration management because the peripheral nodes need not be aware of the network's address structure.

SNA Addressing

Modern SNA implementations include 23-bit and 16-bit address formats. *Extended Network Addressing* (ENA) provides a 23-bit fixed-format network address. Eight bits of the address specify the subarea, and 15 bits identify the element within the subarea. This simple structure evolved from the architecture's complex original approach.

Figure 15-10: SNA Addressing with Boundary Function

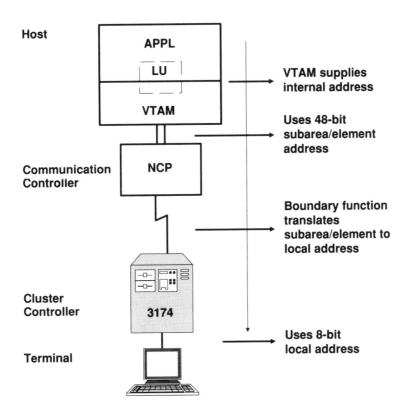

SNA first used a 16-bit network address, which limited a network to 65,535 NAUs. As with ENA, the address contains both subarea and element addresses. However, the width of the subarea address is variable. The subarea occupies two to eight bits of the address, and the element address uses the remaining bits.

Customers must determine this *address split* during network design; every subarea node must use the same address split. For example, a 6/10 split provides up to 63 subareas with 1,023 elements per subarea. When the network grows beyond 63 subareas, the customer must change the split, requiring major changes at each subarea node.

Within its internal data formats, SNA uses a 48-bit network address. Subarea addresses are 32 bits long and element addresses are 16 bits long. Although no product makes full use of this addressing capacity, it provides plenty of growth potential.

Data Links

SNA passes messages between nodes using data links. SNA supports two data link categories: Wide Area Networks (WAN) and Local Area Networks (LAN). The standards used by SNA for data links are similar to well-known industry standards. With few exceptions, the differences between SNA data links and those used by other network architectures are minor.

The most important SNA data links are:

- *Synchronous Data Link Control (SDLC)*   Allows traditional point-to-point or multi-point WAN links through dial-up or leased telephone lines.
- *SNA-X.25 Interface*   Lets SNA use the CCITT X.25 interface to packet data networks. IBM uses standard X.25 packet formats and protocols, but provides extra protocols for sending SNA messages across packet networks.
- *Token-Ring Network*   Provides LAN connections operating at up to 16 megabits per second over short distances. It uses a star-wired ring topology.
- *System/370 I/O Channel*   Connects hosts, communication controllers, and cluster controllers at high speed within a computer room. This special purpose data link isn't part of SAA but is crucial in the System/370 environment.

Chapter 16 discusses the details of these data links. The most important principle is that SNA is independent of physical transmission facilities. Therefore, all the features discussed in this chapter will operate on all the SNA data links listed above. Furthermore, if IBM decides to add data links to SNA in the future, the architecture's character will not change substantially.

Protocol Layers

Systems Application Architecture networking functions divide roughly into four categories:

- *Data Links*   Provide physical connections between nodes
- *Network Services*   Let a network node and its applications communicate with other nodes and applications within the network. This also includes network management

- *Data Streams* Define standard representations for data commonly carried by a network, such as terminal screens, printed output, documents, and electronic mail
- *Application Services* Help programmers write applications that transparently use network services. This includes distributed databases, remote file access, and file transfer

These categories correspond closely in principle to the seven-layer OSI model. Data links correspond exactly to layers 1 and 2, the physical and data link layers. Network services, which encompass many SNA functions already discussed in this chapter, correspond to OSI layers 3 (network), 4 (transport), and 5 (session). Data Streams correspond to layer 6 (presentation). Application services correspond to OSI layer 7 (application).

SNA Layer Descriptions

SNA's layering scheme, shown in Figure 15-11, achieves the same results as OSI's layering, but the SNA layer names are different. SNA layers are a subset of the four SAA communication categories listed above, concentrating mainly in the data links and network services categories. Furthermore, SNA assigns certain functions to different layers from OSI. This is mainly due to differences in routing philosophy. Thus, SNA's layers 3 and 4 are somewhat different from OSI's layers.

The SNA *physical layer* (1) defines the electrical and mechanical interfaces between network hardware devices. It relies on recognized international standards. The SNA data link control layer (2) transmits data between nodes across a physical link. The path control layer (3) routes data through the network from the origin node to the destination node.

The *transmission control layer* (4):

- Keeps track of session status
- Paces the flow of data transmission in the session
- Provides queues that control data flow
- Starts and stops the session

The *data flow control* layer (5):

- Controls the sequence of sending and receiving data
- Defines units of work (for example, starting and ending a transaction) within the session
- Ensures integrity of information exchanged

Figure 15-11: SNA Layers

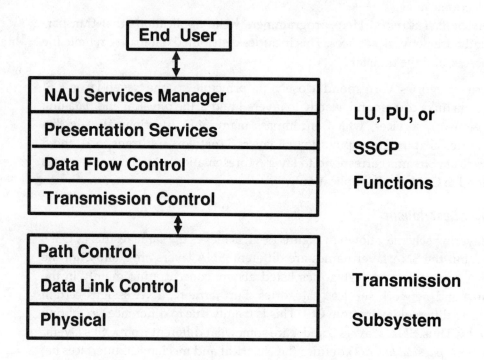

The *presentation services layer* (6) controls the user interface, and provides formatting services and verbs that enable users to access basic network services. The *NAU services manager* (also called transaction services) layer (7) constitutes the boundary to the network and coordinates the activities of layers 4 through 6.

Functional Layers and Peer Protocols

All modern network architectures, including SNA, define two rules for data flow among the seven layers. First, data flows between adjacent layers in the same node. For example, path control always interacts with data link control, but path control never directly interacts with the physical layer. Second, logical communication takes place between the same layer in two different nodes. For example, path control in node X interacts with path control in node Y. However, path control in node X never interacts with data link control in node Y. This approach reduces complexity by limiting the number of possible interfaces.

IBM calls the first rule *functional layers*; it assigns network functions to layers and specifies what information must be exchanged between the layers. This defines the interface between the adjacent layers. The second rule, *peer protocols*, defines how the layers of one node will interact with their peer layers in another node. If both nodes use the same peer protocols, they can run different hardware and software, but they will work together to accomplish a useful result.

Figure 15-12: SNA Peer Protocols

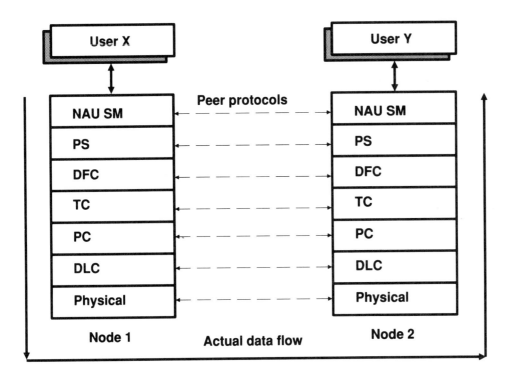

Figure 15-12 shows user X generating data and passing it to the top layer of node 1. This layer does its processing and passes the data to the next lower layer. The network adds a *header* that represents the processing done by layer 7 of node 1. This process repeats for each layer in node 1. SNA doesn't actually add a header at each layer; it uses fewer headers, and appends the headers only in four layers. Figure 15-13 shows the SNA frame structure, including the most important headers.

After the data passes through the physical network, it arrives at node 2. The data link control layer receives the message, performs the peer protocols indicated by the header, removes the header, and passes the remainder of the message up to the path control layer.

The process repeats until the message arrives at user Y.

Figure 15-13: SNA Frame Structure

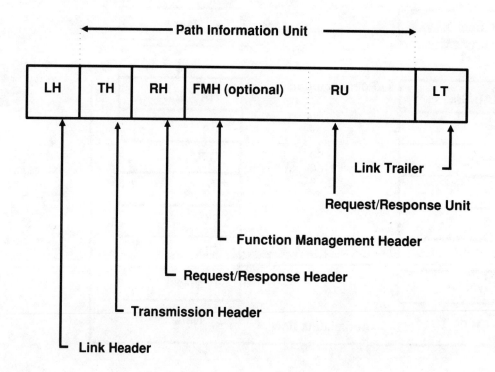

Chapter 16

Data Links

Chapter 15 gave an overview of network architecture from a "top-down" perspective, concentrating on the upper layers. Chapter 16 discusses the details of the lowest architectural layers. Chapters 17 and 18 proceed upward through the details of the middle and upper layers of CCS networks. As the upper layers work closely with SAA applications, the lower layers reliably and efficiently pass information between nodes. Though seldom directly accessed by application programs, SAA data links are crucial to cooperative processing applications.

Data links are part of the lower level of the SNA transmission subsystem. They constitute layer two of network architecture, responsible for controlling the transmission between network nodes. The upper level of the transmission subsystem is path control, which selects the proper data link for transmission, breaks messages into segments, and ensures correct data sequence. Path control relies on the data link layer to recover from errors induced by unreliable transmission media such as telephone lines.

Data link protocols transfer error-free blocks of data between pairs of devices connected to the same physical link. Such protocols usually have comprehensive error detection mechanisms. They allow simultaneous two-way communication (called full duplex) or alternating communication (half duplex) over the link. Modern data link protocols provide *transparency*, in which there are no restrictions on the content or format of the transmitted data. They usually allow several link configurations, connecting many devices to a single link.

The SAA data links are:

- *Synchronous Data Link Control* (SDLC) Allows traditional point-to-point or multi-point links through dial-up or leased telephone lines.
- *SNA-X.25 Interface* Uses the CCITT X.25 interface to packet data networks. IBM uses standard X.25 packet formats and protocols, but provides extra protocols for sending SNA messages across packet data networks.
- *Token-Ring network* Provides local area network connections operating at up to 16 megabits per second over short distances. It uses a star-wired ring topology.

Synchronous Data Link Control

Synchronous Data Link Control (SDLC) is the oldest and most popular SNA data link protocol. IBM introduced SDLC in the mid 1970s as the successor to binary synchronous and asynchronous protocols. Binary synchronous (bisync) protocols became popular in the 1960s, primarily for remote job entry (RJE) and clustered display terminals. Asynchronous (async) protocols first appeared in the 1940s. Oddly, async wasn't common in IBM environments until the mid-1980s, when personal computers fueled its growth.

SDLC offers big advantages over its predecessors, such as:

- SDLC is bit-oriented; async and bisync are character-oriented. Character-oriented protocols aren't inherently transparent because they use special characters to control the link. SDLC treats data as a bit stream and confers no significance to individual characters.
- SDLC checks every message for transmission errors. Normal async protocols provide no error checking; bisync can't check all transmissions for errors.
- Bisync requires one acknowledgement for each data message; SDLC can send up to 127 messages before needing an acknowledgement. This is important for data links with long propagation delays or high data rates.
- SDLC operates on full- or half-duplex links; bisync is inherently half-duplex. Some async protocols require full-duplex and can't operate half-duplex.

Physical Interfaces to Wide Area Networks

An SDLC data link connects to an SNA node through a standard physical interface. The most common physical interface in the United States is EIA's RS-232. Its international counterpart is CCITT's V.24. This interface usually connects the SNA node to a modem (or equivalent device), but it can also can connect two SNA nodes directly. These physical interface standards define a pair of 25-pin connectors, unbalanced electrical circuits, and serial (one bit at a time) bidirectional signalling. They usually transmit fewer than 20,000 bits per second.

Other physical interfaces, such as RS-449 and V.35, provide high data rates (usually above 19.2 kilobits per second) by using balanced electrical circuits. High speed links, up to 2 megabits per second, often connect host computers together in SNA wide area networks. Although customers still use async and bisync protocols at low data rates, they almost always use SDLC on high speed links.

Figure 16-1 shows a typical data link which has two modems, one at each end of the communication circuit. The circuit may consist of conventional voice telephone lines, twisted-pair wire, microwave links, or satellite links. Modems convert digital signals used by the physical interface (such as RS-232) to signalling methods (for example, analog tones) compatible with the physical circuit. Some links, such as those used in digital telephone systems, require special interface devices, which technically aren't modems. Regardless of the type of circuit, all SDLC links use standard physical interfaces.

Link Stations

Link stations are part of the data link layer. They consist of hardware and software inside an SNA node that manage data transmission through the physical interface. SDLC defines two types of link stations:

- *Primary stations* control data transfer, including the sequence of messages exchanged. They tell secondary link stations when to send and receive.
- *Secondary stations* send and receive information upon command from a primary station.

Each link has one primary station and one or more secondary stations. All communication takes place between primary and secondary stations; two secondary stations on the same link can't communicate directly. The primary station *polls* each secondary station. Receipt of a poll constitutes permission to send. Secondary stations can't send unsolicited messages.

Figure 16-1: Typical SDLC Data Link

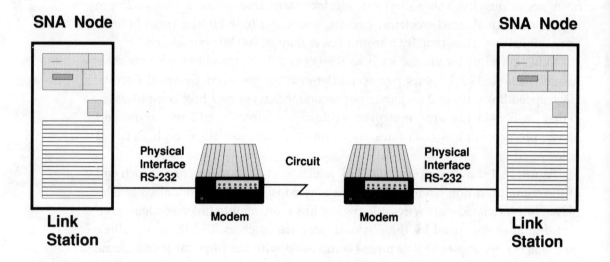

SDLC defines three data link configurations, shown in Figure 16-2. *Point-to-point* links connect one primary station directly to one secondary station. *Multipoint* links (sometimes called multidrop) connect one primary station directly with 2 to 254 secondary stations. *Loops* have one primary station and multiple secondary stations connected in a circular topology. Loops are the forerunners of Token-Ring networks, discussed on the next page.

Link Addresses

Each message sent on a data link contains an eight-bit station address. Every secondary station has one *send address*. When a secondary station sends a message, it places its own send address in the data link header. This is how the primary station determines the origin of every message.

When a primary station sends a message, it places a secondary station address in the data link header. A secondary station has an address to receive messages addressed specifically to it. Secondary stations also respond to a *broadcast address*, which can be attached to messages to be received by every station. A primary station can send messages to a *group address,* to which several secondary stations may respond. Hence, secondary stations have multiple *receive addresses.*

Figure 16-2: SDLC Link Configurations

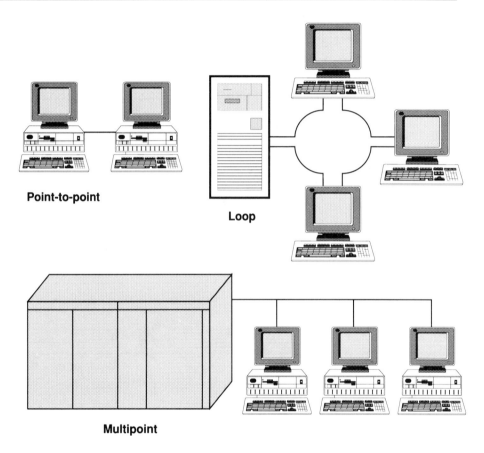

Point-to-point

Loop

Multipoint

Note that addresses at the data link level differ from network addresses and names used in the upper layers of SNA. Applications use network names to identify network resources (such as Logical Units). Each data link protocol uses a different addressing scheme to identify stations on a link. For example, the Token-Ring network's addressing scheme is different from SDLC's. Such differences are not visible to network users because they use names, rather than addresses, to refer to network resources.

Frame Structure

As Figure 16-3 shows, SDLC links carry information in a *frame*, which consists of a link header, an information field (shown as DATA), and a link trailer. The *link header* contains information that controls data transmission and link status. The *information field* (or I-field) usually contains the data to be moved between nodes. SNA sometimes refers to this data as a Basic Transmission Unit (BTU). The *link trailer* mainly contains an error detection code.

Figure 16-3: SDLC Frame Structure

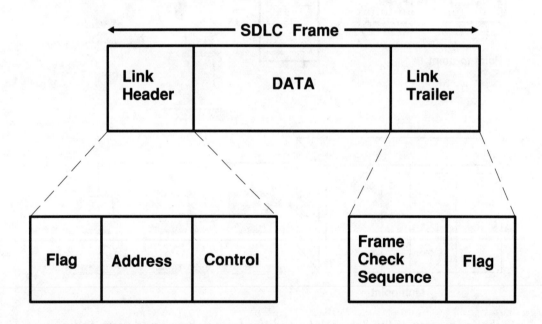

The SDLC frame fields contain:

- *Flag* marks the start of a frame. A flag is eight bits containing the unique bit value 0111 1110 (hex 7E).
- *Address* identifies the secondary station sending or receiving this frame.

- *Control* specifies the frame type, holds a sequence number, and designates polling. Usually this field is eight bits long, but it can extend to 16 bits.
- *Information* contains user data, which follows the headers for the upper SNA layers. Information is variable-length, but it must be a multiple of eight bits. SDLC's bit stuffing approach ensures that the bit configuration of a flag (discussed above) won't appear anywhere inside the frame.
- *Frame Check Sequence* is a 16-bit polynomial code that provides cyclic redundancy checking (CRC) to detect errors in all parts of the frame except the flags.
- *Flag* ends the frame; it uses the same bit sequence as the flag that starts the frame.

Using SDLC

SDLC data link topology and framing are similar to other wide area network standards, such as ISO's High Level Data Link Control (HDLC). SDLC provides high data integrity and good performance for parts of the network that transmit information at nominal rates between 10 kilobits per second and 2 megabits per second. At lower data rates, async protocols usually are more cost-effective; at higher data rates, local area networks are appropriate. SDLC covers the middle ground of data links very efficiently and therefore is very popular.

SNA Interface to X.25 Packet Data Networks

Packet switching is the predominant form of wide area network technology in many parts of the world today. In a few countries, it isn't possible to obtain permanent point-to-point lines; hence SDLC isn't practical for many applications. In the United States, public packet data networks sometimes are more economical or easier to administer than networks that use private lines. Furthermore, some large organizations (such as the U.S. Department of Defense) have set up private packet data networks and mandated their use throughout the organization.

In the 1970s, SDLC was the only SNA data link. As more customers began demanding connectivity through packet data networks, IBM developed an interface to let packet data networks transport SNA protocols. Unfortunately, SNA and packet data networks use routing strategies that differ fundamentally. Development of the SNA-X.25 interface involved many complex issues.

In 1978, IBM announced that it would use the emerging X.25 standard for packet data network connectivity. The first products, delivered in 1980, worked fairly well. The X.25 interface eventually extended to cover most SNA product lines. IBM's X.25 interface strategy treats the packet data network as a data link. This simplifies integration while retaining key SNA features.

X.25 Overview

CCITT recommendation X.25 specifies a three-layer interface between packet data networks and computers or terminals. Readers of X.25 literature must understand three basic terms:

- *Data Terminal Equipment* (DTE) is the user facility, such as a computer or terminal, that connects to the packet data network.
- *Data Circuit Terminating Equipment* (DCE) is the communications access port to the network; to the DTE, it resembles a modem.
- *Data Switching Equipment* (DSE) is the part of the network that routes data packets from origin to destination.

In principle, packet switching is simple. DTE A in Figure 16-4 generates messages to be transmitted to DTE B. DTE A breaks the message into packets. Each fixed-length packet is short; several packet sizes are possible, but usually packets are less than 128 bytes. Hence a single message might require many packets for transmission. DTE A uses DCE to pass each packet to the network. X.25 defines the formats of the packets and procedures for exchanging them with the network.

The network transports the packets using its own internal routing algorithms. Note that X.25 doesn't define how to route packets. The network passes the packets to DTE B via DCE. Again DTE B uses X.25 to connect to the network. When DTE B gets the packets, it reassembles them into the original message generated by DTE A. DTE B then processes the message in its usual way.

X.25 Layers

X.25 defines layers 1 through 3 of the seven-layer OSI model. It uses the following standards for the physical layer:

- *X.21* provides a 15-pin simplified serial interface, intended for digital networks. Customers in the U.S. seldom use this interface.
- *X.21-bis* is compatible with established standards such as RS-232, V.24, and V.35. This interface is popular throughout the world.

Figure 16-4: Packet Switching

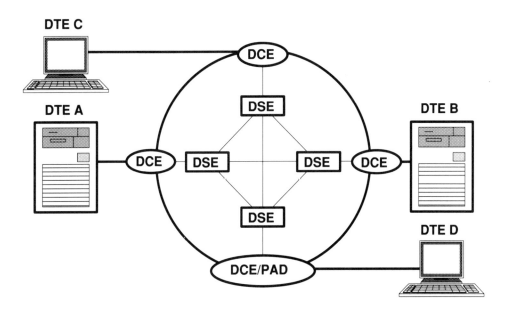

The data link layer is compatible with ISO's HDLC, and therefore is similar to SDLC. X.25 lets network designers choose among three data link protocols:

- *Link Access Procedure (LAP)* is a non-standard HDLC procedure that uses primary-secondary link relationships like SDLC. Nevertheless, IBM doesn't recommend using LAP.
- *Link Access Procedure Balanced (LAPB)* uses HDLC frame structure and combines both primary and secondary link station functions into a single station. This is the primary data link used with IBM X.25 interface products.
- *Link Access Procedure for ISDN (LAPD)* supports the advanced digital telephone network interconnection standard, Integrated Services Digital Network (ISDN). Much discussed, ISDN hasn't been successful in the U.S. market.

The network layer (3) defines the format of packets and procedures for exchanging packets between the DTE and DCE. The packet has user data prefixed by a *packet header.* The X.25 standard provides for several packet sizes, which are fixed within a network, but vary among networks.

Virtual Circuits

X.25 DTEs exchange packets through *virtual circuits,* which are logical network connections between pairs of DTEs. A *permanent virtual circuit* is continuously available for sending packets between two specific DTEs. The DTEs don't take any action to establish the virtual circuit. The network establishes this circuit automatically and maintains its availability. In this respect, a virtual circuit is similar to a leased line.

Switched virtual circuits require a call setup procedure before packets can be exchanged. DTE A sends a call request packet to the network, specifying DTE B's network address. The network informs DTE B that DTE A has called. DTE B sends a packet that accepts the call. The network informs DTE A of the acceptance, and the two DTEs exchange data packets.

After finishing the exchange of data packets, DTE A ends the connection by sending a call clearing packet to the network. The network informs DTE B that the switched virtual circuit is disconnecting. The network then confirms the termination to DTE A. Switched virtual circuits are similar to dial-up lines.

SNA-X.25 Interface Design Strategy

IBM's main objective in designing the X.25 interface was to preserve all SNA features, especially node functions, session protocols, and network management. The company wanted to make it easy to connect SNA nodes through a packet data network. IBM accomplished this by having SNA view the packet data network as a collection of conventional data links.

Rather than connecting two SNA nodes with an SDLC link, customers can connect the nodes to the packet data network. The network provides virtual circuits, which are equivalent to dial-up or leased lines. Each SNA-X.25 node contains software that makes virtual circuits look like real circuits to the path control layer of SNA. This retains all SNA features, except those specifically associated with SDLC.

The essence of this strategy is mapping virtual circuits into real circuits. The architecture treats permanent virtual circuits as leased lines and switched virtual circuits as dial-up lines. The X.25 virtual circuit protocol provides the mechanism to transfer data between adjacent SNA nodes. Hence, X.25 provides similar functions to other data links, and appears at the same architectural level.

SNA-to-SNA Connectivity

To let the network use both SDLC and virtual circuit protocol concurrently, IBM emulated some SDLC functions within a virtual circuit. SNA-X.25 DTEs use a Logical Link Control (LLC) protocol to communicate across a packet data network. Because this approach uses qualified packets to transfer data link commands between the two SNA nodes, IBM calls it *Qualified Logical Link Control* (QLLC).

Qualified packets have the "Q" bit turned on in the packet header. This X.25 feature lets SNA distinguish between data and control packets. SNA uses this bit to mark each packet that contains data link control commands. After establishing the data link, the network sends data using normal unqualified packets.

The SNA-X.25 interface connects SNA peripheral nodes (such as cluster controllers) to subarea nodes. This is useful for communicating from an SNA host computer to remote cluster controllers via the packet data network. As previously mentioned, SNA has *boundary function* in the subarea node to support its peripheral nodes. Thus, BNN QLLC (Boundary Network Node) is the name of the SNA-X.25 protocol used between subarea and peripheral nodes.

The SNA-X.25 interface also connects pairs of subarea nodes. This lets a packet data network operate as a backbone for an SNA multiple host (MSNF) network. Intermediate Network Node (INN) QLLC protocol, which connects adjacent subareas, is more complex than BNN QLLC. The term *Intermediate Network Node* means that a subarea node could receive a message from an adjacent INN and pass it along to another SNA node. This normally happens when a customer connects a pair of communication controllers (such as IBM 3745s) through the packet data network.

SNA to Non-SNA Connectivity via X.25

Many DTEs don't use SNA protocols. For example, remote async terminals often connect to networks through Packet Assembler-Disassemblers (PADs).These PADs receive messages in async protocol from terminals, and turn them into streams of packets. (This is analogous to the function that QLLC performs.) Three interrelated CCITT standards, X.3, X.28, and X.29, define the protocols for async PADs. Most IBM SNA-X.25 products communicate with such PADs.

IBM's SNA-X.25 interface provides three methods of operation for communicating with non-SNA DTEs, including PADs: *Mapped* lets applications use SNA protocols; *Transparent* lets applications use X.25 directly; *Hybrid* combines mapped and transparent operations.

Mapped operation converts X.25 packet-level protocols to similar SNA session types. For example, an SNA application could communicate with a printer using LU-LU session type 1. This requires no changes to SNA applications, but might require special coding in the non-SNA DTE.

Transparent operation lets SNA applications implement X.25 packet-level protocols. The SNA network transparently transports the X.25 packet-level protocols, and passes them to the packet data network. The SNA application therefore must know the X.25 virtual circuit protocol. This mode is useful for interfacing to non-SNA network architectures such as OSI or Transmission Control Protocol/Internet Protocol (TCP/IP).

Hybrid operation combines mapped and transparent operation. An SNA application performs X.25 packet-level operations but also maps X.25 protocols into SNA sessions. In the printer example above, the application might need to establish virtual circuits with selected printers in the network. Hybrid operation lets the application send X.25 call setup packets to connect with the printer, but then use SNA protocols to communicate with it.

Token-Ring Local Area Network

A Local Area Network (LAN) is a data link that lets many independent, dissimilar devices communicate with each other. It's different from other data links because communication takes place within a small area such as a building, factory, or campus. The most important LAN characteristics are:

- Speeds above 1 megabit per second
- Distances under 10 kilometers
- Low error rates
- Network has a single owner; users are in the same organization or company

In contrast, a Wide Area Network spans greater distances, usually has a wide range of users, and uses unreliable transmission media provided by common carriers.

The IBM Token-Ring network is a general-purpose LAN that uses star-wired ring topology, baseband signalling, and token passing protocols. The Token-Ring conforms to the IEEE 802.5 standard; its data link interface also conforms to IEEE 802.2. IBM introduced the Token-Ring in 1984. Today Ethernet (IEEE 802.3) and Token-Ring are the most popular high-performance general-purpose LANs in the world.

Figure 16-5: IBM 8228 MAU with four devices

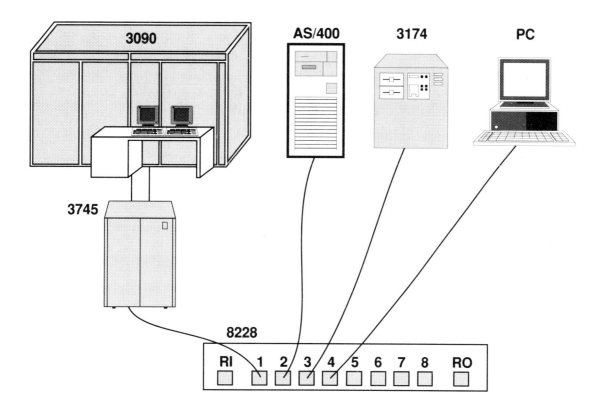

Star-Wired Ring Topology

A ring is similar to a loop; data travels over a closed path. A station on this path receives data from its nearest upstream neighbor. If it is the intended recipient, it copies the message to its internal memory, and then retransmits the data downstream.

Unlike loops, rings use decentralized control mechanisms, in which all active stations are peers. Loops use SDLC-style primary-secondary relationships. SDLC loop users learned from experience that centralized control didn't work well; IBM avoided those problems with the Token-Ring.

The Token-Ring topology combines star-like and ring features. Data flows on a circular path, but wiring flows from each device to a central wiring concentrator. The wiring concentrator is an IBM 8228 Multistation Access Unit (MAU). Customers usually locate MAUs in telephone wiring closets, so that part of the network has the shape of a star.

The cable from a station to the MAU consists of two pairs of wire. This cable terminates inside the MAU at an electromechanical relay, which controls access to the ring. Figure 16-5 shows a MAU with four devices. Although the MAU uses star wiring, the actual data path is a ring.

Each MAU connects up to eight devices. MAUs connect to each other; they form a data path that is a closed circuit. Figure 16-6 shows the actual circuit path. In summary, the MAU provides the following functions:

- Controlling the station's access to the ring
- Joining all stations connected to it
- Simplifying station movement; a station can be unplugged from one location and plugged back into another location
- Expanding the network by chaining together additional MAUs

Figure 16-6: Token-Ring Transmission Paths

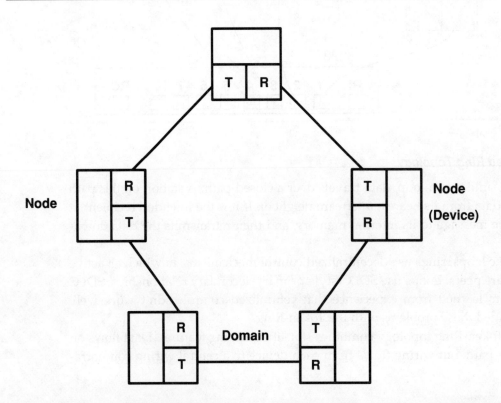

Baseband Transmission

The Token-Ring uses baseband, as opposed to broadband, transmission techniques. *Baseband* transmission puts a signal directly onto a transmission medium without modulating a carrier. Information flows along a single channel. Stations share the channel by allocating time slices for different transmissions. Baseband is the most popular LAN transmission technique today; many others, including Ethernet, also use it.

The transmitted digital signals must be regenerated after traveling certain distances. These distances vary, depending on the transmission medium. For example, the maximum distances for telephone wire, shielded wire, and fiber-optic cable are different. Each station regenerates the signal; this determines the distance between each station and the MAU. Separate repeaters can also regenerate the signal, thereby increasing distance.

IBM offers two nominal data rates for the Token-Ring: 4 megabits per second and 16 megabits per second. All stations on a ring must operate at the same data rate. Token-Ring adapter hardware that operates at 16 megabits per second usually has a switch to select either 4 or 16 megabits per second.

Logical Link Control

The IEEE standards for LANs divide the OSI data link layer into two sublayers:

- *Logical Link Control (LLC)* provides services to layers above the data link, insulating them from the oddities of the various transmission media.
- *Media Access Control (MAC)* defines rules for access to the network's transmission medium.

LLC defines the peer-to-peer protocols that transfer and control the flow of information among stations. The LLC standard, IEEE 802.2, defines two types of services:

- *Connection-oriented service*, which delivers data in sequence and provides error recovery procedures. It requires a connection between two LLCs before exchanging data.
- *Connection-less service*, based on simpler protocols that provide lower reliability, less control, and higher performance.

Service Access Points (SAPs) are entities that communicate at the LLC level. Higher layers use SAPs to get services from the LLC, MAC, and physical layers. SAPs exchange information using the protocol data units illustrated in Figure 16-7, which contain the Destination SAP (DSAP), Source SAP (SSAP), control, and information fields.

Figure 16-7: Token-Ring Frame

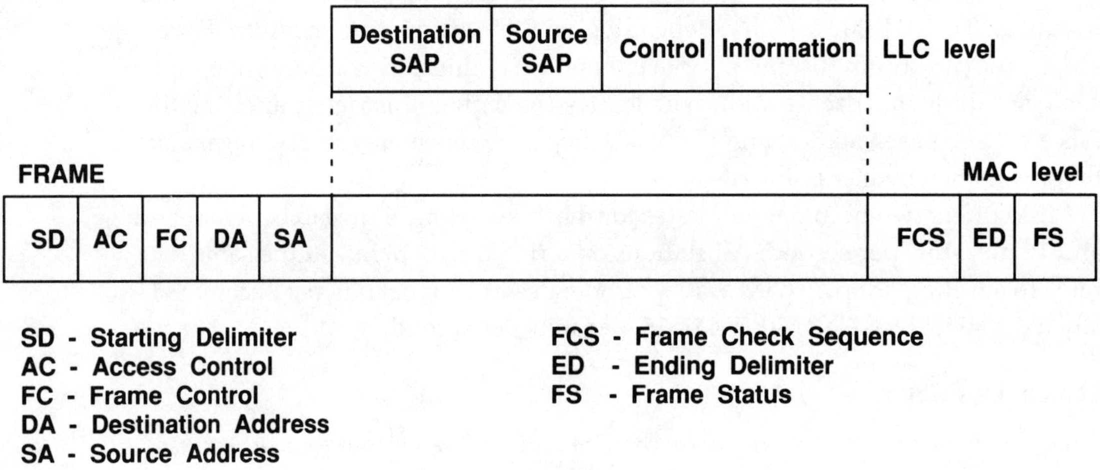

```
                    ┌────────────┬────────┬─────────┬───────────┬──────────────
                    │Destination │ Source │         │           │
                    │   SAP      │  SAP   │ Control │Information │ LLC  level
                    └────────────┴────────┴─────────┴───────────┴──────────────
                      ┊                                            ┊
  FRAME               ┊                                            ┊        MAC level
┌────┬────┬────┬────┬────┬──────────────────────────────────────┬─────┬────┬────┐
│ SD │ AC │ FC │ DA │ SA │                                      │ FCS │ ED │ FS │
└────┴────┴────┴────┴────┴──────────────────────────────────────┴─────┴────┴────┘
```

SD - Starting Delimiter   FCS - Frame Check Sequence
AC - Access Control   ED - Ending Delimiter
FC - Frame Control   FS - Frame Status
DA - Destination Address
SA - Source Address

The DSAP and SSAP provide the same function as the SDLC address. The control field contains commands, responses, sequence numbers, and polling information. It is almost the same as SDLC's control field. IBM calls the connection-oriented data link procedures *link stations*, but IEEE calls them connection components. They accomplish the same functions as SDLC link stations.

Media Access Control

The MAC sublayer defines procedures for accessing the network transmission medium. Such procedures either avoid simultaneous transmissions (called collisions), or recover from them by re-transmitting. Collisions never occur in Token-Ring networks. However, some LANs, including Ethernet, expect collisions to occur, detect them, and retry transmissions until they are successful. The relative merits of these approaches are debatable; in practice they offer similar performance.

The MAC protocols depend on the electrical characteristics of the medium. Hence, IEEE and equivalent standards cover both the MAC sublayer and the physical layer. The IEEE 802.2 LLC standard works with all MAC protocols. IEEE's MAC standards cover three media types: Carrier-Sense Multiple Access with Collision Detection (IEEE 802.3); Token-Bus (IEEE 802.4); and Token-Ring (IEEE 802.5).

The IEEE 802.5 MAC standard for the Token-Ring defines an address for each station physically attached to the ring. IBM implementations use 6-byte addresses. Routing mainly uses the destination address, but the frame also includes a source address. As with SDLC, there is a provision for both individual and group addresses.

The network administrator can assign station addresses (called *locally administered*). Alternatively, each Token-Ring hardware board contains a unique address assigned by the hardware manufacturer. This address is "burned-in" to ROM; it is called a *universally administered* address. The second bit of a locally administered address is "1".

Tokens, Frames, and Monitors

The access control method uses a pre-defined bit pattern, called a *token*, which continuously circles the ring. When a station wants to send, it waits until it receives the token. Because it now holds the token, it can begin sending. The sender inserts the source address, destination address, and information, which transforms the token into a frame. While the frame is circulating, there is no token on the ring. Hence, no other station can transmit.

Each station on the ring receives and retransmits the frame. Only the destination station copies the data to its internal memory. Then it retransmits the frame. Eventually the frame arrives at the sending station. The sender removes the frame, and transmits a new token.

A monitor function checks for error conditions and recovers from them. It detects and corrects such conditions as lost tokens or frames that circulate continuously. The monitor is not always the same station on the ring; the active stations *elect* it (by choosing the highest station address). All stations on the ring must support the monitor function. However, only one monitor is active at any time; the others are *standby monitors*.

Figure 16-8: Circulation of the Token

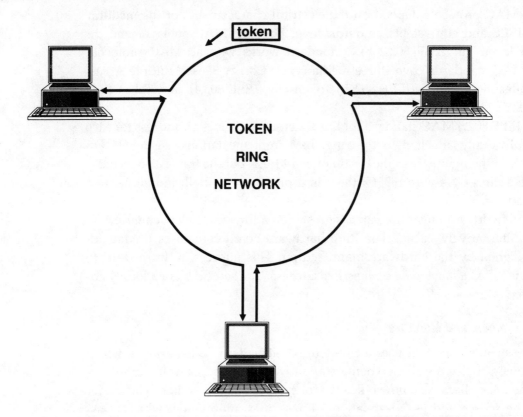

Using Token-Ring Networks

Despite its complexity, the Token-Ring performs as reliably and efficiently as competitive LANs. It is the fastest growing LAN architecture, largely due to IBM's effective marketing effort. Nearly every IBM computer connects to the Token-Ring network, and all SAA environments have solid Token-Ring implementations.

Token-Ring may not be the best LAN architecture for every customer. For example, customers who have substantial Ethernet LANs (such as those connected to UNIX systems) may prefer not to install Token-Ring. Ethernet offers similar performance and reliability to Token-Ring and often costs less. Most major IBM computers also connect to Ethernet. On the other hand, Ethernet isn't part of SAA. Not all SAA communication features are available through Ethernet.

Chapter 17

Network and Application Services

SAA cooperative processing applications require the services of an SNA network to connect user workstations to applications and data on host computers. Although SAA data links physically move the data, applications seldom use them directly. Instead, applications use services provided by the highest layers of network architecture (usually the presentation and application layers). These services, in turn, rely on data links to transmit information between SNA nodes.

Applications need many approaches for exchanging information, including:

- File transfer
- Remote file access
- Document storage, distribution, and retrieval
- Direct real-time conversations between pairs of programs

SAA Common Communications Support (CCS) provides these services for all three SAA hardware platforms across a wide range of network configurations. CCS allows both hierarchical and peer-to-peer network topologies. What's more, the architecture includes services to manage the network, which applications automatically use.

CCS makes a designer's job easier because SAA applications usually don't need to know about physical configuration or network management details. When the need arises, however, applications can explicitly control the network. Applications have the choice of letting SNA manage the network automatically, or doing some of the network management themselves.

This chapter discusses the most important services the network provides to applications. It describes the peer-to-peer network topology, which is essential to nearly all cooperative processing applications. Together, the network and application services form a framework for running cooperative applications involving PS/2, AS/400, and System/370 computers.

Advanced Program-to-Program Communications

Technically, Advanced Program-to-Program Communications (APPC) is the most important service in CCS because it is the foundation for many other powerful services. It is the lowest level network service that applications can easily use. Although APPC concepts will seem foreign to some programmers, its features parallel those found in other modern networks. Programmers familiar with transaction processing or advanced networking will understand APPC easily.

The earliest SNA implementations provided sessions between applications and terminals. Although SNA was powerful enough to communicate between programs, IBM didn't initially provide standard application program interfaces (APIs) or protocols for this purpose. Programmers had to invent their own protocols.

Hence, SNA has a category of non-standard protocols, Logical Unit 0, which supports important functions including Network Job Entry (NJE), bank automatic teller machines, and batch file transfer. Because each had its own unique protocols and interfaces, these functions didn't communicate with each other. This made standardization across product lines difficult.

APPC and the Common Programming Interface for Communications (CPI/C) are long-term solutions to this problem. APPC, also called LU-LU session type 6.2, provides standard protocols; CPI/C provides a single consistent API for all SAA environments. Applications that follow these standards can be portable among SAA platforms. Furthermore, most non-IBM computers support APPC today and CPI/C is becoming an important part of non-IBM SNA implementations.

Conversations

When two applications want to communicate using APPC, they establish a conversation. The conversation consists of a sequence of verbs, some of which send and receive data supplied by the programs. Each conversation takes place entirely within one SNA session. A session carries one conversation at a time. After completing a conversation, the session is ready to carry another conversation. Thus, most sessions handle multiple conversations.

Figure 17-1: APPC Structure

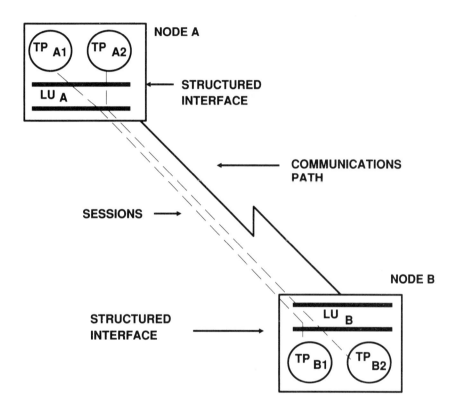

At each end of a conversation, SNA Logical Units (LUs) support the programs. Pairs of LUs communicate via LU-LU type 6.2 sessions. Each LU can support many programs; thus most APPC LUs allow multiple sessions. Furthermore, a given pair of LUs may have several *parallel* sessions. This is necessary when several pairs of programs need to communicate concurrently between two nodes.

Application programs take turns sending and receiving data in a conversation. This *half-duplex* protocol is similar to that used by SNA to communicate between applications and terminals. Figure 17-2 shows the sequence of verbs in a conversation.

- Program A starts the conversation and sends data
- Program A gives program B permission to send
- Program B receives the data and then gets permission to send

- Program B sends its data to program A; then it notifies program A that the conversation is complete
- Program A receives the data and then recognizes that the conversation is over
- Both programs end

Figure 17-2: Verb Sequence in an APPC Conversation

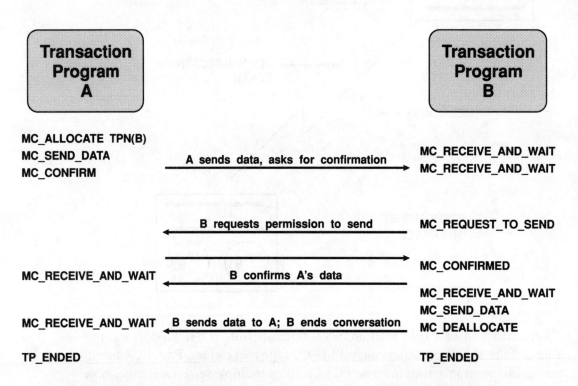

Note that this conversation is short. Alternatively, conversations can be even simpler than this example; often one program only sends and the partner program only receives. Programs often have a separate conversation for each data object.

There is low overhead for starting and stopping conversations. APPC normally operates in a *transaction processing* style, which is common in commercial applications. Each transaction requires two conversations. One program sends a transaction and the partner program processes it and returns a result. This is the most efficient way to use APPC.

Transaction Programs

Not surprisingly, all programs that engage in APPC conversations are called transaction programs. Application Transaction Programs (ATPs) are APPC applications written by customers or vendors. IBM also imbeds some transaction programs in its hardware or software products. These Service Transaction Programs (STPs) provide high-level services within the network. Applications sometimes call STPs, rather than directly using APPC, to accomplish their functions. However, some STPs aren't accessible to application programs.

Figure 17-3: Transaction Programs

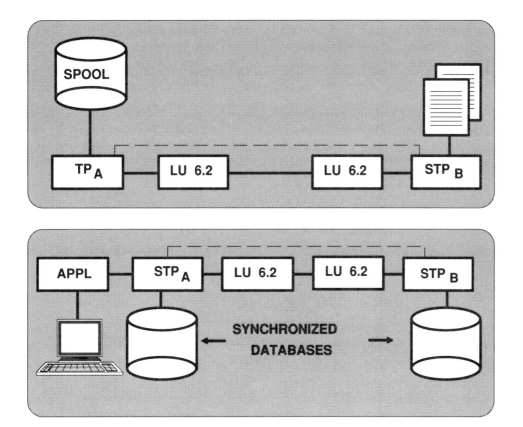

For example, an IBM 3820 laser printer contains an STP. Applications running under MVS on a System/370 write their output to JES spooling queues. IBM's Print Services Facility (PSF) software receives the output from the queues and uses its built-in STP to send the output to the printer. Thus, this pair of STPs provides an important network service, remote printing.

Other STPs offer remote file access and file transfer services. Applications can tap these services by using the STP's API, if it has one. For example, IBM's DISOSS electronic mail system provides an API that lets applications indirectly use the services of its STP. The IBM 3820, mentioned above, has an STP, but no API; customers can't program it.

Verbs

Transaction programs use APPC *verbs* to interact. These verbs and their parameters determine the events that take place in the conversation. When an application calls APPC, it specifies which verb it wants to use. The most important verbs are:

- *ALLOCATE* Begins a conversation
- *SEND_DATA* Moves data to an output buffer
- *RECEIVE_AND_WAIT* Waits for incoming data, then passes it to the transaction program
- DEALLOCATE Ends a conversation.

APPC includes two types of conversations: basic and mapped. Using mapped conversations, applications can be independent of coding schemes or data streams used by any particular product. The network converts all data sent by applications into a standard format, *Generalized Data Stream* (GDS). At the receiving end, the network converts data from GDS to the format required by the application.

In theory, GDS could insulate programs from machine-specific differences, such as ASCII on PS/2 versus EBCDIC on System/370. However, few APPC implementations provide automatic mapping. Applications usually do the code translation themselves.

Basic conversations don't use GDS. APPC performs no processing on the data within basic conversations. Programs that use basic conversations take more responsibility for error recovery than their mapped counterparts. Every APPC implementation must support basic conversations; mapped conversations are optional. However, any product that provides an API must also provide mapped conversations.

APPC provides three types of verbs:

- *Basic Conversation Verbs* Provide a privileged interface intended mainly for STPs. Programs written in low-level languages use this interface
- *Mapped Conversation Verbs* Intended for data exchange between application programs. In theory, these verbs provide mapping of data types and insulate applications from some of the intricacies of APPC
- *Control Operator Verbs* Let applications administer the communication path

The ALLOCATE and SEND_DATA verbs are part of APPC's basic conversation verb set. As with nearly all basic verbs, they have equivalents in the mapped conversation verb set, MC_ALLOCATE and MC_SEND_DATA. Control operator verbs include ACTIVATE_SESSION, CHANGE_SESSION_LIMIT, and DEFINE. The DEFINE verb sets system definition parameters, including LU names, modes, and session limits.

Base and Option Sets

All APPC implementations have specific base-level functions. Besides these, most SAA environments offer option sets (occasionally called *towers*). The base functions include:

- Allocating and deallocating conversations
- Sending and receiving data
- Controlling the direction of data flow
- Confirming successful receipt of data
- Sending error notification to a program

The option sets include:

- *Mapped conversations*, including compatibility with LU 6.1, data mapping, GDS, and simplified error handling
- *Syncpoint*, which defines units of work, provides commitment control, allows transaction backout, and automates resynchronization. This supports distributed databases and complex transaction processing
- *Parallel sessions* allow multiple concurrent conversations between programs

■ *Program Initialization Parameter (PIP) data* lets a program send parameters to its partner program using the ALLOCATE verb

With so many options, APPC's structure seems complex and confusing. Nevertheless, this approach makes it practical to offer APPC in many different computer families with a wide capacity range. For example, System/370 APPC offers nearly the full set of options, but APPC/PC provides only a few. Many hardware products (such as the IBM 3820 printer) have limited capacity, and thus provide only base APPC functions.

Figure 17-4: APPC Base and Towers

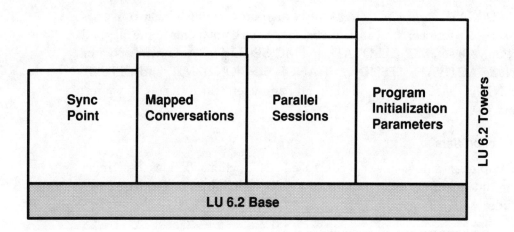

APPC Protocol Boundary

APPC defines the names of the verbs and their parameters. IBM calls this the *protocol boundary*. However, many APIs that implement APPC don't use the same verb names and syntax as the architecture does. Applications using different APIs can communicate, however, because all implementations must use the same protocols to represent the verbs.

For example, one implementation might require applications to call SNAWRITE, but another might require an EXEC SEND statement. Both result in an APPC SEND_DATA request. Although two applications can communicate, they aren't portable between the two environments. It might require a big effort to rewrite the programs when they must move to a new platform.

Figure 17-5: APPC Architecture

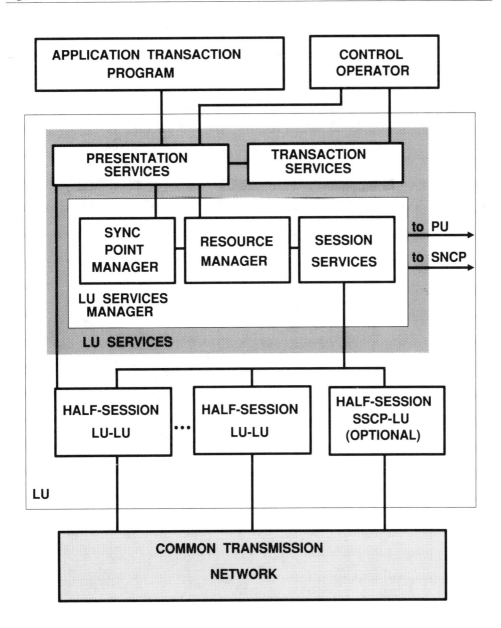

Common Programming Interface for Communications

IBM tightened the protocol boundary definition by standardizing the API. The SAA CPI for Communications (CPI/C) provides libraries of routines that are callable from standard high-level languages. These routines let programmers issue APPC verbs in a portable manner. They provide all APPC base functions plus important option sets.

CPI/C closely resembles the syntax of APPC's architecture. For example the ALLOCATE verb is CMALLC, SEND_DATA is CMSEND, and DEALLOCATE is CMDEAL. CPI/C can coexist with other APIs in the same SAA environment. Existing programs continue using the old APIs, while new programs can take advantage of CPI/C. Hence, CPI/C is a portable APPC protocol boundary for all SAA platforms. Furthermore, the new API is appropriate for non-SAA computer environments, such as UNIX systems.

Peer-to-Peer Network Topology

To support the kind of connectivity promised by APPC, IBM had to provide peer-to-peer networking functions in SAA CCS. In early SNA versions, applications running on System/370 computers could be peers to each other. However, programs running on other systems communicated in a primary-secondary relationship with System/370 applications. What's more, two applications running on small computers couldn't communicate directly; a System/370 computer had to relay the information.

It would have been difficult for IBM to abandon the hierarchical SNA architecture completely. Instead, the company adapted the existing peripheral node architecture to handle peer-to-peer connectivity. This had two major consequences:

- Besides primary-secondary relationships, peripheral nodes must allow peer-to-peer relationships
- Nodes must allow parallel sessions between LUs, which may be directly connected

To provide these features, IBM introduced SNA node type 2.1. As its numbering suggests, it is similar to peripheral node type 2. Although the new node type is a modest enhancement to the peripheral node, it led to important new SNA network topologies. Its common name, Low Entry Networking (LEN), also suggested new directions in IBM's marketing of SNA connectivity.

Node Type 2.1

The type 2.1 node improves on the connectivity of the type 2 node. It functions as a type 2 node within a hierarchical SNA network. But it also provides peer-to-peer communication, multiple sessions, and multiple data links. Many people call this function *PU type 2.1*, but the term *node type 2.1* is more accurate.

Peer-to-peer communication means that LUs in a type 2.1 node can have sessions with LUs in another type 2.1 node without supervision by a central host computer. There is no SSCP; thus there are no SSCP-LU sessions. The two nodes connect and establish direct LU-LU sessions. This provides "any-to-any" connectivity. Though very simple, this approach provides minimal network management.

LUs in type 2 nodes must be secondary LUs and handle only one LU-LU session at a time. LUs in type 2.1 nodes support multiple sessions. For example, an LU can have concurrent sessions with several other LUs in the network. Furthermore, it can have several parallel LU-LU sessions with a single partner LU. LUs in type 2.1 nodes can be primary or secondary. This lets several pairs of APPC applications communicate simultaneously between two peer nodes.

Type 2 nodes have one data link, but type 2.1 nodes can have several. Each of these links connects either to other type 2.1 nodes, or to host computers in the hierarchical SNA network. The dual personality of the node emerges here: simultaneously it supports both peer-to-peer (type 2.1) and primary-to-secondary (type 2) connectivity. On a data link, type 2.1 nodes can be either primary or secondary stations.

Control Points

Within hierarchical SNA networks, type 2.1 nodes connect to a subarea node. *Boundary function* in the subarea node provides routing services. An SSCP is essential for requesting and terminating LU-LU sessions. The SSCP also provides centralized network management, working with the Physical Unit Control Point (PUCP) in the node.

In peer-to-peer SNA networks, type 2.1 nodes connect directly to each other. There is no subarea node or SSCP; the type 2.1 node provides its own routing services. Two nodes communicate directly, but there is no intermediate routing. This means that two LUs must be in adjacent nodes to be able to communicate. This is in sharp contrast to hierarchical SNA networks, where messages may flow through several intermediate nodes before reaching their destination.

Type 2.1 nodes contain a *Single Node Control Point* (SNCP), which provides a subset of SSCP functions. When a 2.1 node is working in a peer-to-peer setting, its PUCP function doesn't operate. The SNCP assists in establishing and terminating LU-LU sessions between directly connected type 2.1 nodes.

Network Topology

There are many possible network topologies involving type 2.1 nodes, considering the data link flexibility mentioned above. Several configurations are possible:

- Single point-to-point link
- Two (or more) parallel links between a pair of nodes
- One node with several point-to-point links to other nodes
- A multipoint link, connecting several nodes
- A hybrid configuration, connecting to a subarea node, but also combining the configurations listed above

The network provides connectivity between LUs in two ways. LUs in type 2.1 nodes connected to the hierarchical network can participate in sessions with other LUs elsewhere in the network. The subarea node provides the routing and boundary function for the type 2.1 node. Alternatively, type 2.1 nodes can connect directly with each other, and any LUs in those nodes can have sessions.

Without the hierarchical network, LUs can establish sessions only between directly-connected (that is, adjacent) type 2.1 nodes. Often, users employ "relay" programs in intermediate nodes. Such programs must provide the routing and queueing functions to bridge the data from its origin, through an intermediate node, and to the destination node. IBM's Advanced Peer-to-Peer Networking (APPN) handles this problem elegantly. But APPN isn't available in many IBM product lines, and it isn't part of SAA.

Document Interchange Architecture

APPC serves as the foundation for many important high-level services in SAA. The remainder of this chapter discusses three such network services, which support office automation and data processing. The first two, Document Interchange Architecture (DIA) and SNA Distribution Services (SNADS), often work together handling documents and electronic mail in IBM office systems. The third, Distributed Data Management (DDM), provides file access through the network.

Figure 17-6: Type 2.1 Node Architecture

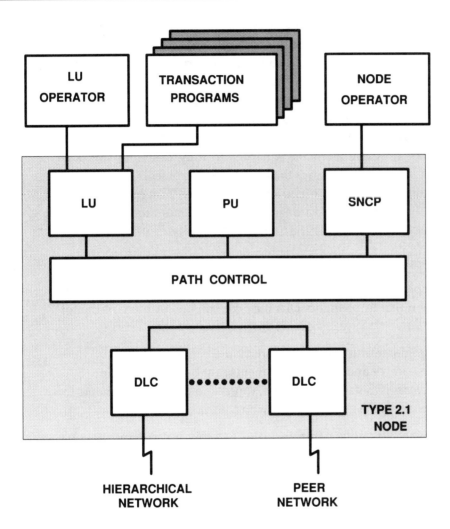

IBM created *office information architectures,* which handle data objects encountered in the workplace. These SAA architectures deal mainly with exchanging information. Such information consists of text, drawings, graphics, images, bar codes, or coded data. The text may represent notes, letters, reports, or publications. Although these items differ in format and usage, IBM treats them all similarly, and calls them *documents.*

An *office system* provides services for creating, storing, revising, distributing, and retrieving documents. It lets users exchange documents within a particular office system and between dissimilar office systems. Users need not worry about differences in document formatting. Both the content and format of the information is preserved when users exchange documents. The office system network provides automatic delivery of documents; when documents arrive at a destination, the network holds them until the recipient asks for them.

Two office information architectures provide these functions: Document Content Architecture (DCA) and Document Interchange Architecture (DIA). DCA defines the formatting of text documents; Chapter 18 fully describes this SAA communication data stream. DIA defines the formats and protocols for the transparent exchange of documents in an office system network. This includes document distribution, filing, retrieval, and deletion. Such services are important in linking SAA office products, especially the OfficeVision family.

DIA Nodes

DIA defines three types of nodes. These node types are separate from SNA node types. An SAA system that implements DIA may contain one or more of the following node types:

- *Source Nodes* originate and control the interchange of documents
- *Recipient Nodes* receive and control documents sent by another node
- *Office System Nodes* (OSNs) receive, store, route, and deliver documents for source or recipient nodes. They also provide a library of documents

Source and recipient functions naturally occur together because most people who send documents also receive them. Therefore, *source/recipient node* (SRN) is the term for nodes that only originate and receive documents. Such nodes can communicate with each other in a peer-to-peer manner. Often they have limited storage capacity and processing power. For example, PS/2s usually serve as SRNs.

In contrast, OSNs store and forward information; they are intermediate nodes that route information through the network. OSNs communicate hierarchically with SRNs. OSNs also communicate with each other. Figure 17-7 shows the relationships among DIA nodes.

Figure 17-7: DIA Node Relationships

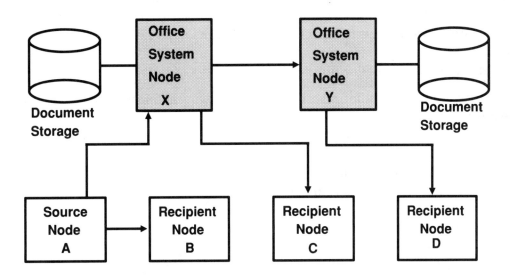

DIA Services

DIA defines network services. Processes in the network's application layer perform these services. DIA also specifies how the processes interact to provide office system functions. The architecture is independent of document content. Many IBM products transmit documents in DCA format, but DIA treats all documents as buckets of bits.

Each DIA service performs functions requested by end users. An end user is the source or recipient of information. The information exchanged by DIA services consists of commands and user data. Examples of DIA commands are:

- Distribute a document to users A and B at node V1
- Search the library for documents meeting specific search criteria
- Retrieve document 1234 from the document library

DIA offers four service categories: document distribution, DIA sessions, document library, and application processing. The next sections describe these services.

Document Distribution Services

Document distribution services deliver documents from a source node to one or more recipient nodes. Such distribution can occur directly between source and recipient nodes. More often, documents flow from the source node to an OSN. The OSN may forward the documents to other OSNs. Finally, an OSN sends the documents to the recipient node.

Important document distribution functions are:

- *Document addressing*, including distribution lists, allowing automatic transmission of multiple copies
- *Confirmation of delivery*, which notifies the sender that the recipient got the document
- Marking documents as *personal*
- Providing services to help users retrieve documents

DIA Session Services

As DIA consists of many processes running in different nodes, the architecture must have rules for them to communicate. DIA session services define the commands to establish a session between two DIA processes. These commands include:

- Establishing the DIA session; agreeing on the scope of work
- Transmitting documents between SRNs and OSNs
- Entering, retrieving, and deleting documents from a library
- Executing an application on an OSN
- Changing the contents of a document profile

IBM grouped DIA commands into *function sets*, which parallel the capabilities of each type of DIA node. Therefore, simple nodes, such as SRNs, implement a small subset of the architecture. OSNs, on the other hand, implement more substantial subsets of the architecture.

Document Library Services

Document library services handle the storage and retrieval of documents in a library, which resides on an OSN. Each document has a profile that contains descriptors such as document name, subject, author's name, creation date, and search keywords. In searching for a document, users specify *search criteria* based on the descriptors in the profile. Note that DIA doesn't search the entire text of documents.

Document library services include:

- Filing documents in the library
- Assigning a unique library-assigned document name (LADN) and returning it to the user who filed the document
- Searching document profiles according to user-specified search criteria
- Retrieving documents
- Maintaining the document library

Application Processing Services

Occasionally, users at an office workstation need to run application programs related to the office system. SRNs usually serve workstations such as PS/2s or 3270s. OSNs run on hosts such as System/370 or AS/400 computers. Application processing services let users at SRNs request execution of programs on OSNs.

IBM DIA implementations provide built-in applications that run batch jobs, print documents, convert document formats, and modify document profiles. Users and product developers can invoke application processing services to run their own office applications.

SNA Distribution Services

Most of the applications discussed thus far use real-time conversations between pairs of programs. These conversations are analogous to a telephone call, in which the programs take turns sending information interactively. However, some applications, such as electronic mail, require a *store and forward* style of data transmission. IBM calls this *asynchronous distribution*, because the sender and receiver don't establish a session, and therefore need not maintain synchronism.

Asynchronous distribution is analogous to a package delivery service. At the origin, users deliver the package to the carrier. At this point, the carrier takes responsibility for the package and routes it to the destination. The package might stop at some intermediate point (perhaps Memphis) along the route to its destination. Users don't need to know about this. At the destination, the carrier delivers the package to the users.

SNA Distribution Services (SNADS) is the carrier. It relies on APPC to transport the data between SNA nodes. SNADS takes responsibility for data at the origin, and delivers it to a destination some time later. Though never explicitly stated by IBM, SNADS is SAA's file transfer protocol. IBM office products, such as DISOSS, use SNADS to send documents between OSNs.

Distribution Service Unit

When an application wants to send a file, it interacts with a *Distribution Service Unit* (DSU). A DSU consists of APPC service transaction programs that connect it to other DSUs. From an application's perspective, there are origin DSUs and destination DSUs. Figure 17-8 shows the SNADS building blocks.

Figure 17-8: SNADS Building Blocks

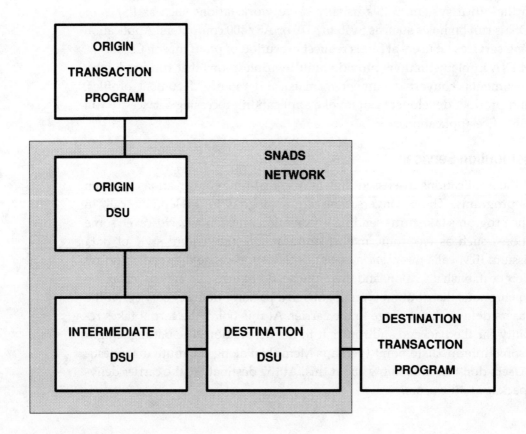

An application passes data to the origin DSU, which may route it through intermediate DSUs, ultimately to the destination DSU. Another application receives the distribution from the destination DSU. Each intermediate DSU stores the entire file, then forwards it. Neither application is aware of the intermediate DSUs.

Applications interface to DSUs using the *distribution protocol boundary*. It is much simpler that APPC's protocol boundary because it has only three verbs, with few options:

- *DISTRIBUTE_DATA*   Sends from the origin DSU
- *RECEIVE_DISTRIBUTION*   Receives at the destination DSU
- *DISTRIBUTE_STATUS*   Inquires about distributions

Directory and Routing

All distributions contain at least the recipient's name. Each DSU has a distribution directory that maps user names into DSU names, for routing purposes. The DSU looks up the recipient's name in the directory and sends the distribution to the specified DSU.

A given DSU's directory might not contain every user's name; wildcards such as SALES.* or *.* are possible. Furthermore, the DSU specified in the directory might not be the destination DSU. Additional routing may be necessary.

SNADS allows for retransmission when a recoverable error (such as temporarily running out of disk space) occurs. It lets a sender check the status of a distribution for each of its recipients. The architecture interacts with *servers* at the DSUs, which provide for access to data objects, formatting, and preparation for transmission.

SNADS provides a general file transfer architecture for SAA, which integrates closely with DIA. The combination of DIA and SNADS provides equivalent (but not compatible) functions to CCITT's X.400 electronic mail interchange standard.

Distributed Data Management

Distributed Data Management defines protocols that let an application running in one computer access files on a different computer. The two computers don't need to use the same operating systems or file systems. DDM has the same goals as the Network File System (NFS), used extensively with UNIX systems.

DDM is attractive to programmers because it can be 100 percent transparent to applications. The other network services described in this chapter require considerable programming effort. A DDM programmer uses normal file I/O operations and the network handles all the communication details.

Although this seems ideal, not all DDM implementations are complete. DDM applications have been successful in the AS/400, System/36, and System/38 environments. Under System/370, DDM works only with CICS; this limits the applications that can use the architecture. Implementations for PS/2s and PCs provide a limited subset of DDM functions.

Source and Target DDMs

DDM consists of two function sets: *source* and *target*. These functions are similar to clients and servers in other architectures. A source DDM supports applications by sending I/O requests (such as READ or WRITE) to a target DDM through the network. The target DDM uses the operating system to perform I/O operations. It sends the results to the source DDM, which causes the results to be passed back to the application. Figure 17-9 shows this process.

IBM operating systems provide a wide range of file structures, allowing sequential, keyed, and random access. Most IBM file systems are record-oriented, with fixed-length or variable-length formatted records. This approach is different from the stream-oriented approach used by PCs and UNIX. DDM provides only record-oriented structures.

DDM Features

DDM supports standard utility functions for files, including:

- Creation, deletion, and renaming
- Loading and unloading
- Clearing files
- Locking, at the file and record levels

DDM uses APPC to communicate between SAA systems. Like APPC, DDM has base functions and options, which differ among implementations. Within each SAA environment, it relies on a local data manager interface (LDMI), which intercepts an application's I/O requests and redirects them to DDM. This is similar to the I/O redirection that occurs in PC-based local area networks involving DOS and IBM's PC LAN Program.

Figure 17-9: DDM Architecture

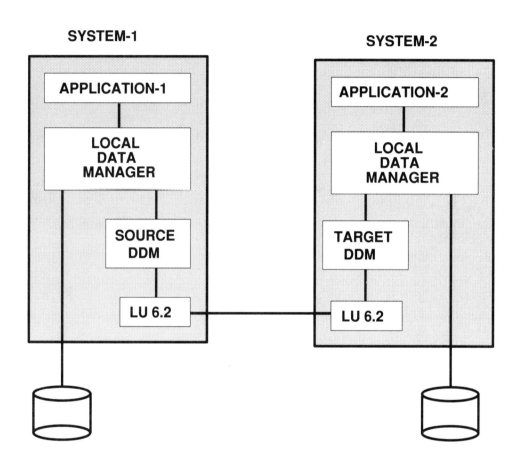

Thus, DDM provides record-level access to files stored in remote systems. This reduces the need to transfer entire files when an application needs to access only a few records. DDM is fully transparent; it isn't necessary to change or re-compile an application program to use the architecture. When writing code, programmers can assume that all files are local to the system.

Chapter 18

Data Streams

You can think of data streams as the back roads of the SAA road map. They define standard ways to represent information within a network. Their services usually involve minor parts of SAA applications. Data streams are only incidental to SAA's cooperative processing theme; mainly they provide consistency among IBM product offerings.

The oldest and most useful of the trio of data streams is 3270 data stream. It primarily connects mainframe application programs to terminals. The terminals may be real or emulated by a program. Considering the wide range of 3270 products and the huge assortment of 3270 emulators, this architecture is very important, despite its ancient technical foundations.

Nearly all System/370 application programs now communicate using 3270 data stream; however, few can do cooperative processing. One possible short-cut to implementing cooperative processing is to have a program on a PS/2 communicate with System/370 programs using 3270 data stream. This would require little or no change to existing code on the System/370. Some customers have found that 3270 data stream provides a useful bridge from older technology to SAA cooperative processing.

Document Content Architecture (DCA) is another data stream that provides compatibility. During the late 1970s and early 1980s, IBM developed several word processing products, including both hardware and software. These included the legendary Displaywriter, and the not-so-famous 5520 and Distributed Office Support Facility/8100 (DOSF).

None of IBM's word processors talked to each other. Each product used a different scheme for representing text documents. DCA solves this problem by providing a standard format for exchanging documents. Today, most IBM and many third-party word processing and electronic mail products support DCA.

Compatibility problems also nagged IBM's printer designers. The company offered many printer product lines that used different formatting approaches. Software products had to know about the idiosyncrasies of each product line. The growing need to print graphics and images, besides text, forced IBM to standardize its language for communicating with printers. Intelligent Printer Data Stream provides this language for IBM's high-end printers.

IBM also adopted Adobe's PostScript page definition language for some of its inexpensive laser printers. PostScript's services are similar to those provided by IPDS, but it uses a different technical approach. Thus, IPDS performs better with high speed printers, but PostScript offers more features and greater flexibility. PostScript is not part of SAA.

3270 Data Stream

The IBM 3270 terminal family is widespread within the IBM world. Emulation of both 3270 display terminals and printers by minicomputers and PCs has been commonplace for over a decade. IBM and many competitors offer 3270 connectivity products with a wide range of functions and configurations. The 3270 data stream is the language of the 3270 product family. It forms the basis for emulating IBM mainframe terminals.

MVS, VM, and their subsystems, TSO, CMS, IMS, and CICS, use System/370 hardware to communicate with 3270 terminals. OS/2 Communications Manager contains complete 3270 emulation that runs on the PS/2. The AS/400 mainly uses the IBM 5250 terminal family as workstations, but also emulates the 3270 faithfully. Given this wide software base, IBM could not ignore the IBM 3270 product family when it developed SAA.

IBM Terminal Philosophies

In the 1970s, IBM developed two distinct terminal product families: 3270 and 5250. As suggested, customers should use the 3270 family with large computers and the 5250 family with small computers. As terminal technology evolved, IBM brought the two families together. For each category of terminal, IBM offers a 3270 version and a 5250 version. Hence, equivalent 3270 and 5250 terminals are hard to distinguish visually; they also have similar model numbers (for example, 3472 versus 3477).

Figure 18-1: IBM 3472 Terminal

The IBM 5250 terminal family connects to System/36, System/38, 5520, and AS/400 computers. These terminals use the 5250 data stream, which defines different protocols from the 3270 data stream. The 5250 data stream is not part of SAA. IBM has reassured customers that its omission of 5250 data stream from SAA doesn't mean that the 5250s are boat anchors.

IBM's approach to communicating with terminals differs radically from that of its competitors. Many modern computers use asynchronous protocols to communicate with inexpensive terminals; such terminals connect to the computer without a network. Both 5250 and 3270 terminals use SNA network services to communicate with host computers. This requires terminals that are complex and sometimes difficult to connect. They are more expensive than equivalent asynchronous terminals.

The 3270 Product Family

The 3270 product line contains display terminals and printers that connect to cluster controllers. Most products emulate the following 3270 display terminal models:

- 3278 display models 2 through 5
- 3279 display models S2A, S2B, and S3G
- 3287 printers

The 3278 is a standard, full-function monochrome terminal; its model numbers denote different screen dimensions. The 3279 is a color terminal with both text and graphic modes. The IBM 3287 is an old dot matrix printer with the same performance as a modern $200 dot matrix printer. Though no longer manufactured, all these devices have become benchmarks; all modern 3270 products are upwardly compatible with them.

Note the peculiar numbering of IBM terminal products. The family name is 3270, but the terminals have diverse model numbers. As the family dates back to the early 1970s, there have been about five generations of display terminals:

- 3277 is a first generation product: simple, heavy, and expensive
- 3278 and 3279 are second generation: more complex, heavy, and expensive
- 3178 and 3179 are third generation: these are the first 3270 terminals with plastic cases; they are much cheaper
- 3180 is a more sophisticated version of the 3178; first terminal that offered both 5250 and 3270 models
- 3191 through 3197 are fourth generation: sleeker than previous models
- 3471 through 3477 are the latest terminals, announced in 1989

These terminals connect to an IBM 3174 or equivalent cluster controller. Such cluster controllers connect directly to S/370 I/O channels or through communication controllers such as IBM 3745s. The data link from cluster controllers to communication controllers is either Synchronous Data Link Control (SDLC) or a packet data network using the SNA-X.25 interface.

Cluster controllers connect to terminals directly through cables. They also connect to programmable workstations through a Token-Ring local area network. The wiring for a direct connection varies, but often customers use coaxial cable or the IBM cabling system. Two interfaces exist for this connection:

- Control Unit Terminal (CUT) mode, for non-intelligent terminals
- Distributed Function Terminal (DFT) mode, which allows up to five concurrent sessions on a single cable

Figure 18-2: IBM 3174 Cluster Controller (Large Model)

3270 Data Stream Functions

The *3270 data stream* defines the data and commands for controlling and formatting information on IBM 3270 display terminals and printers. The data stream offers two levels of functionality: base data stream, which defines simple screen formatting, and extended data stream, which offers seven colors and extended highlighting. Most modern products support both base and extended data streams.

The data stream consists of commands and orders that direct the presentation of information. For example, the data stream can specify that a particular field on the screen is purple, blinking, and reverse video. The data stream lets programs interrogate device model numbers and features. This is useful, for example, in determining whether a particular terminal can display graphics.

Figure 18-3: IBM 3270 Configurations

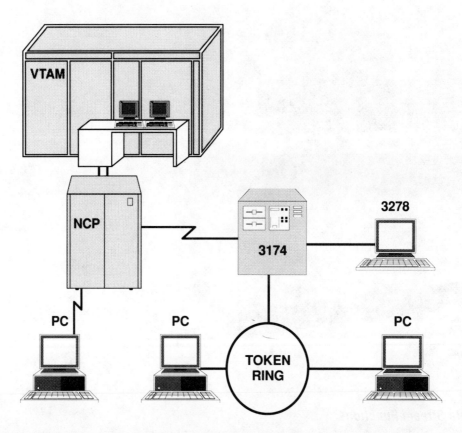

Structured fields let programmers use advanced data stream functions, such as file services. Structured fields vary in length; they always include a code showing the function to be performed. They may also contain parameters that further define the function. The other SAA data streams (DCA and IPDS) also use structured fields.

Figure 18-4: IBM 3174 Cluster Controller (Small Model)

In an SNA network, 3270 display terminals use Logical Unit (LU) type 2 session protocols combined with 3270 data stream. Printers in the 3270 product family occasionally use LU type 3. This LU type uses 3270 data stream exclusively, and it provides for compatibility with printers manufactured in the 1970s.

However, in practice most 3270 printers use LU type 1, which requires SNA Character String (SCS) protocol for formatting. Many other IBM printers, including Remote Job Entry terminals, use LU type 1. SCS is more generic and usually performs better for printing than 3270 data stream. SCS is not part of SAA.

Some products use 3270 data stream without SNA. This provides compatibility with older implementations. Such implementations probably would not be consistent with SAA.

Physical Connectivity with 3270

Products that support 3270 data stream allow a wide range of physical connections. A direct cable from a workstation to a cluster controller is a popular connection. The controller is an IBM 3174 (or the older 3274), which connects to the System/370 by either an I/O channel or a data link.

The connection operates in CUT mode, which emulates a single non-programmable terminal, or DFT mode, allowing multiple concurrent sessions. In DFT mode, workstations handle more high-level SNA protocols than they do in CUT mode. Most terminals operate in CUT mode, but some sophisticated terminals (for example, the IBM 3290) can operate in DFT mode. Virtually all programmable workstations (such as PS/2s) can operate in CUT mode, but they work best in DFT mode.

Because many large companies have wired their buildings for 3270 connectivity, this scenario is convenient. It works especially well for communicating with existing host applications. However, performance often falls short of expectations; the cluster controller or the data link can constitute a bottleneck.

Alternatively, many products emulate an SNA cluster controller and connect to the host via an SDLC link and synchronous modems. This type of product can act as a combined cluster controller and terminal. Thus the product functions as a PU type 2.

Because a single SDLC link carries up to 254 sessions, this configuration can also operate as a LAN-to-mainframe gateway. The data rate of the SDLC link may limit performance; it seldom exceeds 64 kilobits per second. Hence, this scenario provides moderate performance.

The third connection alternative is the Token-Ring local area network. Workstations connect via Token-Ring adapter hardware through the network to the Token-Ring adapter of a 3174 or 3745 controller (or equivalent). These controllers act as a gateway from the Token-Ring network to the SNA wide-area network. This type of configuration offers high performance.

Document Content Architecture

In its simplest form, DCA is a standard document format for word processing and electronic mail. It defines the arrangement and presentation of information in a document to be interchanged within an office system. It provides three document formats: revisable form text, final form text, and mixed object (MO:DCA).

Revisable Form versus Final Form Documents

Documents in revisable form contain text plus control information that determines the formatting of the text. For example, a document might have a particular heading on even-numbered pages. The declaration of this heading appears once, at the beginning of the document. As its name suggests, anyone who receives a revisable form document can edit both the text and the control information. This would be useful, for example, to exchange drafts of a paper being co-authored by two people.

Documents in final form contain text plus control information in a format suitable for viewing or printing by a non-intelligent device. In the example above, the heading appears in final form several times; it prints on every other page. This format is not suitable for editing. For example, it would be the ideal format for sending an luncheon invitation to a colleague. It's not likely the recipient would need to edit such a message.

Users can convert documents from revisable form to final form using utility programs supplied with most products. Figure 18-5 shows this process. Automatic conversion from final form to revisable form will not necessarily preserve all formatting controls; information usually will be lost. Therefore, few products offer this feature.

Figure 18-5: Converting Revisable Form to Final Form

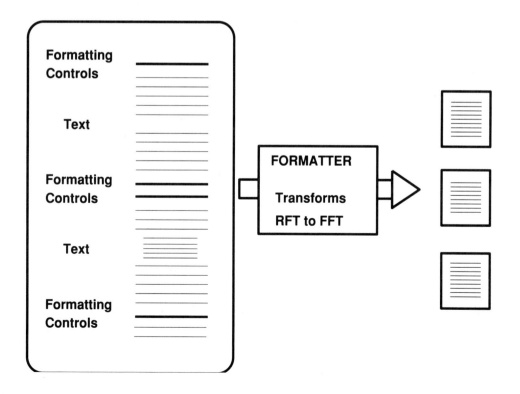

Mixed Object Document Content Architecture

Mixed Object DCA (MO:DCA, pronounced mod-ka) provides a structure for transporting more complex documents among SAA applications. In MO:DCA, the document constitutes the highest level in the data stream hierarchy. A document contains pages, which constitutes the middle level. Pages are composed of *objects*. As in IPDS, each object contains either text, graphics, or images.

As in other SAA data streams, structured fields mark the beginning and end of each document, page, or object. Products can selectively process MO:DCA documents; for example, if a particular product doesn't know about images, it bypasses all image objects in the document. MO:DCA has four subsidiary architectures:

- FOCA Defines fonts
- PTOCA Defines the presentation of text objects
- IOCA Represents and exchanges image data
- GOCA Creates and specifies vector graphics, including lines, arcs, shading, orientation, and color

MO:DCA is the latest addition to DCA. It signals the emergence of graphics and images as important features of office system and data processing products. IBM's ImagePlus product family is now starting to use these architectures for complex document storage, distribution, retrieval, and processing.

Intelligent Printer Data Stream

IPDS provides a protocol to communicate between SAA host computers and high-end IBM printers. The information to be printed may contain several intermixed object types: text, vector graphics, bit-map images, and bar codes. IBM developed IPDS as a result of its experience in developing Advanced Function Printing Architecture (AFPA). Due to its evolutionary nature, IPDS contains many features unique to IBM printers.

All-Points-Addressable Printers

IPDS is appropriate for all-points-addressable (APA) printers that contain substantial computing capacity (such as a microprocessor). The term all-points-addressable means that applications can control printing of each dot of ink. For example, many IBM printers print black images on paper at 240 dots per linear inch. An APA printer lets applications determine the horizontal and vertical coordinates of each dot to be printed. Although all IPDS printers are APA, not all APA printers support IPDS.

Figure 18-6: Sample MO:DCA Data Stream

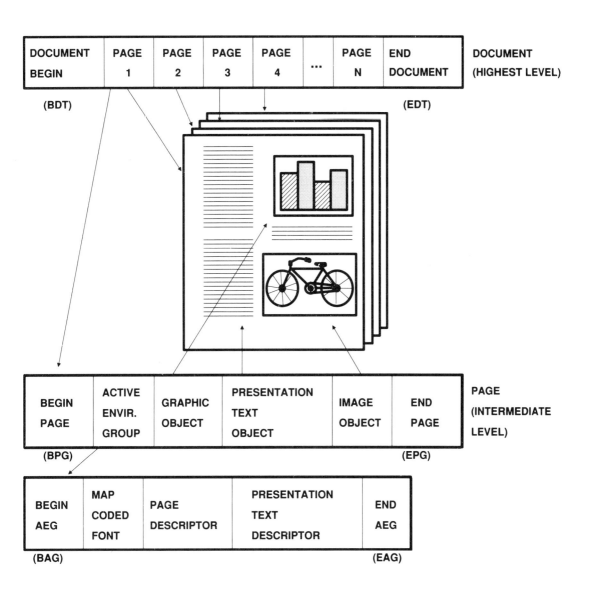

Architecture Structure

IPDS lets different applications create source data independently. For example, a word processor creates the text, a scanner obtains an image, and a graphics package draws a chart. IPDS enables merging the output of these applications at print time to produce a single printed page.

In theory, IPDS does not rely on any particular communication protocol. In practice, most IPDS implementations use APPC (SNA LU 6.2), which is also part of CCS. This lets IPDS operate over all the SAA data links, and allows efficient operation with the System/370 I/O channel. Customers therefore can connect high performance printers through either local area networks or wide area networks.

The architecture defines *objects*, which are independently-defined blocks of data. IPDS represents objects in a manner analogous to that used by the 3270 data stream, which enables using the same objects with both architectures. IPDS sends its data and commands through structured fields that describe the presentation of information on the page. They resemble 3270 structured fields, except that IPDS provides different functions, such as:

- *Device control*, such as paper tray selection, duplex printing, bursting, and collating
- *Management of downloaded data*, such as fonts, page segments, and electronic forms
- *Exception handling*, which lets users control how the printer will handle errors, such as missing fonts.

IPDS provides its own response protocol at the data stream level. This is independent from the response protocols used by APPC or the data link. It allows queries (for example, about device capabilities), synchronizes the printer with the host computer, and handles exception conditions.

IBM divided IPDS architecture into several *function sets*. Each function set contains IPDS commands that represent a major printer capability. Each printer product implements the base IPDS functions plus optional function sets. This is similar to the "base and towers" approach used by other CCS services, such as APPC and DDM.

Printing Subsystem Components

IPDS environments all contain three elements: source applications, presentation services, and IPDS printers. These elements work together in various configurations to provide printing services. The source applications may not know about IPDS. Presentation services convert application output to IPDS, thereby insulating user programs from the details of the printer hardware or the architecture.

Source applications generate *source data* to be printed. Most applications generate this data in a format suitable for non-IPDS printers, such as the legendary IBM 1403. Some applications use 3270 data stream or SNA Character String for output formatting. Other applications, including a few IBM products, use IBM's Advanced Function Printing Architecture (AFPA). Hence, applications use diverse formatting methods, corresponding to the functions of various IBM printer product lines.

Presentation services receive source data and convert it to IPDS. The services require no changes to the source applications, and also can provide features that enhance the quality of the output. For example, programs written for the IBM 1403 could display multiple fonts per page, which was not possible on the original 1403 printer. Customers can add other embellishments, including duplex printing and electronic forms.

IPDS therefore provides compatibility with many of IBM's older printer products and their formatting and control features. The level of compatibility depends on the software implementation; the architecture itself doesn't specify it. The key ingredients are software compatible with IPDS on the host computer and an IPDS printer. Such printers connect to all SAA computer environments.

IPDS Environments

System/370 application programs usually spool print data via JES2, JES3, RSCS, or POWER, as previously described. IPDS presentation services obtains the data from the spool and generates IPDS commands to drive the printer. This *spooled host* configuration is very common, and is easy for programmers to use. Note that spooled host applications do not drive printers directly.

The *Print Services Facility* (PSF) product provides the presentation services for VM, MVS, and VSE operating systems. As most applications use the simple IBM 1403 print formatting approach, PSF converts this to IPDS. A few applications (mostly IBM products) use the more complicated Advanced Function Printing Data Stream (AFPDS), which is not part of SAA. PSF also converts AFPDS to IPDS.

In *interactive host* environments, applications generate IPDS commands directly, without format conversion. The SNA network may send these commands to a cluster controller, such as an IBM 3174, which drives the printer. Inside the host, applications use the Graphical Data Display Manager (GDDM) software product to provide presentation services for printers attached to 3174s. In this environment, GDDM generates the IPDS and sends it directly to the printer; the system does not spool the output.

Figure 18-7: IPDS Configurations

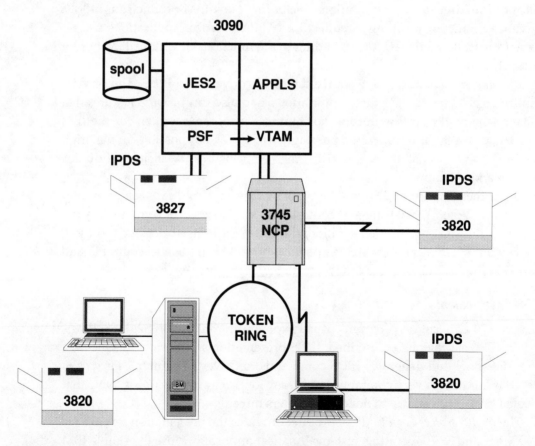

Mid-range computer environments, including the AS/400, operate in a manner analogous to the host environments described above. IBM integrated the presentation services functions into the OS/400 operating system. It converts SNA

Character String data into IPDS and also allows a mixture of text, graphics, and bar codes.

PS/2 workstations can send output to a print server on a local area network. IBM's LAN Manager product provides the connection between the workstation and the server. The server provides format conversion, such as ASCII to IPDS, and drives the printer.

Chapter 19

Communication Products

The products discussed here are practical implementations of the architectural components described in Chapters 15–18. These communication products, combined with operating systems and application enablers (such as CICS, IMS, TSO, and CMS), provide most CCS services. Previous chapters contain details about the operating systems and application enablers; this chapter focuses on the basic system software products that communicate between SAA systems.

The architectural features of CCS don't always correspond neatly to IBM products. The Logical Unit (LU) is a good example of this. It would be convenient to say that the Virtual Telecommunications Access Method (VTAM) provides the LU function in a System/370 host. This isn't true, however; IBM decided to split the LU function between application enablers (such as CICS or TSO) and VTAM. Sometimes the LU also encompasses application programs. Thus, the implementation of a major architectural feature may span three or more products.

When IBM developed its architectures, the company didn't specify how they were to be implemented. Separate product implementation groups within IBM made these decisions. So IBM's products have different structures and relationships in each SAA environment.

In System/370, customers must select and install several products that provide communication services. The first product customers must install on the host computer is VTAM. By itself, VTAM provides no useful ability to communicate. Most System/370 computers require a communication controller, such as an

IBM 3745, to connect to data links. This programmable device requires IBM's Network Control Program (NCP) software.

Figure 19-1: Communication Product Relationships

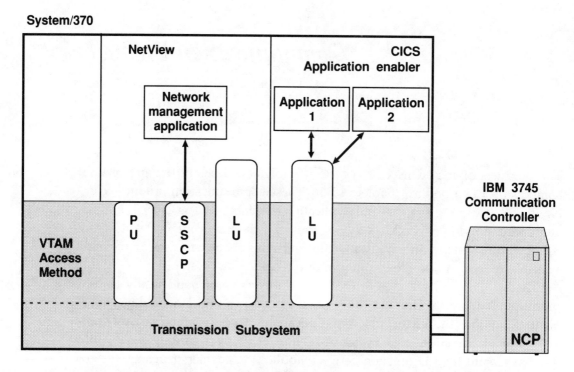

Customers must also install subsystems such as TSO or CICS, and install their applications in those environments. VTAM's network management functions are rudimentary; again customers install extra products, such as NetView, to get comprehensive network management. NetView doesn't manage everything in a network, so it is necessary to buy more software, such as NetView/PC, to manage those items (Token-Ring networks, IBM/Rolm telephone PBXs, and non-IBM modems) not handled directly by NetView.

In contrast, the OS/400 and OS/2 environments are not so fragmented. OS/2 Extended Edition includes the Communications Manager, which provides most of the connectivity a customer will need. OS/400 also has built-in communication functions that serve most common user needs. Although IBM sells extra communication products for these environments, they aren't necessary at every customer site. Due to the similarity between the structure and features of OS/2 and OS/400 communications, this chapter examines only OS/2.

The OS/2 and OS/400 communication functions are easier to operate, simpler to maintain, and much less expensive than those for System/370. However, System/370 provides more features (especially many esoteric ones), and offers extensive tools for tuning the system to peak performance. Customers appreciate these advantages, but some regret the labor-intensive nature of IBM's mainframe networking products.

System/370 Communications Access Methods

In System/370, application programs often read and write information through access methods, introduced in Chapter 7. Accessing disk and tape files is the most common function of access methods. Starting in the 1970s, communication access methods also became commonplace. These software products execute in the System/370 and provide an interface between programs and the network.

The earliest teleprocessing (TP) applications used communication access methods directly. Since all access methods contain APIs designed for assembly language programs, these TP applications were complex and difficult. The APIs weren't accessible to applications written in languages such as COBOL. Furthermore, programmers had to know network protocols to use the access methods effectively.

Starting in the late 1960s, IBM developed a layer of software that insulated applications from the details of the access methods and the network protocols. Previously called teleprocessing monitors (TP monitors) or database/data communications (DB/DC) systems, today they are called application enablers. Products such as IMS and CICS fit this description.

From a programmer's perspective, TP monitors greatly simplified application development because they reduce the level of detail in programming. Programmers who were not technical gurus could be productive after a few weeks of training and practice. This approach worked well, and has become the standard method of developing transaction processing applications in almost every commercial IBM environment.

From the access method's perspective, an application enabler is an application. It is common to say that CICS is a VTAM application, for example. In this context, the term *application* might not refer to programs that provide services to end users. For example, most people think that NetView is system software; nevertheless it is also a VTAM application. Alternatively, customers can write applications that use VTAM's API directly. This is not common, due to the difficulties mentioned above.

The first teleprocessing access method, Basic Telecommunications Access Method (BTAM) made its debut in the 1960s. Still occasionally used today, BTAM is functionally obsolete because it doesn't support SNA. The next access method, Telecommunications Access Method (TCAM) was popular during the 1970s. It supported SNA, but it was unreliable and somewhat strange. IBM phased out TCAM during the mid-1980s.

Hence, only VTAM remains. IBM introduced VTAM in 1974 as the primary SNA access method. Features were steadily added to the product, which has proven to be reliable and efficient. IBM changed the product's formal name to Advanced Communications Function Virtual Telecommunications Access Method (ACF/VTAM), but most people still call it VTAM (pronounced vee-tam or victor-tam; never V-T-A-M). It is a very large software product; VTAM provides all the basic communications and network management functions for System/370 host computers.

Virtual Telecommunications Access Method

IBM has VTAM products for three major operating systems: MVS, VM, and VSE. These products are functionally similar, and only differ in ways related to the underlying operating system. For example, under MVS, VTAM runs in an address space, but under VM it runs in a virtual machine. Distinctions such as these dictate important differences in operating procedures. Nevertheless, the products are more alike than different.

VTAM functions fall into three categories:

- Provide an API to VTAM applications, which include user programs and vendor-supplied subsystems, such as CICS
- Route information between host applications and the network using the System/370 I/O channel to connect control units such as IBM 3174s or 3745s
- Manage the network in a rudimentary way, and provide an API for more sophisticated network management by products such as NetView

VTAM Services

Within its functional categories, VTAM provides many services. These correspond to the SNA functions discussed previously in the host's LUs, SSCP, and transmission subsystem. They include:

- Helping to start, maintain, and disconnect LU-LU sessions
- Controlling data flow within the network
- Interacting with the network operator
- Responding to equipment and software failures in the network
- Establishing and modifying the network configuration
- Maintaining a network directory and allocating network resources, such as LUs, PUs, SSCPs, and data links

VTAM provides two levels of detail in its API. The first is appropriate for low-level programming. It controls SNA sessions by directly or indirectly specifying each bit in the protocol headers. This type of programming occurs within many IBM products, such as TSO, CICS, and IMS. The second type lets programmers specify APPC verbs; this is suitable for customer applications. VTAM automatically generates the necessary protocols and headers.

VTAM's most important job is the transmission of data between applications and local devices attached via channels. These local devices are communication controllers (for example, IBM 3745) and cluster controllers (IBM 3174). In turn, these devices attach to data links, including SDLC, X.25, and Token-Ring. The devices manage the data links at a low level, responding to individual data transmissions. VTAM manages them at a high level, only getting involved in exceptional circumstances, such as repeated transmission failures.

The role of VTAM in network management includes activating and deactivating network resources, such as lines, communication controllers, cluster controllers, and terminals. It provides commands and messages for operators to control the system. VTAM notifies operators of major error conditions within the network. It has an interface for products, such as NetView, that provide more comprehensive network management services.

Functions that support important SNA features, such as Multiple Systems Networking Facility (MSNF) and SNA Network Interconnection (SNI) are part of VTAM. MSNF enables customers to build networks having multiple System/370 hosts, with each host managing a particular domain. SNI provides a gateway function that interconnects multiple MSNF networks. VTAM and Network Control Program (NCP) work together to provide MSNF and SNI functions.

Figure 19-2: Simple SNI Gateway Between Two SNA Networks

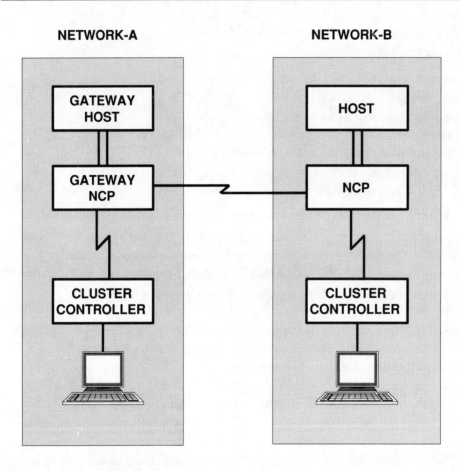

Network Control Program

Each communication controller that connects to a System/370 host contains software that performs SNA protocols. The software product for the IBM 3745 (or equivalent) is Advanced Communications Function Network Control Program (ACF/NCP). As with VTAM, people often omit the ACF part of the name. NCP's main function is to connect data links to the System/370. Usually it does this via an I/O channel, but it also can act as a remote concentrator across an SDLC link or X.25 packet data network.

Figure 19-3: IBM 3745 Communication Controller

NCP contains the SNA transmission subsystem, boundary function, and Physical Unit Control Point (PUCP). At a low level, it controls network data links, including both SDLC and Token-Ring. With the additional Network Control Program Packet Switching Interface (NPSI) product, it also provides the SNA-X.25 interface described in Chapter 16. For data links, NCP does the following:

- Assembles and disassembles messages
- Routes messages to the next node on their path through the network
- Provides SNA boundary function, which does address format translation for peripheral nodes
- Polls, transmits, and handles errors
- Provides the framing structure

- Runs diagnostics to isolate problems
- Sends network management statistics to the host computer

Network Definition

A system programmer creates an NCP by coding macros that specify the configuration of the communication controller. Each data link, PU, and LU appears in the NCP definition. The programmer codes the technical characteristics of each data link, including:

- Data rate
- Treatment of physical interface signals (for example, the DTR pin of the RS-232 interface)
- Data link protocol (such as SDLC)
- Half-duplex versus full-duplex
- SDLC flow control parameters

The NCP definition also covers all attached cluster controllers, communication controllers, and physical terminals. It isn't unusual for this definition to exceed 5,000 lines of code. Hence, NCP coding and maintenance can be laborious.

After coding the NCP, the system programmer executes the traditional two-stage system generation (NCP gen) process on the System/370. (Many 1970s-vintage IBM products use this approach; customers are very familiar with it.) The first stage verifies the configuration and generates a batch job stream. After running the job stream (called "stage 2"), the executable NCP now resides on the System/370's disk. This operation usually takes an hour or two; the network continues to operate during an NCP gen.

Upon command from the network operator, VTAM downloads the NCP to the communications controller. This takes a few seconds, assuming the communication controller is on a channel. The NCP then controls the part of the network assigned to it. Before downloading the NCP, the network operator must be sure that the communication controller isn't active on the network. If it is active, all existing sessions will end abruptly.

Customers make most configuration changes by regenerating the NCP. However, the product allows *dynamic reconfiguration,* in which operators use VTAM commands to change the configuration. This stopgap measure is OK for emergency changes, but is error-prone and difficult to manage in a production environment.

NCP and VTAM Data Flow

NCP and VTAM work together to provide the basis for networking in System/370. They usually exchange information across the channel, at high data rates. The piece of information exchanged is a Path Information Unit (PIU), which contains user data enveloped by SNA addressing and session protocol information (see figure 15-12).

VTAM controls the channel. As with any access method, VTAM uses System/370 channel programming to write information to NCP. NCP receives all PIUs sent by VTAM, and decides how to process them. NCP sends incoming PIUs across the channel whenever VTAM issues a read command.

Upon receiving a PIU from VTAM, NCP decides where it should go. If the PIU is destined for the NCP's subarea, NCP sends it to the boundary function for the destination node. If its destination is for another subarea, NCP looks up the subarea in its path table. Based on the path table, NCP decides which data link will get the message to the next node in the message's route. It then sends the message across the data link.

NetView

NetView is a network management subsystem that runs in System/370 host computers. NetView evolved from several individual products that IBM developed in the 1970s and 1980s, including:

- *Network Communications Control Facility (NCCF)* Automates network operations, providing a better operator interface than VTAM does
- *Network Management Productivity Facility (NMPF)* Automates certain routine operator functions
- *Network Problem Determination Application (NPDA)* Helps operators solve network problems
- *Network Logical Data Manager (NLDM)* Tracks SNA connectivity and reports response time
- *VTAM Node Control Application (VNCA)* Automatically reactivates failed nodes, and displays network status

NetView represents IBM's first step in integrating diverse network management functions into a single cohesive product and architecture. The product implements SNA Management Services, which are part of SAA and define the network management protocols for all IBM communication product lines. IBM has enhanced this architecture to handle alerts and error conditions generated by non-IBM network equipment.

NetView attempts to bring a consistent user interface to its disparate parts. The user interface isn't consistent with SAA; it uses a character-based 3270 line-oriented command and menu approach. However, recent products let customers control NetView from workstations using a CUA-like graphical user interface. This type of graphical interface is quickly becoming the industry standard.

The most important NetView components are the command facility and the hardware monitor. IBM derived these from NCCF and NPDA, respectively. NetView also provides a session monitor, based on NLDM, and a status monitor, based on VNCA.

Figure 19-4: NetView Product Structure

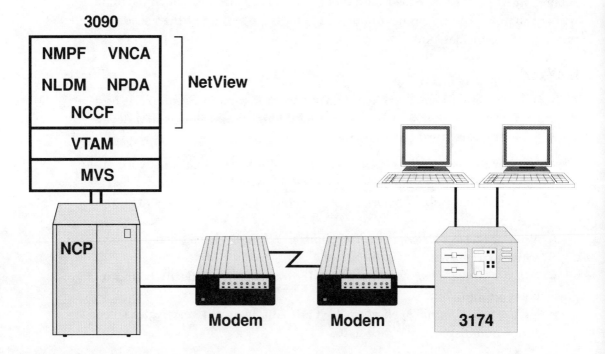

Command Facility

The NetView command facility is the foundation for all other NetView functions. It lets operators use any 3270 terminal as a master console to control any domain in an SNA network. The product can also distribute responsibility for network management among many 3270 terminals, which can be located anywhere in a network. Besides running all other NetView applications, the command facility:

- Executes command lists (CLISTs) written in REXX or NetView's own CLIST language
- Sends messages to other network operators
- Provides security features to limit the span of control of particular network operators
- Maintains a disk log of all VTAM messages
- Executes network commands in other hosts

NetView provides extensive services for running network management applications. You could think of it as the "CICS of network management." It provides a simple database for storing network error records, and functions for collecting, retrieving, and displaying error information. It also provides the foundation for file transfer services, using the SNADS architecture in combination with the NetView Distribution Manager product.

Hardware Monitor

As its name suggests, the hardware monitor keeps track of the reliability of network hardware components. It collects network error notifications and stores them on a database. When a critical error occurs, or the error rate exceeds a threshold, it sends an alert to a network operator. The hardware monitor displays error records on an operator's screen, and suggests possible actions to correct a problem.

The hardware monitor supports practically all recent IBM communication hardware products. What's more, it handles generic alerts, which any network equipment can generate. Many network product vendors provide hardware and software features that communicate with NetView. Such communication can take place directly (using a standard SNA SSCP-PU session), or through the NetView/PC product.

NetView/PC

Most IBM communication products contain a microprocessor (or equivalent device) that handles the details of networking, including network management. Most such products can communicate directly with NetView, using SNA Management Services protocols. Such products include the IBM 3174, 3745, 3708, and

AS/400. However, some devices, including many non-IBM products, can't communicate directly with NetView. NetView/PC provides a mechanism to do this.

NetView/PC collects alerts from network devices and forwards them to the host computer. It supports IBM devices, including the Token-Ring local area network and the IBM/Rolm 9751 telephone PBX. It also provides an API that lets network management applications run on the PC and send alerts to the host. The customer's application can collect the alert in any manner, for example, by receiving information through the PC's serial port. This lets vendors and customers interface virtually any network equipment to NetView.

Figure 19-5: NetView/PC Structure

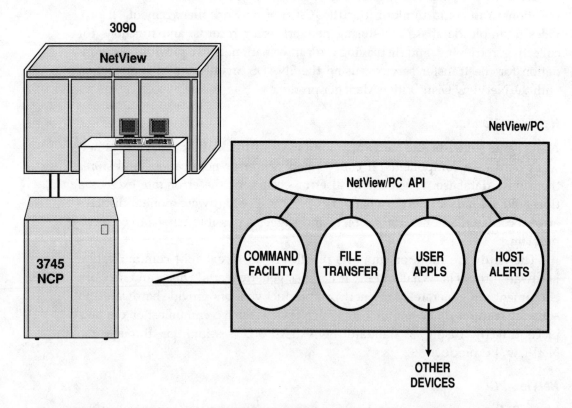

NetView/PC runs on AT-compatible personal computers and PS/2s with Micro Channel Architecture. It requires a co-processor board, which runs part of the software. IBM supplies either DOS or OS/2 versions of NetView/PC. The product uses SNA Management Services, which is part of SAA, to communicate with VTAM and NetView on the System/370 host computer.

OS/2 Communications Manager

OS/2 Communications Manager is an integral part of OS/2 Extended Edition, introduced in Chapter 5. The product provides complete Application Programming Interfaces (APIs) for SAA communication protocols. It supports many SAA features, including:

- IBM 3270 terminal emulation
- SNA server functions
- SNA-X.25 interface
- IEEE 802.2 Logical Link Control
- Advanced Program to Program Communications (APPC)

Communications Manager has other features, including:

- IBM 5250 terminal emulation
- Network Basic Input/Output Support (NETBIOS)
- Server-Requester Programming Interface (SRPI)
- Asynchronous terminal emulation

Communications Manager expands the usefulness of OS/2 by letting it work as a database and application server. OS/2 lays the foundation for the use of intelligent communications subsystems, in which a separate, dedicated CPU handles network protocols. OS/2 eventually will allow true multiprocessor configurations, with multiple CPUs available to execute any task in the system. This will provide high performance network services.

APIs, Servers, and Gateways

OS/2 provides consistent APIs for each of the major communication protocols. As with other OS/2 APIs, programmers can call them directly from any application. Because OS/2 provides a 16 megabyte address space, large applications are possible. The presence of communication software doesn't limit the memory usage of applications, as it did in DOS.

OS/2's architecture is ideal for applications acting as servers, especially those performing communications. Client applications could run under DOS on a local area network and communicate with the OS/2-based server. In turn, the server communicates with the mainframe. This is a practical way to use Communications Manager, but is not strictly within the realm of SAA.

Figure 19-6: Communications Manager Connectivity

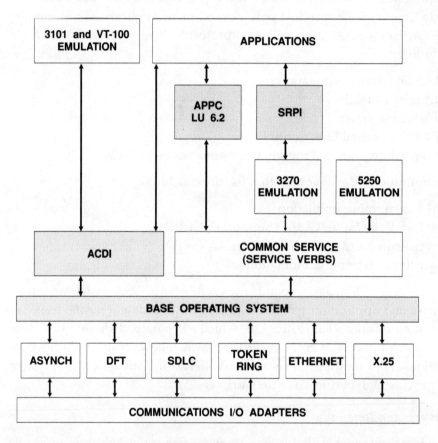

Communications Manager provides a gateway between a LAN and the host system. The *gateway* translates the network protocols of the local area network to the protocols of the SNA wide area network. PS/2s communicate across the LAN to the gateway, and the gateway communicates with the host using SDLC or SNA-X.25 data links.

Multiple 3270 or APPC connections between workstations and host applications can pass through the OS/2-based gateway. User workstations can be running either OS/2 or DOS. Each gateway will support up to 254 Logical Units, and each workstation on the LAN can have up to four active sessions. The gateway does not need to be dedicated to communications; with sufficient capacity it can act as a file server or application processor. A single local area network can have more than one gateway.

Data Links

Communications Manager offers three SAA data links: SDLC, Token-Ring local area networks, and CCITT X.25 packet data networks. Furthermore, Communications Manager provides IEEE 802.3 Ethernet local area network connectivity. With additional products, it allows Transmission Control Protocol/Internet Protocol (TCP/IP) network services. TCP/IP and Ethernet are not part of SAA; nevertheless, they are becoming important in IBM customer environments.

IBM supports CCITT's X.25 packet switching interface using two complementary approaches. OS/2 has an API that contains the full set of X.25 DTE (data terminal equipment) functions, intended to support non-SNA connections. The product also provides full SNA support via IBM's Qualified Logical Link Control (QLLC) protocol.

Communications Manager's X.25 implementation is compatible with a wide range of IBM products, including System/370 and AS/400. Although there is limited demand for such connectivity in the United States, X.25 is a necessity in Europe, Canada, and Japan.

3270 Terminal Emulation

Communications Manager contains the OS/2 counterpart of IBM's DOS-based 3270 emulators, such as Personal Communications 3270. The 3270 display emulator runs in Presentation Manager windows. The Communications Manager provides a separate window for each communication session, and can have several different protocols active concurrently. For example, a workstation can have three concurrent 3270 sessions and one asynchronous terminal emulator running simultaneously; the user can access four windows.

Communications Manager itself doesn't use Presentation Manager. It runs in its own screen group, and therefore occupies the entire display when it appears on the screen. It operates in the same manner as a full-screen (non-Presentation Manager) OS/2 command processor.

The keyboard re-mapping feature of the 3270 emulator redefines the keyboard layout in the 3270 session. This facility allows key swapping, key disabling, and assigning a string of keystrokes to a single key. Users can select from multiple keyboard profiles, but only one can be active at a time; it applies to all active 3270 sessions.

Anyone who has ever used any of IBM's 3270 emulators will immediately understand the usefulness of this feature. IBM's default keyboard mapping is more challenging than playing a Liszt sonata on the piano; it gives new meaning to the term "chord." A normal user is almost obligated to redefine the keyboard, but, alas, there is no standard re-definition that works for everyone.

Figure 19-7: X.25 Connectivity

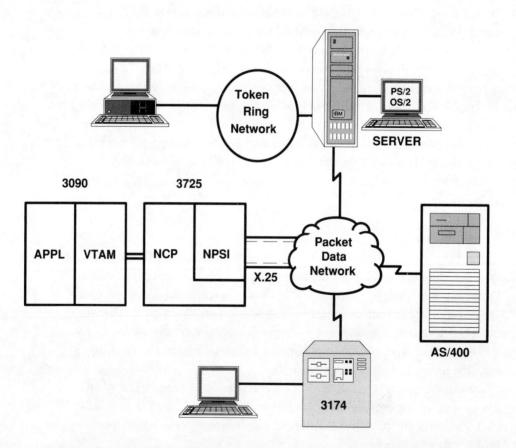

OS/2's implementation of 3270 data stream includes Double-Byte Character Set (DBCS) language translation. DBCS is part of SAA Common User Access. It specifies rules for supporting languages other than English, including those in which writing is right-to-left. DBCS handles languages that do not have Latin characters, including Japanese (Kanji), Korean, and Chinese.

File Transfer Using 3270 Data Stream

Communications manager supports the IND$FILE file transfer protocol, which the IBM 3270 Personal Computer previously used. IND$FILE is compatible with CICS, TSO, and CMS. Users can start file transfers either from the OS/2 command line, using the SEND and RECEIVE commands, or from the Communications Manager main menu. When transferring files, users can specify a file transfer profile, which they created during the installation of the Communications Manager. It specifies ASCII/EBCDIC translation, code pages on the host and PS/2, the name of the file transfer program, file attributes, and disk space allocations on the host.

Although not specifically part of SAA, IND$FILE uses 3270 data stream. It works with many System/370 and PS/2 software products, and performs reasonably well in practice. Hence, customers often use it as a PC-to-mainframe file transfer tool.

Emulator High Level Language API

Another 3270 feature of the Communications Manager is Emulator High Level Language API (EHLLAPI). EHLLAPI lets applications control an active 3270 session. In effect, it substitutes a program for a human terminal operator.

Customers use EHLLAPI to simplify the interaction between a user and a host-based application. Data can be pre-processed at the workstation before transmission to the host, and the host's response can be reformatted for presentation to the user. Some customers have used EHLLAPI as the first step in migrating from central processing to cooperative processing.

Application designers have used EHLLAPI to perform automatic logon, intercept host messages, and generate an appropriate response. It can also coordinate input from the workstation to multiple concurrent host applications. It is compatible with EEHLLAPI (EE stands for Entry Emulator) which IBM used in its older 3270 emulation products that ran under DOS.

5250 Emulation

The 5250 workstation feature emulates up to five print and display sessions. It emulates the 5292-1 and 3197-C20 display terminals. Emulated printers include the 5219, 5224, and 5256. The product connects to the AS/400 using several SAA data links: SDLC, Token-Ring, and X.25. It also connects via twinaxial cable and the IBM 5394 remote control unit. The programming interface is EHLLAPI, which is identical to that provided for 3270 emulation.

Advanced Program-to-Program Communications

IBM included both APPC (LU 6.2) and LEN (PU 2.1) in the Communications Manager. Programmers don't need to be aware of LEN, but APPC has an elaborate API for programs written in C, Pascal, and assembly language.

Communications Manager's APPC implementation is much better than IBM's APPC/PC product for DOS. In DOS, a programmer had to build a parameter block and issue a software interrupt, which was difficult in high-level languages. In OS/2, programs issue APPC verbs using a standard API call.

Under APPC/PC, programmers had to write an *application subsystem*, which performed extensive communications management functions. The operating system handles this in Communications Manager. Programmers no longer need to imbed the details of the system configuration in applications. Menus in the Communications Manager handle SNA parameter definitions.

The Communications Manager gateway function lets APPC sessions pass transparently from LANs though the SNA wide area network to System/370 hosts. It also supports concurrent 3270 sessions. This improves connectivity for cooperative processing applications.

Enhanced Connectivity Facilities

Considerably simpler than APPC, Server-Requester Programming Interface (SRPI) also provides connectivity between programs running on different machines. SRPI's focus is much narrower than APPC's. It supports only the PS/2 and System/370 TSO and CMS environments. SRPI provides fewer features than APPC.

With only two verbs, SEND_REQUEST and SEND_REPLY, programming is simpler, but many powerful features are missing. SRPI subscribes to the client/server model, with the restriction that PS/2 applications must be clients and System/370 applications must be servers.

Figure 19-8: SRPI Program Interaction

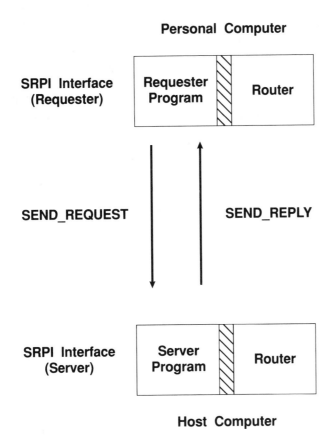

Personal Computer

SRPI Interface
(Requester)

Requester
Program

Router

SEND_REQUEST

SEND_REPLY

SRPI Interface
(Server)

Server
Program

Router

Host Computer

SRPI is part of a larger architecture called Enhanced Connectivity Facilities (ECF). ECF contains a set of IBM-developed requesters for the PS/2 and servers for System/370 that perform the following functions:

- Access to DB2 and SQL/DS data from the PS/2
- Transformation of data to several data formats used on the PS/2
- Virtual disk, file, and printer
- File transfer
- Executing host commands from the PS/2

OS/2 Communications Manager provides all SRPI requester functions. It has an API for OS/2 applications to request services from mainframe programs. On System/370, TSO and VM provide the SRPI server functions. Customers must purchase one of the two ECF products: IBM TSO/E Servers or IBM CMS Servers. Both these products include an *ECF requesters feature*, which runs under OS/2.

Any OS/2 application may call SRPI. The application specifies a server name, which the operating system uses to route the request to the appropriate 3270 session. One of the Communications Manager's profiles defines the routing, which must be set in advance.

Before using SRPI, users must establish a link to the CMS or TSO server program using one of the available 3270 sessions. While SRPI is active, this session cannot be used for any other purpose. SRPI is an extension of the operating system and thus multiple applications can use it concurrently. However, each 3270 session handles only one call at a time; SRPI queues additional callers and services them sequentially.

Although SRPI now uses the 3270 data stream, IBM intends to use APPC as a transport mechanism for SRPI in the future. SRPI will route requests over an APPC conversation to the appropriate server. The interface will be fully compatible with the SAA communication interface. SRPI will continue to use 3270 data stream, to promote compatibility with existing configurations.

SRPI with APPC will be much cleaner from an architectural perspective, and may simplify the design of some applications. APPC may not be as convenient for users as 3270. But SRPI cannot provide the full power of APPC's verb sets, and IBM provides it for the PS/2 and System/370 only.

It isn't clear whether ECF and SRPI comply fully with SAA. Under the heading "ECF-SAA participation," an IBM announcement says "ECF release 2.0 provides a link for three of the participants in SAA—MVS TSO/E, VM CMS, and OS/2 EE." Notwithstanding this vague prose, many observers believe that ECF and SRPI will be important in developing cooperative applications.

Chapter 20

SAA's Future

The fanfare accompanying the SAA announcement in 1987 showed IBM's renewed interest in the application software market. IBM claims that the consistency introduced by SAA will improve the efficiency of end users and programmers. Customers are trying to decide whether they believe this. Although SAA is now more than three years old, many observers aren't sure whether it will be important in the future. Few customers have made tangible commitments to the architecture.

Without question, IBM will benefit from SAA. The architecture is the company's best response to repeated criticism that its diverse computer product lines don't work together. SAA will help sell a wide variety of IBM products. It might even compel IBM's own programming staff to make their application software products more consistent.

Large IBM customers may benefit from SAA. The architecture provides clear guidance in selecting the tools for building cooperative processing applications. Cooperative processing will, in the long term, cut total hardware cost because it will let customers use cheaper computers in place of mainframes. Software costs may rise, however, because customers will need to redesign and rewrite major applications to take advantage of the technology.

Improvements in consistency will reduce the cost of learning to use new applications. However, it is not certain whether SAA is the best way to improve staff efficiency or to reduce hardware costs. Competing technology, such as the UNIX operating system with the X Window System and TCP/IP networking, claims similar benefits. Customers will evaluate the competition before adopting SAA.

SAA in 1991

SAA's goal is to standardize most technical aspects of application design, including look and feel, programming languages, coding style, graphics, windowing, database, and communication protocols. However, for other than demonstration purposes, the architecture is not usable. Significant ambiguities exist throughout SAA.

Whether product developers will use SAA widely is a question that involves technical, marketing, and economic considerations. Technically, SAA must efficiently perform the functions developers need, without greatly complicating the application code or compromising ease of use. From a marketing standpoint, developers must be certain that prospective customers desire the benefits of SAA and are willing to pay for them. The answers to these questions remain unclear.

SAA promises to let customers migrate applications to distributed processing, thereby generating sales of a wide range of IBM hardware and software. Because of the architecture's enormous scope, a customer may need to install a dozen or more system software packages as prerequisites for SAA application execution. IBM intends to sell its customers many database, graphics, application enabling, and communication products. Customers are buying some of these products to be prepared for SAA.

Just as Systems Network Architecture fueled the sales of IBM communications products since the late 1970s, SAA will drive the sales of countless systems software products. In mainframe systems software, SAA may simply expand IBM's dominance of the field. But in the more competitive mini- and micro-computer arena, IBM is seeking competitive advantages over its well-entrenched rivals. The company must also face the challenge presented by UNIX, which is a growing force in the commercial marketplace.

Is SAA a Lock-in Strategy?

Application portability, if it can be achieved, will simplify moving code from one environment to another. In the past, such conversions have been difficult and frequent, forcing programmers to start from scratch in learning new computer environments. Nevertheless, some observers fear that SAA is a lock-in strategy, which will make it more difficult to convert to non-IBM hardware. Nevertheless, some customers are already locked in, and thus are not overly concerned.

If SAA is to be successful, many third-party software developers must embrace it. IBM will convince this group to use the new architecture. SAA's portability features let developers write applications once, then freely port them to other IBM computers. Vendor products offered for multiple environments are useful to customers who operate dissimilar IBM systems, or who plan to migrate to other IBM product lines in the future.

If SAA is a lock-in strategy, developers will have difficulty porting their software to non-IBM computers. Furthermore, IBM could change SAA in the future to favor its own software products at the expense of competitive products. Most competitors are familiar with the IBM tactic of adding proprietary features to its "open" architectures.

Short-Term Expectations

SAA is an ambitious effort to integrate several divergent IBM systems into a consistent and cohesive programming environment. Considering the complexities and differences among System/370, AS/400, and PS/2, observers should expect SAA implementation to take a few years, even for a company as big as IBM. It was no surprise that SAA was not complete at its initial announcement date. However, it surprised many people that the architecture isn't usable after three years.

System/370 and PS/2 SAA implementations will mature by 1993; this is good news for cooperative processing application developers. However, portability between System/370 and PS/2 will remain less than perfect. Also, there will be major differences in user interaction techniques among all SAA environments.

Mainframe SAA applications that perform transaction processing in CICS and IMS will not be able to use all SAA features, including the procedures language, dialog manager, and presentation interface. However, applications running on PS/2s will communicate with CICS or IMS applications using CCS.

The outlook for SAA on the AS/400 is unclear. Though mentioned in SAA documentation, details about the AS/400 remain scarce. AS/400 is very different from System/370 and PS/2; this makes portability difficult to achieve. In the past, the AS/400's predecessors, System/36 and System/38, presented major portability hurdles. The AS/400 offers few SAA-compatible facilities today; this will prevail for a long time.

SAA's Common Applications represent major long-term opportunities for IBM. The first release of the first application, OfficeVision, arrived with much fanfare, but had severe limitations. IBM delayed the next OfficeVision release. There have been hints that the second SAA product family, AD/Cycle, may also disappoint.

As certain as death and taxes, there will be new architectures. Many of these will relate to applications, and they will be specific to particular industries. The architectures will include data models tailored to the needs of the business. IBM will concentrate on its traditional strongholds. There is speculation that a new offering, Financial Applications Architecture (FAA), will address IBM's premier vertical markets: banking, securities, and insurance.

Less likely are new SAA environments. IBM already has been careful to make clear that UNIX is not part of SAA. Changing customer preferences might force IBM to change its tune; UNIX could be added to SAA in the future, if the market dictates. However, this would give many competitors a better entrée into IBM's most important strategic architecture.

SAA Compliance

Judging SAA compliance will be difficult. In many respects, the standard is not absolute, especially in Common User Access. Though SAA contains many mandatory requirements, they are not always stringent, and many features remain optional because of architectural differences among SAA environments. For example, a user interface of programs running on the AS/400 will have a different "look and feel" from those running on the PS/2.

Furthermore, an application might conform to SAA only in some respects. Virtually all applications will have functions not defined by SAA. For example, operating system command languages and job control languages are not part of SAA, but are necessary to run an application. The presence of such functions will not disqualify an application from SAA compatibility.

Suppose a vendor develops a product that conforms to CUA, but also uses asynchronous communications. Is it compatible with SAA or not? There is no official "SAA stamp of approval"; product marketers can claim SAA compatibility, and purchasers will either believe it or not.

Room for Improvement

For the next several years, IBM will be busy delivering SAA software products. However, the company may pause to consider possible enhancements to the architecture, to address a few obvious shortcomings.

It seems odd that IBM didn't provide a complete implementation of SAA in the IMS and CICS transaction processing environments. These products support cooperative processing, but it will take a long time to migrate the large body of existing applications to this new technology. IBM should allow traditional (mainframe only) transaction processing under SAA. This would provide an immediate migration path to SAA, which customers would welcome.

Some of the SAA documentation is verbose, redundant, ambiguous, heavy with marketing rhetoric, but light in useful information. "Many other IBM systems and products will be offered outside the Systems Application Architecture, ensuring that customers with environment-specific business requirements will continue to have those needs satisfied," says one of the manuals. Fortunately, even though they do contain such double-talk, some manuals are well-written and can be understood by people who are unfamiliar with IBM jargon.

SAA must provide more practical connectivity. APPC, SNADS, and DIA have been available for several years, but have not become popular, partly because they are difficult to use, and do not fit well into the PC and PS/2 environment. The 3270 data stream is popular, but its performance and functions are limited. Distributed Data Management doesn't support important file organizations and subsystems.

Thus, for many customers, these architectures are just theory; they aren't useful in a day-to-day production environment. IBM must make the individual parts of SAA useful in a practical setting before customers will believe that the entire architecture is worthwhile. Customers need better implementations that will solve ordinary problems. SAA must lead to working products that actually deliver high-level services such as distributed database and comprehensive file sharing.

Summary

The new architecture has the potential to improve portability and consistency of IBM and other application software. It offers many benefits to IBM and its customers, with few risks. Third-party application developers are weighing the risks and rewards to determine whether they should use SAA. Many will decide in favor of the architecture.

While SAA is suitable for many corporate applications, some customers will find alternatives, such as UNIX, to be more appropriate. Nevertheless, IBM has a strong track record and the marketing muscle to make SAA very successful.

Glossary

ABEND   Abnormal end; an IBM operating system function that abruptly ends the execution of a program after an error.

action bar   A list of action keywords, such as FILE, VIEW, EXIT or HELP, that appears at the top of a panel in SAA Common User Access.

actions language   Defines the responses entered by the user through a keyboard or a mouse in SAA Common User Access.

ACF   Advanced Communications Function; a term used by IBM to describe a certain set of enhancements to a group of communications products. ACF is prefixed to the names of some products. *See also* **NCP, SSP** and **VTAM.**

AD/Cycle   Application Development/Cycle; a strategy and set of tools to handle the entire application development life cycle.

ADT   Application Development Tools; a collection of tools for the AS/400 that includes Program Development Manager, Source Entry Utility, Screen Design Aid, Data File Utility, and Advanced Printer Function.

AFPA   Advanced Function Printing Architecture; a protocol to communicate between IBM computers and printers.

AIX   Advanced Interactive Executive; IBM operating system product family that is compatible with AT&T's Unix. AIX products are offered for PS/2, RS/6000, and System/370 computers.

Amdahl   A company that produces computers and peripherals compatible with IBM System/370 architecture. Gene Amdahl, founder of Amdahl Corporation, was one of the original architects of System/360.

ANSI   American National Standards Institute; a voluntary organization that co-ordinates standards implemented in the United States. Important ANSI standards cover computer languages and data base interfaces.

APA   All-Points-Addressable; the surface of a graphic device, such as a terminal or printer, can be viewed as a two-dimensional matrix of points (which may be called dots or pixels). An APA device allows each point to be directly illuminated individually.

API   Application Programming Interface; the rules that govern an application's interaction with system software. An API defines the services offered to an application and the procedures for the application to request those services.

application generator   A product, such as IBM's Cross System Product, that generates application software from high-level user specifications, rather than requiring detailed coding. Some application generators are called fourth generation languages (**4GLs**).

application software   Computer programs that are designed to perform specific user-oriented or business-oriented functions, such as accounting or word processing. Application software is different from system software, which provides a foundation for running applications.

APPC   Advanced Program to Program Communications; a set of SNA protocols for communication between programs, also called LU 6.2.

APPN   Advanced Peer to Peer Networking; a set of SNA node protocols to enable two systems to communicate on a peer basis. APPN is an improvement to Low Entry Networking (LEN).

architecture   Defines the parts of a system and the interaction of those parts. Contains technical details, including data formats, rules, protocols, or interface standards, to which hardware and software products must conform.

ASCII   American Standard Code for Information Interchange; a method of representing letters, numerals, and special characters in a seven-bit code. This method is frequently used in non-IBM computers and terminals, but is not used extensively in IBM products. EBCDIC is the usual standard for IBM products.

async   Asynchronous; a data transmission protocol that does not require a separate clock signal for reception of data. The transmitter and receiver establish synchronization for each character of data using start and stop bits. Also called start/stop.

AS/400   Application System/400; a series of IBM mid-range computers introduced in 1988, that replace the System/38 and System/36 product lines.

AT   Advanced Technology; refers to the IBM Personal Computer AT, no longer manufactured.

AT&T   A major communications and computer firm, developer of the Unix operating system.

ATP   Application Transaction Program; an APPC application written by a customer or vendor.

baseband   Baseband is a transmission technique that puts a signal directly onto a transmission medium without modulating a carrier.

batch   A group of transactions or bulk data that is not processed in an **interactive** manner.

BIND   In SNA, a session control command that activates an LU-LU session. Under DB2, bind means converting the DBRM into a set of instructions to DB2.

BIOS   Basic Input/Output Support; microcode on a Personal Computer that handles I/O and other system services.

Bisync   Binary synchronous communications; an IBM synchronous communications protocol used for remote job entry, bulk data transmission, and interactive data communications. Bisync was popular in the 1960s and 1970s, but usage is now declining.

BMS   Basic Mapping Support; routes messages, provides terminal paging, and promotes device independence under CICS.

BSAM   Basic Sequential Access Method; a software function in the MVS operating system intended to perform input/output for standard computer peripheral devices including disks, tapes, printers, and card readers.

BTAM   Basic Telecommunications Access Method; an IBM communications software product for interfacing between applications software and the communications network. BTAM was popular until 1980, but it is now declining because it does not support SNA.

BTU   Basic Transmission Unit; the set of path information units within a basic link unit; contains the data to be moved between SNA nodes.

bus   A single connective high speed link among multiple processing machines where any machine can transmit to any other, but only one can be transmitting successfully at any time. In the IBM I/O channel interface, one of the cables is called **bus**, and the other is called **tag**.

C   A concise "third generation" programming language that is used to build system software and complex applications. C was originally developed with AT&T's Unix operating system and now is included in SAA.

cache   A storage area, intended to speed up access to data. Usually a cache is invisible to the hardware or software that is using it. Cache memory is offered in disk controllers. In a CPU, it is called a **high speed buffer**.

CBX   Computerized Branch Exchange, same as **PBX**.

CCITT   Comité Consultatif International de Télégraphie et Téléphonie; an international standards organization for communications and computer networks, organized under the International Telecommunications Union, which is an agency of the United Nations. CCITT standards, such as V.24 and X.25, are used with SAA.

CCS   Common Communications Support; a component of Systems Application Architecture that defines data communications standards for data links, application services, network management, and data streams.

CDRM   Cross Domain Resource Manager; in VTAM, a part of the SSCP that tracks and manages resources owned by SSCPs in other domains.

channel   In System/370, a component of the processor complex that supervises the system's Input/Output functions. A single System/370 can have up to 256 channels.

CICS/VS   Customer Information Control System/Virtual Storage; a popular IBM system software product that schedules and manages the execution of transaction programs under the MVS, VM, and VSE operating systems.

CISC   Complex instruction set computer; a computer architecture with a wide variety of powerful instructions; contrast with **RISC**.

CL   Control Language; a language that executes user programs under the OS/400 operating system. CL is similar in concept to Job Control Language (JCL) on System/370.

CLC   Cluster controller; a semi-intelligent device, sometimes located at a remote site, that allows several non-intelligent terminals or similar devices to connect to a data link. Example: IBM 3174.

CLIST   Command List

CMS   Conversational Monitor System; a software component of IBM's VM operating system, which is used for interactive computing, time sharing, and program development.

CNM   Communications Network Management; a systematic method of managing and controlling a complex network. This term also refers to a group of IBM product functions.

COBOL   Common Business-Oriented Language; a programming language used for developing business application software, which is included in SAA.

Communication Control Unit   Generic term for a processing device that controls data communications links. Also called a **front end processor**.

conversation   A logical connection between two transaction programs, which is defined by **APPC**.

Cooperative processing   A technique for dividing the processing tasks of an application among multiple computers. This may include virtual disks, virtual printers, access to distributed data, and off-loading the user interface.

CP   Control Program; a component of the VM operating system which provides basic system services, including dispatching and spooling. Also, a generic IBM term for **operating system**.

CPF   Control Program Facility; operating system for the IBM System/38.

CPI   Common Programming Interface; a component of SAA that defines rules for programming and use of system services by applications.

CPI/C   Common Programming Interface for Communications; an SAA component that defines a standard interface for applications for communication services, especially SNA LU 6.2.

CPU   Central Processing Unit; the heart of a computer system, which performs arithmetic, logic, and short-term data storage. Also called a **processor**.

CSMA   Carrier Sense, Multiple Access; a technique for media access control used by some local area networks, including Ethernet and the IBM PC Network/Baseband.

CSP   Cross System Product; an IBM application generator, included in SAA, which builds portable applications based on high-level specifications supplied by the user.

CTCA   channel-to-channel adapter; connects two block multiplexer channels together; each system appears as an I/O device to the other.

CUA   Common User Access; a component of SAA that defines a standard user interface.

customer   An organization or person that buys computer products or services; contrast with **user**.

CUT   Control Unit Terminal mode; a direct connection between a cluster controller and a non-intelligent terminal.

DASD   Direct Access Storage Devices; magnetic disks, used for medium- and long-term data storage.

database   An organized collection of data, usually managed by a data base management system, such as DB2 or IMS.

Data Flow Control   Layer five of SNA, which is responsible for defining requests, responses, send/receive states, brackets, chains, and other related protocols.

data link   A data communications connection between two machines (i.e., nodes) on a network. SAA has several data links: SDLC, QLLC, and Token-Ring.

data stream   A sequence of bits in a communications session that directs the presentation or formatting of information. Data streams format information on a terminal screen, define graphic objects or control device functions such as pagination, color, and reverse video.

DBCS   Double-byte character set; part of SAA CUA, it specifies rules for supporting languages other than English.

DBMS   Data Base Management System; software, such as DB2 or IMS, that manages a data base.

DBRM   Data Base Request Module; a set of syntax-checked SQL statements, which is input to the bind process.

DB2   Data Base 2; an IBM relational data base management system for the MVS operating system.

DCA   Document Content Architecture; defines data formats representing documents and electronic mail messages that are compatible among dissimilar office systems.

DCE   Data Circuit Terminating Equipment; hardware installed at the user's premises that provides all the functions required to establish, maintain, and terminate a communications connection. It also defines the signal conversion and coding between data terminal equipment and the common carrier's line (e.g., modems).

DDM   Distributed Data Management; SAA communication protocols that provide access to files on remote systems. For example, DDM lets an AS/400 application access a System/370 CICS VSAM file.

DEC   Digital Equipment Corporation; a major computer vendor, one of IBM's most important competitors. DEC developed the VAX architecture, which defines a successful family of mid-range computers.

demand paging   The movement of pages containing programs and data between disk and real storage.

DFP   Data Facility Product; a product that contains access methods and other file system functions.

DFT   Distributed Function Terminal; a direct connection between a cluster controller, which allows up to five concurrent sessions on a single cable.

DHCF   Distributed Host Command Facility; a product that lets host terminals act as terminals on a mid-range computer such as an AS/400; reverse terminal emulation.

DIA   Document Interchange Architecture; defines protocols and data streams to interchange documents and messages among dissimilar office system products in a consistent manner.

Dialog Manager   A function of the SAA Common Programming Interface that controls the interaction between the user and an application. ISPF is a product that implements the dialog manager interface.

DISOSS   Distributed Office Support System; an IBM product that provides store-and-forward services for documents and electronic mail messages. It executes under CICS in a System/370 host.

DisplayWrite   A set of compatible IBM word processing products for major IBM computer families.

distributed processing   A technique of dividing the work of an application among multiple machines. Distributed processing is the predecessor of cooperative processing.

DL/I   Data Language One; the interface between IMS and application programs that provides access to data bases, terminals and message queues.

DLC   Data Link Control; layer two of network architecture which defines the procedures for exchanging messages using a data transmission medium.

DMT   Dictionary Model Transformer; a product that helps in the transition from existing IBM information bases to the AD/Cycle repository.

domain   In SNA, all communications resources managed by a particular host computer.

DOS   Disk Operating System; the primary operating system for the IBM Personal Computer. Also called PC-DOS and MS-DOS.

DOS/VSE   *See* **VSE**.

DSE   Data Switching Equipment; in CCITT X.25, a packet switching data network.

DSU   Distribution Service Unit; consists of APPC service transaction programs that provide asynchronous data distribution through SNADS.

DTE   Data Terminal Equipment; a machine that is the data source or data sink, which provides communications functions and protocols. A communication path begins or ends at a DTE.

dyadic   A configuration of System/370 processors having two processors in one box, which provides the appearance of a single system.

EBCDIC   Extended Binary Coded Decimal Interchange Code; the character coding system used on many IBM computers, including System/370. Similar to, but incompatible with, **ASCII**.

ECF   Enhanced Connectivity Facilities; an IBM product family that exchanges data between PCs and System/370s, which provide access to host files, disk space, data bases and printers.

ECL   Emitter Coupled Logic; an electronic circuit topology, used in integrated circuits (ICs), which are building blocks of computer hardware. Similar to **TTL**, but faster.

ECS   Electronic Customer Support; tools to help customers service and support their AS/400 systems and networks and to provide remote access to IBM marketing information and service facilities.

EDX   Event Driven Executive; an IBM operating system used on the Series/1.

EHLLAPI   Emulator High Level Language Application Programming Interface; a feature of Communications Manager that lets applications control an active 3270 session.

EIA   Electronic Industries Association; a computer industry standards group, responsible for RS-232, RS-366, etc.

ENA   Extended Network Addressing; 23-bit fixed-format network address structure that contains 8-bit subarea and 15-bit element addresses.

enterprise   A term that refers to an IBM customer's entire organization. *See also* **establishment**.

EP   Emulation Program; IBM software that makes IBM 3705, 3720, 3725, or 3745 communications control units operate like IBM 2701, 2702, or 2703 teleprocessing control units.

ER   Explicit Route; a direct physical path connecting two adjacent subareas in an SNA network. A host computer or a communications control unit may constitute a subarea.

ESA   Enterprise Systems Architecture; an enhancement to System/370 architecture and IBM operating systems to allow expanded address spaces, up to 16 terabytes.

establishment   A term that refers to a single location within an IBM customer's organization. *See also* **enterprise**.

Ethernet   A Local Area Network standard, similar to IEEE 802.3, supported by a wide range of vendors, including IBM.

EXCP   Execute channel program; a function in IBM's MVS operating system that lets an application execute device-level input/output operations.

Extended Architecture   *See* **XA**.

family   Related IBM products are called a family.

FDX   Full duplex; a facility or protocol that can be used for simultaneous two-way communications.

FEP   Front-End Processor; Same as **Communications Control Unit**.

FFT   Final-Form Text; in Document Content Architecture, a method of representing a text document in non-editable form. FFT documents are suitable for printing on paper or viewing on a screen, but cannot be modified by a word processor.

FIFO   First In, First Out; a procedure for processing entities in a queue sequentially.

FI.FMD   Function Interpreters for Function Management Data; layer six of SNA, a set of functions that interpret the data being exchanged in a session. *See also* **PS** (Presentation Services).

FMH   Function Management Header; a header in the SNA frame that supports the FI.FMD layer.

FOCA   Font Object Content Architecture; an architecture that defines fonts.

FORTRAN   Formula Translator; a programming language, included in SAA, mainly used for scientific applications.

4GL   fourth generation language; any non-procedural programming language or application generator; contrast with **3GL**.

frame   In SNA, a unit of information consisting of a link header, an information field, and a link trailer.

gateway   A facility that interconnects multiple networks.

GCS   Group Control System; a multi-tasking virtual machine supervisor that runs communications software under VM.

GDDM   Graphical Data Display Manager; an IBM product that provides graphics and advanced printing functions on System/370. It provides many of the presentation and graphic functions of SAA.

GDS   Generalized Data Stream; a standard format data stream used in mapped conversations.

gigabyte (G)   About one thousand megabytes. Exactly 2^{30} bytes.

GOCA   Graphic Object Content Architecture; an architecture that creates and specifies vector graphics.

HASP   Houston Automatic Spooling Program; spooling software for the IBM OS/360 operating system. IBM adapted HASP for modern operating systems and renamed it to JES2. HASP had its own bisync data communications protocol, which is still used today.

HCF   Host Command Facility; System/370 software that works with DHCF to provide reverse terminal emulation.

HDLC   High-level Data Link Control; an ISO standard family of data link protocols.

HDX-FF   Half Duplex Flip-Flop; a send/receive state protocol used in SNA LU-LU sessions.

hiper   high performance.

host   A computer that runs applications on a network. Often refers to an IBM System/370 on an SNA network.

HSB   High Speed Buffer; memory inside an IBM processor, intended to improve performance. Sometimes called a **cache**.

IBM   International Business Machines Corporation; the largest computer vendor in the world, developer of SAA.

ICCF   Interactive Communications Control Facility; a limited time sharing facility for VSE. Runs under CICS and performs text editing, job submission, and output retrieval.

ICU   Interactive Chart Utility; part of the Presentation Graphics feature of GDDM, ICU graphically presents data retrieved by QMF.

IEEE   Institute of Electrical and Electronics Engineers; a professional society with chapters throughout the world, whose work in local area network technology (including the 802 standards family) is regarded as definitive.

IMS/VS   Information Management System/Virtual Storage; an IBM product that performs data base and data communications functions.

IND$FILE   A file transfer protocol, which usually uses 3270 data stream.

interactive   Describes computer workload that takes place in *real time*, and usually requires a dialog between a person and a computer. Opposite of **batch**.

interface   A set of rules defining the interaction between two systems or products.

I/O   Input/Output.

IOCA   Image Object Content Architecture; an architecture that represents and exchanges image data.

IOP   Input/Output Processor; a system that manages all devices connected to a computer, such as disk units, tape units, terminals, and printers.

IPC   Interprocess Communication; an operating system function that allows cooperation and synchronization between processes and threads. IPC includes pipes, queues, semaphores, and signals.

IPDS   Intelligent Printer Data Stream; an IBM protocol for formatting complex text, graphics, images and bar codes on a microprocessor-based printer.

IPL   Initial Program Load; activation of an operating system in an IBM computer.

ISAM   Indexed Sequential Access Method; a method of accessing data via an index by specifying the key, rather than the physical location, of a record. ISAM's successor was VSAM.

ISO   International Organization of Standardization; developer of technology standards. ISO membership is voluntary, and each member country is represented by its national standards organization, such as ANSI. ISO is responsible for standards including encryption, computer networks and languages such as FORTRAN and COBOL.

ISPF   Interactive System Productivity Facility; an IBM software product that executes under TSO and CMS and allows applications to use full-screen menus with 3270 terminals.

IWS   Intelligent Work Station; same as **Programmable Work Station**.

JCL   Job Control Language; defines the sequence of programs and the data to be processed in jobs executed under the MVS and VSE operating systems.

JES2, JES3   Job Entry Subsystems; IBM software products that perform spooling, manage physical input, control printing, and schedule batch workload.

kernel   A kernel is the part of a multi-layer operating system that provides most operating system services and uses devices drivers as the hardware interface.

LAN   Local Area Network; a series of connections among computers, allowing high-speed (over 1 megabit per second) communications over short distances (under ten kilometers).

LAP   Link Access Procedure; a subset of HDLC that includes unbalanced (master/slave) data link control procedures.

LAPB   Link Access Procedure, Balanced; a subset of HDLC that includes balanced (peer-to-peer) data link control procedures.

LEN   Low Entry Networking; an SNA function that enables direct peer-to-peer connections between two machines. LEN is a marketing term; equivalent technical terms are node type 2.1 or PU 2.1.

LIC   Licensed Internal Code; firmware or microcode that provides a layer of functions positioned between the operating system and hardware in the AS/400.

LLA   Library Lookaside; a service of MVS/ESA that stores frequently-used programs in a data space.

LLC   Logical Link Control; the upper sub-layer of a network's data link.

LSI   Large Scale Integration; refers to the density of packaging of integrated circuits (ICs).

LU   Logical Unit; a network addressable unit that is the logical port through which end users access SNA network services.

LU 6.2   A technical SNA term, same as **APPC**.

MAC   Media Access Control; a sublayer of a LAN data link; MAC defines procedures for accessing the network transmission medium.

MAU   Multistation Access Unit; the wiring concentrator on a Token-Ring.

MCA   Micro Channel Architecture; a microcomputer bus standard, introduced with the PS/2.

MCH   Multiple Channel link; a data link driven by NPSI in the communications control unit, connected to an X.25 packet switching data network.

MFI   Mainframe interactive; in SAA Common User Access, a style of user interaction that can be used with a non-intelligent terminal, such as the IBM 3270 or 5250 families. Opposite of **Programmable Work Station**.

MFS   Message Format Services; a service of IMS that lets application programmers work with logical messages, rather than device-specific data streams. MFS also provides automatic paging for display devices.

MIPS   Millions of Instructions Per Second; *also* Meaningless Indicator of Processor Speed. A unit of measurement of computer performance.

mnemonic   In SAA, a mnemonic is the underlined character (an abbreviation) in an action bar.

MO:DCA Mixed Object Document Content Architecture; an architecture that provides a structure for transporting complex documents among SAA applications. FOCA, PTOCA, IOCA, and GOCA are its subsidiary architectures.

modem Modems convert digital signals used by a physical interface (e.g., RS-232) to signalling methods (e.g., analog tones) compatible with the physical circuit.

MP Multiprocessor; a computer system employing multiple CPUs and a single shared main memory.

multiprogramming The technique of executing multiple programs concurrently in a computer system.

MSNF Multiple Systems Networking Facility; a feature that allows multiple host computers to participate in an SNA network.

MVS Multiple Virtual Storages; a large, general purpose IBM operating system, which is used extensively for general data processing, batch processing, moderate volume transaction processing, and interactive time sharing.

NAU Network Addressable Unit; a generic SNA term representing a Logical Unit, Physical Unit, or System Service Control Point.

navigation SAA dialogs have two parts: requests to process information and requests to navigate through the application. Navigation leads the user through a sequence of steps to the desired function in an application.

NCCF Network Communications Control Facility; monitors, controls and automates the operation of an SNA data communications network. A component of NetView, NCCF is also called the Command Facility.

NCP Network Control Program; an IBM software product that controls the operation of an IBM 3705, 3720, 3725 or 3745 communications control unit. Also called ACF/NCP/VS.

NetView IBM's SNA network management product, which executes on System/370 computers. NetView/PC, an extra-cost product, runs on a PC and provides network management interfaces to non-IBM networks.

NLDM Network Logical Data Manager; a component of NetView that supervises SNA logical resources, including sessions and response time statistics.

node   An intelligent component of an SNA network; it usually contains a Physical Unit. Alternatively, this term refers to a logical unit or a part of the VTAM system definition.

NPDA   Network Problem Determination Application; a component of NetView to assist the network operator to investigate and manage network troubles.

NPSI   Network Control Program Packet Switching Interface; an IBM software product that works with NCP to interface SNA to an X.25 packet switching data network.

object   On an AS/400, objects are programs, documents, databases, and other resources; they include anything that users focus on and manipulate as a single item; objects are similar to files on other systems. In IPDS, an object is an independently defined block of data.

object-action principle   In SAA Common User Access, allows users to select an object from the panel body first, and then to select an operation from the action bar or function keys to work on that object.

OCL   Operations Control Language; the control language for the System/36 SSP operating system. Similar in concept to **JCL**.

OfficeVision   A family of SAA-compatible office automation software products, the first SAA common application announced by IBM.

OS/2   Operating System/2; a multiprogramming operating system for IBM's Personal System/2 and other equivalent microcomputers.

OS/400   Operating System/400; operating system for the AS/400 mid-range computer. It supports SAA and simplifies migration from the System/38 and System/36 computers to the AS/400.

OSI   Open Systems Interconnection; a seven layer reference model developed by the International Organization of Standardization (ISO), which describes the logical structure of all modern communication systems.

OSN   Office System Node; a node in DIA that receives, stores, routes, and delivers documents for source or recipient nodes. It also provides a library of documents.

PAD Packet Assembler/Disassembler; a function that provides the necessary conversion between a user's data transmission and a packet data network by assembling and disassembling messages to packets.

page Pages are 4,096-byte blocks of virtual storage.

paging *See* **demand paging**.

panel A predefined set of information arranged in a specific way and displayed on a screen.

PBX Private branch exchange; equipment to connect the user's telephone equipment to a common carrier's facilities. Same as **CBX**.

PDF Program Development Facility; a companion product to **ISPF**, PDF provides a text editor and tools for application program development.

PDM Program Development Manager; part of the AS/400 Application Development Tools package. PDM displays lists of libraries and objects and manipulates them using standard operations, such as copy, delete, and rename.

PDS Partitioned Data Set; in the MVS operating system, a data organization method that subdivides files into multiple individual members.

peer Refers to a system that is equal in function to another. In networking, a balanced relationship between two nodes, which does not use a master/slave approach.

PEP Partitioned Emulation Program; a software configuration of both Emulation Program (EP) and Network Control Program (NCP) in the same communications control unit.

pipe IPC mechanism that passes information between processes; operates like a file.

PIU Path Information Unit; part of the SNA data structure exchanged by VTAM and NCP across a channel.

PLU Primary Logical Unit; in an SNA LU-LU session, the LU that is responsible for setting the session parameters and for performing error recovery.

PL/I Programming Language One; a "third generation" programming language, used for commercial and scientific applications. PL/I is popular in Europe.

PostScript   PostScript is Adobe's page definition language for laser printers.

presentation language   In SAA Common User Access, an application's method for giving information to the user.

Presentation Manager   A component of the OS/2 operating system that provides a graphical user interface and an applications program interface.

processor   A machine that performs arithmetic and logic. Also called a **CPU**.

PROFS   Professional Office System; an IBM electronic mail and personal productivity software product that operates under the VM operating system. PROFS is not compatible with SAA, but the successor product, OfficeVision, is.

Programmable Work Station   A machine, having substantial computing capacity, which is located in a person's work space. This generic term often refers to a personal computer. SAA Common User Access contains a style of user interaction tailored for Programmable Work Stations. Opposite of **Mainframe Interactive** (MFI).

protocol   A method adopted by two systems for controlling the exchange of information between them.

PS   Presentation Services; a component of SNA layer six, responsible for editing, formatting, and presenting data to end users.

PS/2   Personal System/2; successor product line to the IBM Personal Computer series.

PSDN   Packet switching data network; a network in which messages are divided into packets to improve transmission efficiency. CCITT standard **X.25** interfaces a computer or terminal to a packet data network.

PSF   Print Services Facility; a product that provides the presentation services for VM, MVS, and VSE operating systems; converts IBM 1403 printer formatting approach and AFPDS to IPDS.

PTOCA   Presentation Text Object Content Architecture; an architecture that defines the presentation of text objects.

PU   Physical Unit; a network addressable unit responsible for managing physical configuration in SNA.

PUCP Physical Unit Control Point; part of an SNA node that activates and de-activates the node.

PVC Permanent Virtual Circuit; a permanent logical connection between DTEs in an X.25 network.

QBE Query By Example; a tabular language that uses a pattern technique to extract data from a relational database.

QLLC Qualified Logical Link Control; a SNA data link protocol used with an X.25 network, implemented by NPSI software, and the 3710, 3174, and 3274 cluster controllers.

QMF Query Management Facility; an IBM software product, offered for the MVS and VM operating systems, that composes queries of a relational data base and creates reports containing the answers.

QSAM Queued Sequential Access Method; MVS access method for sequential files on disk or tape.

RACF Resource Access Control Facility; IBM's standard security software for MVS and VM.

relational data base A type of data base that is viewed as a set of tables. Information is organized into rows and columns, similar to records and fields. Applications access data by performing operations on tables.

request In SAA Common User Access, to initiate an action. Several methods can be employed to initiate the action: pressing a function key, typing a command, or selecting a choice in a pull-down menu.

REXX Restructured Extended Executor; the procedures language in SAA, which lets the programmer code statements in the operating system's command language, as well as conventional programming logic.

RFT Revisable-Form Text; defines a standard representation of a document in editable form. A recipient of the document can easily modify it because all word processing control commands remain intact.

RISC Reduced instruction set computer; a computer architecture with a small repertoire instructions, most of which can be executed in one machine cycle; contrast with **CISC**.

RMF Resource Measurement Facility; IBM's performance measurement software for the MVS operating system.

RJE Remote Job Entry; a communications technique for transmitting batches of input data and printed output from a terminal to a computer.

RPG Report Program Generator; a programming language often used on IBM System/36 and System/38. Also called RPG-II, RPG-III, and RPG/400.

RPS Realtime Programming System; an IBM operating system for the Series/1.

RS-232 A standard of the Electronic Industries Association (EIA) for the mechanical, electrical, and procedural interconnection between DTE and DCE. It is a popular data communications standard in North America.

RS-449 A standard of the Electronic Industries Association (EIA) for mechanical, electrical, and procedural interconnection. It provides high data rates by using balanced electrical circuits.

RS/6000 RISC System/6000; An IBM computer family that includes workstation and rack-mount computers that run the UNIX operating system.

RSCS Remote Spooling and Communications Subsystem; IBM software component of VM that communicates with RJE terminals and other VM systems. Supports transmission of files, input, and output.

RSP, +RSP, -RSP In SNA, responses, either positive (+) or negative (-).

RT PC An IBM computer family that uses the Reduced Instruction Set Computer (RISC) architecture and runs the AIX operating system. This product family is now obsolete; IBM replaced it with the RS/6000.

SAA Systems Application Architecture; an IBM architecture that defines tools and techniques for application development.

SAP Service Access Point; entity that communicates at the Logical Link Control level of the data link layer. SAPs get services from the LLC, MAC, and physical layers.

SCP System Control Program; generic IBM term for **operating system**.

screen In SAA Common User Access, the surface of the workstation or terminal on which information is displayed to users.

SCS   SNA character string; a set of character codes defined in SNA to map the text data to the presentation space of the intended device.

SDA   Screen Design Aid; part of the AS/400 Application Development Tools package; it interactively designs, creates, and maintains application screens and menus.

SDLC   Synchronous Data Link Control; the standard data link control (layer two) protocol used in SNA; a set of procedures for exchanging information on a data link.

semaphore   IPC mechanism that tells which thread is in control of a serially-usable resource; they insure that only one thread at a time modifies a critical resource.

Series/1   Mid-range computer, open system, now obsolete

session   In SNA, a temporary logical connection between two Network Addressable Units, for a exchange of information, following agreed-upon rules. In OS/2, a group of processes that can occupy the screen, which constitute a single application.

SEU   Source Entry Utility; part of the AS/400 Application Development Tools package; it provides full-screen editing and syntax checking of source programs.

signal   IPC mechanism that notifies processes that an event has occurred.

SIO   Start I/O; in System/370, the machine instruction that begins an input/output operation. The operation is handled by the channel, and proceeds independently from activity on the CPU.

SLU   Secondary Logical Unit; in an SNA LU-LU session, the partner to a primary logical unit (PLU).

SMF   System Management Facilities; in MVS, a component of the operating system that collects computer resource statistics, typically used for accounting.

SMP/E   System Modification Program Extended; an IBM software product used for installing software error corrections and new software functions.

SNA   Systems Network Architecture; IBM's master blueprint for communications, which defines sets of communications functions that are distributed throughout a network and formats and protocols that relate these functions to one another.

SNADS   SNA Distribution Services; a set of protocols in SAA Common Communications Support to provide store-and-forward communications services for files and documents.

SNCP   Single Node Control Point; part of an SNA type 2.1 node that provides a subset of SSCP functions.

SNI   SNA Network Interconnection; an IBM software product that provides a gateway between two dissimilar SNA networks.

SPOOL   Simultaneous peripheral output, on line; a technique to store printed output on a disk while a program is running, then later to transfer the output to a printer. This is a primary function of a **Job Entry Subsystem**.

SQL   Structured Query Language; provides interface services to define, retrieve, insert, delete, and update information in a relational data base.

SQL/DS   Structured Query Language/Data System; an IBM SAA relational data base management product, which is similar to DB2, but operates under the VM operating system.

SRN   Source/Recipient Node; a node in DIA that only originates and receives documents.

SRPI   Server/Requester Programming Interface; a communication tool for connecting PC applications, which act as requesters, to System/370 applications, which act as servers. SRPI is the foundation for **ECF**.

SSCP   System Services Control Point; a SNA network addressable unit (NAU) that provides network management and control functions.

SSP   System Support Programs; an IBM software product that is needed to generate Network Control Program or Emulation Program. It has many utility functions such as NCP load, dump, and trace formatting programs. Also called ACF/SSP/VS.

STP   Service Transaction Program; transaction programs written by IBM and imbedded in hardware or software products. They provide high-level services within a network.

subarea   In SNA, each host computer and each communications controller is assigned a subarea number for routing and addressing purposes.

SVC   Switched Virtual Call; a temporary logical connection between DTEs in an X.25 network.

SYSGEN   System generation; a procedure for configuring certain IBM software products, including most operating systems.

System/3X   A term that refers to both IBM System/36 and System/38.

tag   One of the cables in the System/370 channel interface. *See also* **bus**.

TCP/IP   Transmission Control Protocol/Internet Protocol; a network architecture that is not part of SAA.

terabyte (T)   About one thousand gigabytes, or one million megabytes. Exactly 2^{40} bytes.

TCAM   Telecommunications Access Method; an obsolete IBM software product for controlling communications lines, terminals, and applications programs. Also called ACF/TCAM.

TCM   Thermal Conduction Module; the basic unit of hardware packaging in IBM 308X, 3090, and some 9370 computer models.

TCU   Teleprocessing Control Unit; a hardware device attached to IBM System/360 and 370 computers to interface them to communications lines and terminals.

3GL   third generation language; a high-level procedural programming language, such as COBOL, FORTRAN, or PL/I; contrast with **4GL**.

thread   Basic units of work that are scheduled on a CPU.

time sharing   A type of computer workload in which programs can be executed interactively from terminals. Time sharing often is used by professional programmers for writing and debugging programs. TSO and VM/CMS are examples of time sharing environments.

Token-Ring network   IBM's strategic local area network (LAN), which uses a star-wired ring topology. The architecture of the Token-Ring is defined by the IEEE 802.5 standard, which is included in SAA Common Communications Support.

TP   Teleprocessing; a term describing the integration of telephone and computer technologies.

TP monitor   A generic term for software products that interface applications programs to a data communications network. TP monitors, such as CICS, provide a variety of application development, data base management, file management, and communications session services.

TPF   Transaction Processing Facility; a specialized operating system for high volume transaction processing.

transaction   A logical unit of work, performed by an application program.

transaction program   A program that processes transactions in cooperation with other similar programs on a computer network.

TPF   Transaction Processing Facility; a high performance and high volume IBM transaction processing operating system, used primarily by airlines, banks and large retail companies. TPF was previously called Airline Control Program (ACP).

TSO   Time Sharing Option; a function of IBM's MVS operating system that provides text editing, program development, and program execution services.

TTL   Transistor-Transistor Logic; *see* **ECL**.

TTY   Teletype; a machine with a keyboard and printer that is used for data communications. This term also describes the protocols used by such machines.

T-1 carrier   A common carrier digital data communications facility that operates at 1.544 megabits per second, full duplex; the lowest level (lowest speed) of the Bell System digital hierarchy.

Unix   An interactive operating system, originally developed by AT&T Bell Labs, now offered by many computer vendors, including IBM.

user   A person who actually uses a hardware or software product. Usually a user is employed by a **customer**.

VIO   Virtual Input/Output; directs disk I/O operations for temporary datasets to memory.

virtual circuit   A logical connection between two DTEs in an X.25 network.

virtual disk   A function of a computer or network that acts like a disk, but no such disk is physically present. This is sometimes used to simplify access to data on remote systems.

VLF   Virtual Lookaside Facility; a service of MVS/ESA that lets privileged programs store data objects in data spaces.

VM   Virtual Machine; an IBM operating system that provides a simulated System/370 processor to each user. In combination with Conversational Monitor System (CMS), it provides time sharing services. Most other IBM operating systems can operate under VM as guest virtual machines. Also called VM/SP, VM/IS, VM/XA and VM/370.

VR   Virtual Route; a predefined path between any two subareas in an SNA network.

VSAM   Virtual Storage Access Method; a file access method used in MVS, VSE and CMS that supports sequential, random, and indexed file structures.

VSE   Disk Operating System/Virtual Storage Extended; an entry-level operating system intended for small System/370 computers. Also called **DOS/VSE**.

VS1   Operating System for Virtual Storage 1; an obsolete IBM operating system, primarily used for batch processing and low volume transaction processing.

VTAM   Virtual Telecommunications Access Method; an IBM software product that provides SNA control functions in the host computer system and interfaces the SNA network to applications. Also called ACF/VTAM.

V.24   A CCITT communications standard similar to EIA RS-232.

V.35   A CCITT standard for the physical interface on high speed (above 20,000 bits per second) data links.

WAN   Wide Area Network

window   A function that allows users to divide the screen into multiple independent areas, each containing one panel. Windows can be scrolled, resized, and moved. Windows are provided by the operating system and related presentation tools or by the application.

XA   Extended Architecture; extensions to System/370 for bimodal 24/31 bit addressing and an improved channel subsystem.

XI X.25 SNA Interconnect; a product that enables the SNA network to act as a carrier for X.25 virtual circuits.

XT Refers to the IBM Personal Computer XT, which is no longer manufactured.

X.21 A CCITT communications standard for physical interface using a fifteen pin connector, intended for digital networks.

X.21-bis A CCITT communications standard similar to EIA RS-232.

X.25 A CCITT communications standard that defines the procedures for exchanging packets and control information between a computer or terminal and a packet switching data network.

4GL Fourth Generation Language; a class of programming languages that are intended to develop business applications quickly. Some 4GLs are also called **application generators**.

Numbered IBM products

AS/400 Mid-range computer, successor to S/38

Series/1 Small computer system

System/3 Small business computer

System/34 Small business computer

System/36 Small business computer

System/38 Mid-range computer, advanced architecture

System/88 Fault-tolerant computer, built by Stratus

2701 Teleprocessing control unit

2702 Teleprocessing control unit

2703 Teleprocessing control unit

2740 Keyboard/printer terminal (bisync)

2741 Keyboard/printer terminal (async)

2770 Remote job entry terminal (bisync)

2780 Remote job entry terminal (bisync)

303X	Family of large computers
3031	Processor complex
3032	Processor complex
3033	Processor complex
308X	Family of large computers
3081	Processor complex
3083	Processor complex
3084	Processor complex
3088	Multisystem channel communication unit
3090	Processor complex
3101	ASCII CRT terminal
3151	ASCII CRT terminal
316X	ASCII CRT terminal
3174	Cluster control unit (3270 family)
3178	CRT terminal (3270 family)
3179	CRT color terminal (3270 family)
3180	CRT terminal (3270 family)
319X	CRT terminals (3270 family)
3262	Printer (3270 family)
3268	Printer (3270 family)
3270	Family of terminals
3271	Cluster control unit (remote)
3272	Cluster control unit (local non-SNA)
3274	Cluster control unit
3275	CRT terminal (bisync)
3276	CRT terminal/cluster control unit

3277	CRT terminal
3278	CRT terminal
3279	CRT color terminal
3284	Printer (3270 family)
3286	Printer (3270 family)
3287	Printer (3270 family)
3288	Printer (3270 family)
3289	Printer (3270 family)
3290	Plasma gas display terminal (3270 family)
3299	Terminal multiplexer (3270 family)
3380	Disk unit
3390	Disk unit
3420	Tape drive
3480	Tape cartridge unit
3600	Financial (banking) terminal family
3650	Retail store control unit
3704	Communications control unit
3705	Communications control unit
3708	SNA protocol converter
3710	SNA protocol converter
3720	Communications control unit
3721	Expansion unit for 3720
3725	Communications control unit
3726	Expansion unit for 3725
3728	Communications matrix switch
3727	Operator terminal for 3725

3737	Channel to T1 communications adapter
3745	Communications control unit
3746	Expansion unit for 3745
3767	Keyboard/printer terminal (asynchronous or SNA)
3770	Family of remote job entry terminals
3800	Laser printer
3803	Tape control unit
3814	Matrix switch for System/370 peripherals
3827	Laser printer
3830	DASD control unit
3834	Modem
3835	Laser printer
3864	Modem
3880	DASD control unit
3990	DASD control unit
4300	Family of medium size computers
4321	Central processing unit
4331	Central processing unit
4341	Central processing unit
4361	Central processing unit
4381	Central processing unit
4700	Financial (banking) terminal family
4954	Processor, Series/1
4956	Processor, Series/1
5080	Graphics system
5250	Low cost SNA display terminal

5360	Processor, System/36
5362	Processor, System/36
5364	System/36 PC
5381	Processor, System/38
5382	Processor, System/38
5520	Office computer system
58XX	Modems, DSU/CSUs, etc.
6670	Laser printer
7171	Asynchronous protocol converter
8100	Distributed processing computer system
8503	CRT monochrome, for PS/2
8512	CRT color, for PS/2
8513	CRT color, for PS/2
8514	CRT high performance color graphics, for PS/2
8775	CRT terminal/controller (3270 family)
9370	Mid-range computer system, System/370 architecture
9375	Processor, 9370 family
9377	Processor, 9370 family
9402	Processor, AS/400
9404	Processor, AS/400
9406	Processor, AS/400
9751	Telephone PBX (Rolm)

Bibliography

ACF/NCP/VS General Information	GC30-3058
Advanced Function Printing Software General Information	G544-3415
AIX/370 General Information	GC23-2062
An Introduction to Local Area Networks	SC20-8203
AS/400 Information Directory	GC21-9678
AS/400 Introduction	GC21-9766
CICS/VS General Information	GC33-0155
CMS Introduction	GC20-1800
Data Communication Device Summary	GA27-3185
DDM Architecture, General Information	GC21-9527
DDM Architecture, Reference	SC21-9526
DB2 General Information	GC26-4373
Document Content Architecture (DCA)	SC23-0758
Document Interchange Architecture (DIA)	SC23-0759
DISOSS General Information	GC30-3085
DXT General Information	GC26-4241
Electronic Customer Support	G580-0993

Network Program Products General Information	GC27-0657
Network Program Products Planning	SC30-3351
NPSI General Information	GC30-3189
Office Information Architectures: Concepts	GC23-0765
Office Systems Architecture Primer	GG24-1659
PROFS Specifications	GH20-6803
QMF General Information	GC26-4229
RSCS General Information	GH24-5055
SAA An Overview	GC26-4341
SAA CPI Application Generator Reference	SC26-4355
SAA CPI C Reference	SC26-4353
SAA CPI C Reference - Level 2	SC09-1308
SAA CPI COBOL Reference	SC26-4354
SAA CPI Communications Reference	SC26-4399
SAA CPI Database Reference	SC26-4348
SAA CPI Dialog Reference	SC26-4356
SAA CPI FORTRAN Reference	SC26-4357
SAA CPI Presentation Reference	SC26-4359
SAA CPI Procedures Language Reference	SC26-4358
SAA CPI Query Reference	SC26-4349
SAA RPG Reference	SC09-1286
SAA CUA Advanced Interface Design Guide	SC26-4582
SAA CUA Basic Interface Design Guide	SC26-4583
SAA Writing Applications: A Design Guide	SC26-4362
SDLC General Information	GA27-3093
Series/1 Selection Guide	GA34-0143
SNA Concepts and Products	GC30-3072
SNA Formats and Protocols, Reference Manual	SC30-3112
SNA Formats and Protocols, Architecture Logic for LU 6.2	SC30-3269

SNA Formats and Protocols, Architecture Logic for type 2.1 nodes	SC30-3422
SNA Formats and Protocols, Distribution Services	SC30-3098
SNA Introduction to Sessions Between Logical Units	GC20-1869
SNA Logical Unit Types	GC20-1868
SNA Management Services Overview	GC30-3429
SNA Reference Summary	GA27-3136
SNA Technical Overview	GC30-3073
SNI Planning and Design	GG24-1630
System/36 Introduction	GC21-9016
System/370 Bibliography	GC20-0001
System/370 to PC ECF Introduction	GC23-0957
System/370-XA Principles of Operation	SA22-7085
System/38 Introduction	GC21-7728
Systems and Products Guide	G320-6300
Token Ring Network Architecture Reference	6165877
Transaction Programmer's Reference for LU 6.2	GC30-3084
TSO/E General Information	GC28-1061
Virtual Machine/System Product	GC19-6200
Vocabulary for Data Processing	GC20-1699
VM/SP General Information	GC20-1838
VSE/SP General Information	GC33-6176
VTAM General Information	GC27-0608
The X.25 Interface for Attaching SNA Nodes to Packet-Switched Data Networks	GA27-3345
X.25 Primer	GG22-9103
X.25 Protocol	GA27-3345
3270 Data Stream Programmer's Reference	GA23-0059
3745/3746 Introduction	GA27-3608

4381 Guide   GC20-2021

9370 Planning Guide   GA24-5055

Black, Uyless: *Physical Level Interfaces and Protocols*, The Institute of Electrical and
   Electronics Engineers, 1988, ISBN 0-8186-8824-6

Bratz, A. E., et. al.: *SNA Networks of Small Systems, IBM Corporation, 1985*

Cypser, R.J: *Communications Architecture for Distributed Systems*, Addison-Wesley,
   1978, ISBN 0-201-14458-1

Gillin, Paul: *SAA: Looks Like A Winner*, Computerworld, October 1989

Halliday, Caroline M. and Shields, James A.. *IBM PS/2 Technical Guide*, Howard
   W. Sams & Company, 1988, ISBN 0-672-22628-6

Hoskins, Jim: *IBM AS/400: A Business Perspective*, John Wiley & Sons, Inc., 1989,
   ISBN 0-471-62149-8

Killen, Michael: *IBM—The Making of the Common View*, Harcourt Brace
   Jovanovich, 1989, ISBN 0-15-143480-8

Letwin, Gordon: *Inside OS/2*, Microsoft Press, 1988, ISBN 1-55615-117-9

Martin, James and Chapman, Kathleen: *SNA: IBM's Networking Solution*, Prentice
   Hall, 1987, ISBN 0-13-815143-1

Index

A

Access method, 112, 142, 317

Action, 168, 170, 177

Action bar, 40, 145, 170, 174

AD/Cycle, 204, 208, 234

Address space, 109

Address split, 253

Advanced Function Printing Architecture, 308

Advanced Function Printing Data Stream (AFPDS), 311

Advanced Interactive Executive PS/2 (AIX PS/2), 69

Advanced Interactive Executive/370 (AIX/370), 24

Advanced Peer-to-Peer Networking (APPN), 288

Advanced Printer Function (APF), 159

Advanced Program-to-Program Communications (APPC), 52, 133, 278, 332

base and towers, 283

basic conversation, 54, 282

control operator verb, 283

conversation, 278

mapped conversation, 54, 282

verb, 282

All-Points-Addressable (APA), 308

American National Standards Institute (ANSI), 35

Apple Computer, 81, 131

Application development, 159

Application development information model, 211, 215

Application development platform, 211, 214

Application Development Tools (ADT), 159

Application enabler, 173

Application generator, 48, 205, 212

Application object, 170